WINNING THE GLOBAL TALENT SHOWDOWN

HOW BUSINESSES AND COMMUNITIES CAN PARTNER TO REBUILD THE JOBS PIPELINE

EDWARD E. GORDON

BK

Berrett–Koehler Publishers, Inc.
San Francisco
a BK Business book

Berrett-Koehler Publishers, Inc.
235 Montgomery Street, Suite 650
San Francisco, CA 94104-2916
Tel: (415) 288-0260; Fax: (415) 362-2512 www.bkconnection.com

Ordering Information

Quantity sales. Special discounts are available on quantity purchases by corporations, associations, and others. For details, contact the Special Sales Department at the Berrett-Koehler address above.

Individual sales. Berrett-Koehler publications are available through most bookstores. They can also be ordered directly from Berrett-Koehler: Tel: (800) 929-2929; Fax: (802) 864-7626; www.bkconnection.com.

Orders for college textbook/course adoption use. Please contact Berrett-Koehler: Tel: (800) 929-2929; Fax: (802) 864-7626.

Orders by U.S. trade bookstores and wholesalers. Please contact Ingram Publisher Services: Tel: (800) 509-4887; Fax: (800) 838-1149; E-mail: customer. service@ingrampublisherservices.com; or visit www.ingrampublisherservices.com/ Ordering for details about electronic ordering.

Berrett-Koehler and the BK logo are registered trademarks of Berrett-Koehler Publishers, Inc.

Printed in the United States of America.

Berrett-Koehler books are printed on long-lasting acid-free paper. When it is available, we choose paper that has been manufactured by environmentally responsible processes. These may include using trees grown in sustainable forests, incorporating recycled paper, minimizing chlorine in bleaching, or recycling the energy produced at the paper mill.

Library of Congress Cataloging-in-Publication Data

Gordon, Edward E.
    Winning the global talent showdown : how businesses and communities can partner to rebuild the jobs pipeline / Edward E. Gordon.
        p. cm.
    Includes bibliographical references and index.
    ISBN-13: 978-1-57675-616-4 (hardcover : alk. paper)
    ISBN-13: 978-1-60509-303-1 (pbk. : alk. paper)
    1. Job creation. 2. Ability. 3. Globalization. I. Title.

    HD5713.3.G68 2009
    331.12'042—dc22
                                                                    2009002121

First Edition
12 11 10 09   10 9 8 7 6 5 4 3 2 1

Cover design: Irene Morris Design
Cover photos: People: Amana Images / Hiroshi Yagi / Getty Images
Map: Dustin Steller / Images.com

To my wife, Elaine, whose love is matched only by her thoughtfulness and intelligence.

CONTENTS

PREFACE

A round the world, jobs and labor markets are undergoing a radical transformation. Between 2010 and 2020, much of the world will experience a watershed era of rapid technological, economic, social, and cultural change. This new era will offer more people the promise of high-skill/high-wage careers that also will support broader global economic development—if we can find better ways to create the talent needed to fill these jobs.

Between 2010 and 2020, nations all over the globe will experience profound changes in employment because of scientific and technological advances. *Winning the Global Talent Showdown* shows how the great majority of businesses around the world are underperforming precisely because their most significant assets—their employees' knowledge and talent—are unwittingly being suppressed or underdeveloped. It then reviews specific means that businesses and communities can use to unleash the potential of this untapped talent.

After exhausting all the short-term fixes, business and community leaders are just beginning to face the reality that this is not their parents' workforce anymore. How can business profitably participate? Where will the new career systems first appear? Who will take the risk to introduce them? When will these new job support systems be adopted by a community, state, or nation? How much will taxpayers, businesses, unions, and governments be willing to invest in more effective education-to-employment systems? These are some of the basic questions we will explore in what follows.

What you are about to read in *Winning the Global Talent Showdown* are stories from the firing line, where individuals and groups are waging a successful battle to replace the broken education-to-employment system. The introduction outlines the three major economic and cultural forces that have combined to produce the forthcoming talent showdown: a globalized economy, the combined demographic pressure of massive boomer retirements and falling birthrates, and a breakdown in the global education-to-employment system that has not kept pace with twenty-first-century skill needs and employment aspirations. The clash of these forces has triggered a seemingly contradictory situation in which significant numbers of workers are seeking employment (or even dropping out of the job market) while many employers have trouble filling open positions.

Part 1, "Making Sense of the Talent Shortage Around the World" will show how an imminent global talent shortage now threatens much of the industrialized world. In chapters 1 through 3, we will take a quick trip around the world to better understand the interlocking nature of these problems. Business, community, and government leaders need to understand that the talent shortage is not local, but global. Demographics, the globalized economy, and broken education-to-employment systems are problems around the world. There is no hidden pool of talent out there somewhere.

Because the competition for all kinds of talent is truly world-wide, leaders have to solve the global talent problem in their own countries. We cannot outsource our way out of this shortage. Those days are over. Countries like India that in the past have provided resources for outsourcing are now experiencing their own talent shortages. Nor will immigration solve the problem, because countries like China, once sources of skilled talent, are now luring their expatriate workers home to take advantage of higher wages and a growing economy.

On our world tour we will focus on twenty-five countries that need to play in the new game of global talent successfully if they are to maintain their economic momentum through the next decade. In chapter 1 we will look at the Western Hemisphere, where North,

South, and Central America are experiencing a growing mismatch between popular cultural expectations for employment and the on-rushing jobs revolution that underpins today's tech-based economies. From the heartland of the United States, across Canada, to the cities of Brazil, the future engines of economic growth will be powered by rising numbers of talented cyber-mental workers, but businesses are increasingly having trouble finding them.

Chapter 2 follows the impact of 2 billion low-cost, and mainly low-skill, Indian and Chinese workers flooding the world markets with cheap goods. As millions of jobs are outsourced to Asia, low-skill U.S. and European workers collect unemployment. But recent quality and technology demands reveal that the talent pools of these third-world economies are running dry as they play catch-up with Japan, Korea, and Singapore, their better-educated, higher product-quality neighbors. Many factories in China and India are now installing modern technology that requires maintenance by talented workers with advanced technical and engineering skills. Other high-tech sectors in these economies are also growing.

We will see why raw population numbers and recent explosive economic growth in China and India are misleading indicators of high-tech employability. National pools of available skilled technical talent are surprisingly shallow. Both India and China allegedly graduate about 400,000 engineers each year. Yet according to India's National Association of Software and Service Companies (2005), only about 25 percent are considered suitable for employment. A 2005 McKinsey & Company report found the situation to be similar in China, where only 10 percent of each year's engineering-school graduates meet world-class multinational employment standards.[1] The challenge of the technology paradox for much of Asia is to develop the range of talent needed for modern knowledge-intensive economies from their current weak education critical mass.

Chapter 3 explores how Europe, the United Kingdom, and Russia are now struggling to remain competitive in areas of sophisticated technology and design while low-wage countries make cheaper, more basic products. We will examine population and workforce shrinkages that are driving up wages across Europe, as well as how immigration has strained Germany's educational system to the breaking point. The key issue for the European Union (EU) will be to find a combination of policies that address the root issues of a growing talent meltdown. We will look at both the EU nations that have prospered—like Ireland—and those that have not. In Scandinavia the "Nordic Model" is said to deliver strong growth and low unemployment. However, Norway, Sweden, Denmark, and Finland all have trouble attracting and keeping talented workers. Unlike the rest of Europe, Eastern Europe has a burgeoning population and some of the most motivated and best-educated workers, but low wages and open borders are causing a brain drain and a talent shortage. Finally, we will consider Russia, where plummeting population, a collapsed education system, and a health crisis have produced a rapidly shrinking workforce.

Part 2, "Harnessing the Power of Public-Private Partnerships," focuses on solutions. The major economic shift from basic-skill jobs to knowledge-based jobs requiring higher thinking skills means that knowledge and talent creation have to become every business's business. In this section you will find inspiration and answers from programs around the world that are finding and creating talent.

Chapter 4 offers ways to take advantage of talent that might otherwise be underrepresented or wasted—retiring boomers, women with young children, people with disabilities, former prisoners, and others. For example, in the United Kingdom employers have begun special programs to target at-risk groups currently seen as unemployable. Another U.K. effort, "Target Chances," helps talented graduates with their applications to top employers. "Pure Potential" also helps disadvantaged inner-city youth tap financial aid to study at Britain's leading universities.[2] Chapter 4 also looks at the generational differences affecting the workforce and examines ways to address the work attitudes and career aspirations of Generation X and Generation Y.

Chapter 5 provides compelling case studies of secondary education career initiatives now under way around the world. It focuses on career academies that are preparing students for twenty-first-century careers by combining a strong background in science, technology, and mathematics with components of a liberal arts education. We will see how businesses are providing apprenticeships and other on-the-job experience to expand students' future career opportunities, as employers are no longer waiting passively for additional high-quality talent to emerge. Many businesses are using innovative programs to encourage student interest in careers in science, technology, engineering, and mathematics.

Finally, chapter 6 explores practical ways of creating momentum for local business and community renewal. Businesses have concluded that combining their expertise with the broader influence of local community-based organizations (CBOs) or nongovernment organizations (NGOs) are the best way of addressing the talent sustainability challenge across the United States and around the world. From California to North Carolina to Singapore, local business and community leaders are rebuilding workforce pipelines that retain and attract businesses to their communities. Many of these case studies offer a rich variety of business and broader workforce solutions that can be adapted to local cultures and economies anywhere in the world.

Winning the Global Talent Showdown draws on interviews with diverse experts on the future of jobs and the world economy to probe into the implications of this global shift. These thought leaders represent business, labor, education, and government at local, national, and international levels. They include professionals, managers, and technical or scientific experts drawn from many fields.

But experts are not the only ones who are concerned about the talent pipeline. These leaders are joined by parents and students, who increasingly want to become better informed about the radically changing job and career environment. I have also spoken with community activists engaged in the reinvention of their local labor-market economy. They have shared with me a growing sense of renewal and hope in the values of democratic self-governance and active citizenship as they mobilize their communities to change cultural perspectives and forge new talent pathways to prosperity in the twenty-first century.

My book *The 2010 Meltdown: Solving the Impending Jobs Crisis* was published in 2005. Since then I have networked with leaders from the United States, Canada, Latin America, Europe, and Asia to discuss the book's central theme—the implications of imminent baby-boomer retirements and the smaller, less well-prepared cadre now entering the workforce. I have seen a near-universal consensus forming that the current "education-to-employment system" is badly broken. This is the talent-building process we have all experienced in which K-12 education, career education, and the world of work are sharply compartmentalized, with little communication between those engaged in each sector. There are increasing shortages of talented people inside service businesses, the professions, manufacturing, and other industrial sectors. Different economic factors (for example, oil, housing, inflation, and immigration) may periodically minimize these trends, but over the next decade they will not reverse this global talent showdown. During the past several years, I personally have observed a true transformation of individual cultural attitudes concerning the risk of a worldwide talent crisis.

We are slowly beginning to witness an increase in employee training and development inside businesses. A substantive refocus of community efforts has begun to raise the quality and to diversify education content so that many more students will meet the talent demands of a global technology-based economy.

Economic change is a messy process, and in practice, countries and businesses are still struggling to make it work in this transitional talent era. We all know how this story is going to end. Sometime in the future, the world's talent pool will begin catching up to the economic realities of the twenty-first century. But history teaches us that nations are wiser to defuse such anxieties with transformational change of "the system" rather than waiting for a "big bang" collapse. *Winning the Global Talent Showdown* will show you how to tackle the talent shortage now.

INTRODUCTION:
What's Causing the Global Talent Crunch?

We live in a moment in history when change is so speeded up that we begin to see the present only when it is already disappearing.

—R. D. Laing

Experts are beginning to say the same thing: Where is the talent? Numerous reports have clearly documented the growing talent crunch in the United States and many other countries.

Through economic ups and downs for companies of all sizes, talent availability has remained a major issue. In April 2006 the National Federation of Independent Business reported that 31 percent of its members had one or more unfilled positions for which they could not find qualified applicants. In November 2008 as a world economic crisis dominated media headlines, 100 CEOs of top U.S. corporations still identified obtaining an educated workforce as one of their highest priorities.[1]

Talent shortages are not confined to the United States. A 2008 Manpower Inc. Annual Talent Shortage Survey polled 43,000 employers in thirty-two nations and reports that "31 percent of employers world-wide are having difficulty filling positions due to the lack of suitable talent available in their markets."[2]

Manpower's CEO and chairman, Jeffrey Joerres, agreed: "The talent shortage is becoming a reality for a larger number of employers around the world. . . . This is not a cyclical trend, as we have seen in the past, this time the talent crunch is for real, and it's going to last for decades."[3]

THE CYBER-MENTAL AGE

This is not the first time in human history in which there has been a gut-wrenching transformation in the nature of work. There have been at least five previous labor-market eras: prehistory, the Agricultural Age, the Industrial Age, the Computer Age, and the emerging Cyber-Mental Age. (See Figure 1.) There often has been significant turmoil in labor markets during past watershed transition periods. Such turmoil is increasingly apparent today as many individuals struggle to make the transition from low-tech to high-tech and from low-skill to higher-skill occupations.

Yet today there are significant differences from the previous

Figure 1: Five Labor-Market Eras

	I	II	III	IV	V
Era	Prehistory	Agricultural Age	Industrial Age	Computer Age	Cyber-Mental Age
Time	100,000– 5,000 BC	5,000 BC– 1850 A.D.	1850–1970	1970–2010	2010–?
Focus	Survival	Food	Machines	Automation	Innovations
Result	Subsistence agriculture	Farming	Mass production	Data/robotics	Intelligent machines
People	Irregular labor	Hand labor	Semiskilled labor	Skilled labor	Knowledge labor

Source: Edward E. Gordon, 2009.

eras. As Figure 2 shows, the time span of each labor era is dramatically compressing. Agricultural labor dominated most of recorded human history. The age of industrial mass production lasted only about 120 years. The Computer Age brought hardware and software that structured the rapid retrieval of stored data for myriad uses; this has transformed almost every industry and spawned the development of numerous new ones. Yet this age has lasted only around forty years. The information technology (IT) industry is now undergoing a revolution larger than any we have ever seen.

An emerging Cyber-Mental Age will give the well-educated person the power to innovate products and services by using very advanced technologies to precisely locate and combine data, rather than drowning in a rising sea of random or ill-organized raw information. This assumes that people have the knowledge and preparation to use such technologies—that is, a great liberal arts education plus specific career education and skills in a professional or technical area.

WHAT IS CAUSING THE TALENT SHORTAGE?

What is behind these deep talent shortages that now confront much of the world? Three major economic and cultural forces have combined to produce this global talent showdown: a worldwide demographic shift, globalization, and a broken talent-preparation system.

Workforce Demographics

Between 1946 and 1964, following World War II, the baby boomer generation swelled populations around the globe. This generation constitutes a vast cohort that is aging. Soon baby boomers will begin retiring.[4]

In contrast, fertility ratios have declined in the generations following the boomers. This is particularly the case in many wealthy, upwardly mobile nations. Many of these nations are not even at a replacement birthrate (2.1 births per woman).

According to United Nation projections, by 2020 the number of people over age sixty in the United States, Japan, and Europe will equal the working-age population. Between 22 percent and 34 percent of the population will be age sixty and over.[5] As these nations have grown more affluent over the past fifty years, birthrates have halved. It is projected that because of immigration the U.S. population will continue to grow until 2050 and then stabilize. But Japan and much of Europe will experience an absolute population decline of between 10 percent and 25 percent.[6]

Both population decline and aging pose massive fiscal and cultural challenges that business and political leaders have been slow to grasp. In Finland, for example, the aging population is the fastest-growing in Europe. As a result, over the next decade Finland will be caught between rising pensions and health care costs, while it faces a shrinking workforce and competitive pressures in many industrial sectors. By 2015 even China faces falling off the same demographic cliff.[7]

In the United States, baby boomers are reaching age sixty at the rate of 8,000-plus a day and are retiring from the workforce even faster. On October 15, 2007, Kathleen Casey-Kirschling, a retired New Jersey teacher, applied for Social Security benefits, the nation's first baby boomer to do so. Born one second after midnight on January 1, 1946, she initiates the coming avalanche of generational changes. The U.S. Department of Labor predicts that between 2010 and 2020, 70 million Americans will retire, but only 40 million will enter the workforce.[8]

The basic message is twofold. First, do not exaggerate the impact of demographic change alone. The people who will enter the workforce from now until 2025 are already in the pipeline. Beyond then, birthrates can alter rapidly. During America's Great Depression of the 1930s, birthrates plummeted. It was predicted that the U.S. population would begin declining by 1946. World War II changed everything: instead, the baby-boomer generation began in

1946. This generation forms the greatest population bulge in recorded history.

The governments of many developed nations have recently responded to the current "baby bust" with "baby bonuses" to boost birthrates. Italy pays about $5,000 annually. Other countries—including Australia, Canada, Germany, the United Kingdom, Cyprus, and Singapore—are also beginning to offer such subsidies. France recently reported an uptick in the birthrate that, at least in part, is credited to this program.[9]

Secondly, demographics may not be destiny. I agree with author Joel Garreau when he says, "But the numerical study of who we are and how we got that way does have a refreshing habit of focusing our attention on what's important, long-term, about our culture and values—where we're headed and what makes us tick."[10] Significant population decline may give us an opportunity to rethink how we will raise the next generation.

The Globalized Economy

The second force driving the worldwide talent shortage is globalization. For many people, globalization means sending low-skill jobs overseas. Others think it helps the United States import high-skill foreign talent using special H 1-B visas. Some in business see globalization as the means of owning and investing in overseas high-skill production facilities through foreign direct investment.

Globalization is all of these and more. Its current spread has become intertwined with the information and communication revolution that occurred just as the Communist bloc was dissolving in the early 1990s.

Over the last twenty years, we have witnessed the sudden entry into the global economy of two vast new sources of hard-working, cheap labor—India and China. China alone has 50 percent more people than the combined population of today's advanced nations.[11]

But demographics alone do not predict economic destiny. According to a 2005 McKinsey and Company report, less than 10 percent of the 1.6 million young Chinese engineers are suitable to work for a foreign company in fields such as engineering, finance, and the life sciences. In the same way, a 2005 study by India's National Association of Software and Service Companies and McKinsey & Company found that only about 25 percent of engineering graduates and 10 percent to 15 percent of general college graduates have acceptable business skills for employment in international companies.[12]

As the demand for skilled workers in China and India increases faster than the supply, wages are rising rapidly. More high-skill Chinese and Indian immigrants in the United States are now returning home. In Bangalore, India, alone, 30,000 to 40,000 Indians have gone back in the past decade. For the past twenty years, H 1-B visas for these foreign high-tech and other professional workers have helped fill significant skilled-talent shortfalls across U.S. business. What will happen now as the United States and other countries compete to attract foreign talent as replacement workers for their shrinking workforces?[13]

Though globalization has meant increased mobility for businesses and workers, the regrettable truth is that a finite pool of talent exists worldwide and it falls significantly short of meeting worldwide demands. Not enough workers in the United States and elsewhere are equipped for today's pace of change in which jobs come and go and skills can quickly become obsolete. This means the U.S. labor-market-preparation system must equip more people with the general and career technical skills that make them mobile. None of this comes cheap, and much of it takes years to reach fruition.[14]

The Education-to-Employment System

Technology shows no signs of slowing down. Breathtaking developments seem just over the horizon. Nanotechnology is producing innovations on a molecular scale. Service robots already paint cars and scrub out nuclear reactors, and nearly 2 million of them were in private and domestic use in 2005. Virgin Galactic promises space planes that will travel from one side of the planet to the other in ninety minutes. Plastic chips herald a new area of very cheap, "intelligent" electronics.[15]

Technology is great—when it works. When it fails, we need skilled people who can fix it fast. Increasingly, support for our sophisticated technological and physical infrastructure is in short supply because the global labor-market preparation system has not kept pace with twenty-first-century skill needs.

In 2005 and 2006, for example, Los Angeles and New York experienced widespread blackouts blamed on technician errors. Across the United States refineries are breaking down with unusual frequency. Though BP and other refiners are making major safety changes, the breakdowns frequently stem from technician error due to increasing shortages of trained workers. In the Kansas City area, new homeowners are being hit by huge house repair bills because "a less-skilled work force" has not "kept pace with new technologies." Two-thirds of New York City's subway elevators in 2007 had at least one breakdown that trapped passengers inside. The system's 169 escalators averaged sixty-eight breakdowns or repairs each. This is after New York City Transit spent about $1 billion to install new elevators and escalators. The problem: they do not have enough competent people with proper training.[16] "More and more it seems that the world will end, not with an explosion, but with a slow grinding halt as everything just stops working," muses Arnold Brown, chairman of the World Future Society.[17]

More complex technology demands more talent in the workforce. However, just as universal demand for more talented people in the workforce is developing, a major shortage of appropriately skilled people is taking hold around the world.

We are beginning to run out of younger, skilled, entry-level workers particularly, but not exclusively, in careers related to science, technology, engineering, and mathematics (STEM). The Organisation for Economic Co-operation and Development's (OECD) 2007 annual labor study of thirty leading industrial countries shows that the spread of computer technology is the chief cause of the widening gap between the incomes of low-skill and high-skill workers.[18]

Too many job-seekers lack literacy, experience, education, and specialized career training. A rising tide of applicants does not meet the minimum qualifications for an increasingly sophisticated world of work. The 2008 Manpower survey reported that the hardest-to-fill jobs worldwide included engineers, technicians, machinists, mechanics, and IT staff.

Over the next decade, the talent creation and distribution system will need to be seriously overhauled. Recruiting, retaining, and developing skilled people will become so challenging that increasing numbers of businesses will be forced out of existence.[19]

The Effect of Computers on the Job Market

In the 1950s and early 1960s, the introduction of computers into the workplace led to the popular outcry that "automation" would lead to mass unemployment. In 1964 the Ad Hoc Committee on the Triple Revolution sent a fourteen-page memorandum signed by several Nobel-Prize-winning scientists warning President Lyndon Johnson that "a new era of production has begun. . . . The cybernation revolution . . . results in a system of almost unlimited productive capacity which requires progressively less human labor."[20]

However, computers did not create mass unemployment. From the 1950s until today, the IT revolution created myriads of new products and services. But computers also created a major upheaval in the nature of human work.

According to Frank Levy and Richard J. Murname, authors of *The New Dimension of Labor: How Computers Are Creating the Next Job Market*, the end result of computerization has been that the number of "middle jobs" in offices and manufacturing companies (that is, filing, bookkeeping, order taking, installing windshields on automobile bodies, and so forth) is shrinking. On the other hand, the more complex jobs that require analysis and higher levels of thinking, literacy, and specialized career and technical knowledge are growing in number. This has caused a jobs revolution in almost every workplace.

As an example, look at the heavy-equipment manufacturer John Deere in Peoria, Illinois. About half of Deere's salaried employees are engineers, but this company also needs hundreds more technicians who know about satellite guidance, artificial intelligence, telematics, and other leading-edge technical processes. Then there are Deere's hourly employees who operate a computer- or robotic-driven assembly-line to manufacture tractors and other heavy equipment. Because of the increasing use of technology over the past thirty years, fewer people now operate that line, but these automotive manufacturing technicians must know more and be able to adapt the technology to make a greater diversity of products. What this means is that Deere now has to compete with other high-tech companies for the same shrinking technical talent pool.[21]

The technology metamorphosis that hit farming in 1900 has now moved on to revolutionize U.S. manufacturing employment. This helps explain the development of the myth of America's so-called postindustrial economy. Do not believe this myth. According to the Bureau of Economic Analysis, the output of American manufacturing has more than doubled to a total of $1.6 trillion in the past twenty-five years. The United States produces 25 percent of the world's manufactured goods, and more than 60 percent of U.S. exports are manufactured goods.

Though U.S. manufacturing employment has dramatically fallen since the 1970s (from 25 million to 14 million), manufacturing has experienced much of the same productivity gains as the American farm industry through applied technologies and rapid innovation. This is due to a 36 percent shift in manufacturing to higher skill levels between 1982 and 2002. As a result, between 1985 and 2005, manufacturing productivity increased 94 percent, as opposed to just 38 percent for services and other business sectors. This has caused a fall in the price of manufactured goods relative to services throughout the U. S. economy. Future economic growth will hinge to a large extent on the ability of U.S. manufacturing to employ new technologies and increase innovation.[22]

All of the above shifts are affecting the rest of the world. Today China and India are struggling to resolve the issue of what to do with the peasant farmers who make up the bulk of their population. How can China and India create new jobs for them as technology raises agricultural productivity and transforms agricultural practices?

In Europe newer technologies are transforming industries. Yet, new tech breakthrough product or services industries are lagging behind due to significant talent shortages. Fewer younger workers are enrolling in educational programs that prepare them for these emerging careers and jobs opportunities.

Technology will also enable work to be digitalized and moved anywhere on the planet. As a result, the countries of the world will have to become increasingly reliant on the quality of their workers' knowledge to compete. It is impossible for any nation to sustain economic development without an appropriately talented workforce.

The world has entered a time of historic transformation—a Cyber-Mental Age. To a large degree, today's talent showdown has been triggered by the unprecedented speed at which we are moving into this new Cyber-Mental Age. How fast can we speed up society's cultural adjustment to these new realities? We need to fix a broken education-to-career system that is out of sync with the practical need to develop all forms of student intelligence. People need to be better prepared for a different cultural reality: jobs that are built upon a knowledge economy.

How can businesses and the communities in which they operate best be mobilized to effect these changes? As the later chapters of *Winning the Global Talent Showdown* will show, community-based organizations (CBOs) or nongovernment organizations (NGOs) are being formed in the United States and many other nations to address the dramatic labor imbalance. What are these CBOs and NGOs doing? At least in part they are supporting training and education for the new global tech economy fashioned to the special needs of employers, communities, and the diverse talents of people in the workforce. To find talented people, businesses are increasing their commitment to higher-quality education across cities, regions, and nations in both the liberal arts and math and sciences to create a broader and deeper talent pipeline. They are also working with students as young as kindergarten-age to encourage them to consider careers in science and technology.

Businesses around the world have come to the conclusion that combining their expertise with that of CBOs and NGOs is the best way to create sustainable talent for the future. CBOs and NGOs are culturally bound together by something more than just self-interest, the pursuit of private economic advantage. This is the true secret behind the CBO and NGO success story.

The basic message of *Winning the Global Talent Showdown* is that community action can make this happen. Everyone can participate in some meaningful way. We need your hands-on leadership.

UNLOCKING THE FUTURE

Throughout the world, labor markets are seriously out of sync with global technological realities. The business community can avoid this talent catastrophe by finally getting serious about the overhaul of the entire education-to-employment system. This business role will be critical in helping labor markets adjust to escalating national and global talent requirements.

Changing this system will take time and will not be cheap. Technology will continue to alter the nature of work and the knowledge that people will need.

CONCLUSION

In the long run, the worldwide labor market will probably adjust to the three economic and cultural forces we have just reviewed: the demographic shift, globalization, and an outdated talent-preparation system. But when will this adjustment be completed? What will be the ultimate cost for business? How many Americans will have higher-wage jobs? Where can business begin to make these transitions? Who will provide the local community and business leadership? Why can we not just muddle through all this, as we have always done before?

This global talent showdown may be a source of anxiety for some in businesses. It should not be. For in the chapters that follow you will discover not only the depth of these issues, but also the new economic opportunities for businesses and communities of all sizes that are willing to invest in developing the minds, spirit, and hearts of ordinary people.

MAKING SENSE OF THE TALENT SHORTAGE AROUND THE WORLD

After our review of the three principal issues driving the global talent showdown, we are ready to embark on a talent exploration around the world—first across the Americas, then to Asia and Europe. We seek to discover how business and society will address shortfalls in their current and future local and national talent pool.

What criteria can we use to select specific nations for our itinerary? In each region, we will focus on the current most successful players in the new game of global talent. These twenty-five countries have a great deal at stake if they are to maintain their economic momentum through the next decade.

We will examine succinctly the current business climate, the talent pool, and the outlook for the future, then look at how the three major forces—demographics, globalization, and the education-to-employment system—are affecting skill demands in the region. Where is the country's talent coming from? How effective is a nation's current talent system at satisfying current and future talent requirements? These are a few of the pertinent questions that we will need to answer while on our tour.

Be prepared for some unexpected bumps along our talent road. The ways in which culture and talent blend in each nation can at times offer business many unique challenges.

CHAPTER 1

THE AMERICAS

Latin America faces a critical choice. It is a choice between the past and the future . . . a commitment to sustainable human development.

—Felipe Calderón, President of Mexico

We will begin our world tour with the Western Hemisphere as we examine how the global talent showdown is affecting North, Central, and South America. The United States will be our first stop. In late 2007 the World Economic Forum, a Swiss-based think tank, gave the United States the top spot in its annual report on global competitiveness. It praised the United States' market efficiency and ability to innovate. This ranking may not last, however, because the U.S. talent pool is drying up. An obsolete twentieth-century education-to-employment system can no longer cope with the realities of a twenty-first-century global labor market.

Until 2010 overall growth in the U.S. workforce will be sustained by importing foreign workers and by members of the echoboom generation (the children of the baby boomers, sometimes called Generation Y or the Millennial Generation) who have reached working age. However, in 2008 labor-force growth began dropping to near zero and is predicted to remain there until 2030. Labor shortages have begun to grow across the country in a broad range of employment sectors, leading to wage inflation as employers compete for fewer and fewer talented people to fill vacant critical positions across the entire economy even as many are left unemployed.

To the north, Canada's economy is booming, but over the next decade (2010 to 2020) the Canadian labor market is expected to experience a serious talent shortage of up to 1 million workers. Already, the Canadian Federation of Independent Business reports that 60 percent of its Alberta membership has been experiencing "the highest level ever" in unfilled jobs. Until now, Canada has depended on skilled immigrants from China and India, but the expanding economies and opportunities in those countries are luring their workers back home.[1]

The Canadian talent squeeze will also be driven by education and generational career issues. More than 40 percent of all workers in both Canada and the United States have basic workforce education skill deficiencies that contribute to decreased personal on-the-job performance, productivity, innovations, and quality.

After Canada, we will travel to Latin America to look closely at how the global talent shortage is affecting the economies of four countries: Brazil, Chile, Mexico, and Costa Rica. Economic stability and a new middle class have brought new prosperity to the region. Regional poverty has been reduced to 35 percent of the people, and unemployment in 2007 fell by 8 percent. Child labor has plummeted, and more children are being educated. But is all of this good enough?

Though Latin America's recent economic progress has been encouraging, its rate of growth has been far less than that achieved by many Asian nations, where we will continue our journey in chapter 2. For now, we will examine the workforce challenges confronting the United States.

THE UNITED STATES

The forces of globalization and technology have raised most Americans' standard of living, increased worker productivity, and boosted business profits, and they continue to drive the future's job picture. However, most Americans do not yet accept the "price" of this growth. Twenty-first-century technology requires even larger cohorts of American workers who are both well educated and possess specialized technical career knowledge. Regrettably, only about 25 percent of America's current eligible workers comfortably meet these criteria.

Since the 1950s, unskilled jobs have been disappearing from the U.S. economy. Even before globalization and the outsourcing of these jobs had picked up steam, unskilled jobs began a steady decline (from about 60 percent to slightly more than 20 percent of all jobs). Simultaneously, skilled occupations requiring specific technical knowledge have steadily increased (from about 28 percent to 68 percent by 2000).

This trend will only accelerate during the next decade. Seventy-five percent of U.S. jobs will begin to require the minimum of both a good liberal-arts-based general education plus postsecondary technical training (for example, four- or two-year degrees, two- or one-year certificates, or apprenticeships).

Workforce Demographics

The massive retirement of the baby-boomer cohort and an end to the rise in the employment rate of women will combine to produce a dramatic drop in long-term U.S. workforce growth beginning in 2008 and extending to 2020 and beyond. The influx of immigrants will have only a limited impact on these trends. The United States does not attract nearly enough high-skill foreign talent to keep pace with the demands of both new job growth and the massive number of replacement workers needed for the departing boomers. The showdown for talent will reach across every state in America.

The U.S. Department of Labor's occupational employment projections help explain what is happening. Between 2006 and 2016, 50.8 million job openings are expected across the economy. But new jobs will number only 17.4 million, whereas replacement jobs will be nearly twice as many at 33.4 million. This means that retirements will account for 66 percent of the jobs to be filled.

Many occupations face a steep job replacement curve. In 2007, 52 percent of U.S. engineers and scientists were over age fifty. About half of all government workers were also approaching the same age. This was also the case for skilled machinists and metal workers.[2]

Globalization

If all this is true, skeptics might ask, how does the United States remain the world's leading high-tech economy? The answer is foreign-born students. The annual survey of the National Opinion Research Center at the University of Chicago found that foreign students constituted 44 percent of received science and engineering doctorates in 2006. U.S. citizens earned only 32 percent of engineering degrees and 47 percent in the physical sciences. It would seem that U.S. culture is not into science anymore.[3] There are broad economic ramifications to this cultural decision.

Whether it is cell phones, computers, automobiles, CDs, DVDs, medicine, or aerospace, advanced manufacturing applies cutting edge concepts in electronics, computers, software, and automation performed by highly educated technicians. A 2007 Manpower Survey, the National Association of Manufacturers, and the Manufacturing Institute all report that STEM jobs are the hardest to fill. Wages are rapidly rising. More dollars will chase less talent over the next decade.

Joel Leonard, a technical jobs expert, explains that "Many complain that our society's view of the mechanic of yesterday hasn't caught up with the realities of today, and as a result, business growth is stalled." We are caught in a technological dead-end scenario, "since thus far automated machines don't repair themselves," Leonard reminds us.[4]

For some, this forthcoming "labor shortage can be a blessing, not a curse," says Michael Lind, Whitehead senior fellow at the New America Foundation. "Where labor is scarce and expensive, businesses have an incentive to invest in labor-saving technology which boosts productivity growth by enabling fewer workers to produce more." This is the current Japanese business model, found in a government white paper, "A Strategy for Growth." Japan's aim is to become the world leader in developing sophisticated new products that have big price tags by having manufacturers focus on high-value production, in contrast to their low-cost Chinese rivals.[5]

U.S. high-tech manufacturers want to follow the same strategy. Yet they fail to recognize a fundamental difference between Japan and the United States. For decades Japan's business community has heavily invested in continuous workforce training. Also, Japan's schools may be largely rote-learning machines, but every high school senior studies calculus. High-value production using the latest advanced labor-saving technology requires a highly skilled workforce. Japan has attained one; the United States has not.

The Education-to-Employment System

More than 90 million U.S. workers currently lack the reading, writing, and math skills to do their jobs properly. Finding competent people is very difficult. Both U.S. and international studies have repeatedly confirmed that the Achilles heel of America's economy is its undereducated workforce.

National Adult Literacy Assessments were conducted by the U.S. government in 1992 and in 2003. They showed little, if any, literacy improvements between those years, and even some declines at the highest levels of literacy. About 95 million adults are reading at or below the eighth-grade level of reading comprehension, disqualifying them for most well-paying jobs. Even more disturbing is the finding that among recent college graduates, prose proficiency (advanced reading comprehension) dropped from 91 percent in 1992 to 72 percent in 2003.[6] This means that their critical competencies (critical thinking skills) are weak.

The Organisation for Economic Co-operation and Development (OECD) has conducted the Programme for International Student Assessment (PISA), testing fifteen-year-olds from OECD nations and others every three years. In 2003 American students ranked twenty-fourth out of twenty-nine developed nations in math literacy and problem solving.[7]

Aligned to these dismal results is the gradual decline of SAT and ACT college entrance exam scores since the 1970s. Though 64 percent of high school graduating seniors enter some form of postsecondary education, only 25 percent of those beginning postsecondary education eventually graduate with a college degree. This is the lowest "survival rate" in any of the major developed countries.[8]

Forty years ago the United States was the undisputed leader in educating its population. Even though America's technological progress increased the demand for talented people, the U.S. education system increased the supply of them even faster. But over the last few decades the education-to-employment system has begun to fray. Technology has increased its pace, whereas educational advancement and talent creation have slowed down.[9]

If U.S. competitiveness is to continue growing, more business profits need to be placed back into raising worker productivity through investing in a renewed education-to-employment system.[10] Many of the jobs going begging require considerable education or specialized technical training, certification, or apprenticeship.[11]

Even the U.S. Pentagon is increasingly importing software and hardware from non–U.S. companies. The so-called Berry Amendment requires the Pentagon to purchase specialty metals from U.S. sources. For national security reasons, national defense contractors must also employ U.S. citizens to build aerospace and military hardware. With an increasing shortage of qualified U.S. tech workers, many Pentagon staffers and defense contractors would like Congress to jettison these restrictions. U.S. defense and aerospace are one of the few bright spots left in U.S. foreign exports. Unless steps are taken, this U.S. industrial base is running the risk of being seriously eroded.[12]

By 2020 the United States needs to accomplish a serious overhaul of its entire education-to-employment system. If it stays on its present course, the alternate scenario might divide the United States into two classes—the first, college-educated managers, professionals, and technicians; the second, the poorly educated, dropouts, immigrants, and others without special career skills who will be trapped in low-wage service jobs. As we shall see, we could write the same message for other developed nations around the world.[13]

But none of this grim scenario has been fixed in the stars. A positive future economic course is already being plotted in many communities in the United States and other nations.

About 15 percent, or 2,000, of U.S. high schools produce about 50 percent of its dropouts. Researchers at the University of Pennsylvania and the Philadelphia Education Fund termed them "dropout factories." Half of these academies to nowhere are in big cities. The rest are mainly in the American South and Southwest. "What we do know is that the number of high schools with weak promoting power (to the next grade level) has nearly doubled in the last decade," these researchers concluded.[14]

The long-term consequences of doing nothing over the next decade to reduce this immense U.S. techno-peasant underclass will be catastrophic for the future talent needed by the high-tech U.S. economy.

American high school graduation rates are bleaker for minority populations: 52 percent for Hispanic students, 56 percent for African-American students, and 57 percent for Native American students, as opposed to 78 percent for white students (Alliance for Excellent

Education). The U.S. Census Bureau tells us that between 2010 and 2020, most of the population growth (from 282 million in 2000 to 336 million in 2020) will occur within minority populations. Patrick Kelly, senior associate at the National Center for Higher Education Management Systems, foresees an overall decline of 2.5 percent in the number of U.S. adults ages twenty-five to sixty-four attaining a high school diploma or higher, if current dropout trends are not corrected. The talent pool will constrict further rather than expand. There will be 7 million more adult dropouts in 2020 than in 2010.[15]

Fortunately for the United States, most of its teenagers do graduate from high school. The great cultural irony is that these young people are eager consumers of technology, but not interested in working in technology careers. Ask the question, "What do you want to be when you grow up?" It is very unlikely that "systems analyst," "software engineer," or "industrial/civil engineer" will appear high on a list of career interests.

The unpleasant cultural fact for the U.S. tech-based economy is that careers in IT and other STEM professions are not as popular among schoolchildren as they were twenty years ago. Teens are more interested in careers in law, finance, marketing, graphic design, professional sports, and communications. Many STEM career areas will need considerably more workers over the next decade. Yet, a 2007 survey of fourteen- and fifteen-year-olds conducted by the Institution of Engineering and Technology showed that 90 percent of these teens knew "little or nothing" about careers in STEM.

On average, dwindling numbers of students enroll every year in STEM-related course areas in secondary schools and colleges. Between 2000 and 2004, the number of computer science majors dropped 60 percent. Andrew Herbert, head of the Microsoft Research Cambridge Laboratory, said, "As an industry, we have an image problem, and it's time we recognized that, so we can start putting it right."[16]

Considerable evidence exists that young adults who go into

STEM-based careers generally learned to love science when they were children, says Rena Dorph, the lead researcher of a new survey from the Lawrence Hall of Science at the University of California, Berkeley and WestEd, a San Francisco education think tank. Yet ten times as many teachers say they feel unprepared to teach science than say they feel unprepared to teach math or reading. In a 2007 survey of 923 San Francisco Bay Area elementary school teachers, 80 percent said they spent less than an hour each week teaching science. Just as the U.S. economy is increasingly science based, these schools have cut science instruction in half over the past seven years. This seems a disconnect with reality. It is hardly surprising that fewer than half of Bay Area fifth-graders scored at or above grade level in science on the 2007 California Standards Test.[17]

What the Business Community Can Do

The U.S. business community has been slow to recognize the need to fix the education-to-employment system. A consensus is lacking among business leaders and other experts.

Balancing short-term and long-term profits has to be set in the context of acknowledging that U.S. business has a wider corporate social responsibility in society. A practical solution is broader investment by large and small businesses in updated community education. A number of businesses are already playing a leading role in helping to expand the proportion of highly skilled Americans who can fill the widening talent shortfalls of every U.S. community.[18] In part 2 we will examine some of the ways they are doing this.

Corporate leadership in these areas was more prominent in the past. Large corporations like RCA, Xerox, and AT&T operated large internal research laboratories. Bell Labs, part of the old AT&T, created the world's first transistor. According to Stanford professor G. Pascal Zachary, "These corporate labs were essentially research universities embedded in private companies, and their employees published academic papers, spoke at conferences, and even gave away valuable breakthroughs." They also encouraged the development of a technical workforce consisting of not only scientists, but also specialized technical assistants. Victims of cost cutting, few corporate labs are left. Microsoft, however, continues to increase its research labs and gives free rein to the scientists in them. The company has labs in six locations, including the United States, China, India, and England.[19]

More recent arrangements are formal partnerships between companies like Intel and laboratories at Berkeley, the University of Washington, and Carnegie Mellon. This newer model of marrying research and markets is in its infancy. Besides the ability to deliver real benefits, can it also encourage an interest in STEM-related careers in local communities across the United States?

The real issue is a U.S. corporate culture dominated by "short-termism." According to "Built to Last: Focusing Corporations on Long-Term Performance," a report by the Committee for Economic Development, preoccupation with the short term was responsible for an excessive focus on the next quarter's profits at the expense of the organization's long-term viability.[20] In many more cases, short-termism has led to cuts in vital areas of long-term investment.[21]

Businesses may proudly proclaim that "In an age of technology, people make the difference." Yet investment in companies' human capital still remains a low priority. More executives and small business owners need to make the connection between the radical changes under way in the national talent pool and how they might be addressed through human capital investment.

CANADA

Let us now journey to the United States' northern neighbor and consider how Canada is responding to these complex talent issues.

By 2007 the Canadian economy was running well above capacity, causing widespread labor shortages. That year, the Canadian

Federation of Independent Business reported job vacancies at an all-time high in many Canadian provinces, with more than 251,000 long-term unfilled jobs in both small and medium-size business sectors. Vacancies grew from 2004 onward. They included positions requiring a college education or specialized technical or apprenticeship education.[22]

With a population that is slightly more than 10 percent than that of the United States, Canada has the world's second-largest land mass. This translates into high infrastructure costs to support a modern, high-tech economy. Canada contributes a mere 3 percent to world scientific and technology research. But in 2007 Canada exceeded China in exports to the United States—$261 billion to $260 billion, providing the United States with more than 2 million barrels of oil daily. It has become the number one source of oil for the United States. With the expansion of Canada's gigantic deposits of oil sands in the Athabasca region of northern Alberta Province, the key to the country's future economy will be energy in all of its forms.[23]

Workforce Demographics

Between 2010 and 2025, the number of Canadians over age sixty-five will rise considerably. As retirements escalate, the overall size of the workforce will shrink. In addition, different sectors of Canada's economy (for example, health care and energy-related industries) will experience rapid growth. Others will seek large numbers of replacements for aging baby boomers who are retiring (for example, highly skilled metal workers and machinists). These business sectors will have significant difficulties in filling their job vacancies.[24]

Globalization

Even more than the United States, Canada has had an immigrant-driven workforce, and today's immigrants are increasingly non-European. Canada's immigration policy is based on a points system, tilted toward attracting highly skilled foreigners to fill its vacant jobs.

According to the OECD, 18.2 percent of Canada's 33 million inhabitants were born outside the country. (This compares with 12.2 percent for the United States.)[25]

Yet relying so heavily on immigrants to underpin Canadian workforce growth has grave dangers. In the global war for talent, most developed nations in Europe and Asia are also easing restrictions on the entry of skilled workers. As we will see, some are going even further and offering economic incentives.

Immigration will not be the magic bullet that solves Canada's workforce talent needs. A preponderance of Canadian immigrants have come from India and China, and these nations are now successfully attracting them to return home. As their economies continue to expand, India and China too are seeking to fill higher-skilled jobs with higher wages that by 2010 will often reach parity with the West.[26]

Canada as a whole desperately needs more workers. One example is Alberta's plan to accelerate crude oil production from oil sands. This is being threatened by an increasing shortage of skilled energy workers. In 2007 unemployment hovered at a thirty-three-year low of 6 percent nationally, and in Alberta at 3 percent. The energy industry, in particular, is in a bidding war for labor. It is getting ever more difficult to locate technical staff for oil-and-natural gas operations not just in Alberta, but also for energy fields off of Nova Scotia and Newfoundland, as well as in Saskatchewan. Canadian operations have embarked on recruiting campaigns in the United States, and as far afield as Venezuela and South Africa to ease this talent shortage.[27]

The Western oil boom is also having the unwelcome effect of draining other Canadian provinces of their workforce. Nova Scotia has been particularly hard hit. Net migration to Alberta has tripled since 2004. Though some workers spend one week a month back home, many others, especially young men, never return to Nova Scotia. The irony is that the development of oil-and-gas fields between Nova Scotia and Newfoundland has also created a demand for technical workers. Frank Corbett, a member of the Nova Scotia legislature assembly, has seen his constituency shrink by 20 percent over the past decade. "We're seeing highly skilled people leaving [Nova Scotia] on an education we paid for. Alberta is getting a great deal here," he laments.[28] The current recession will only temporarily relieve some of these worker shortages. With a resurgence in energy demands, skilled worker shortages will increase over the long term.

The Education-to-Employment System

Canada's education-to-employment system is in need of a serious shake-up. Two international literacy surveys conducted by the OECD and ABC Canada provide some startling statistics. Of the 18.5 million adult Canadians (ages sixteen to sixty-five), about 42 percent read below the eighth-grade level. These adults are at greatest risk of losing low-skill jobs that are readily outsourced or replaced by technology. They are also at a disadvantage in facing complex job demands such as problem solving, prioritizing, multitasking, learning new job skills, or working on a team.[29]

Yet, as in the United States, Canada's literacy problems are not simply confined to the adult population. An alarming 30 percent of high school students drop out of school in Ontario, Canada's industrial heartland, points out Mary Anne Chambers, the province's minister of training.[30] Like their U.S. counterparts, very few Canadian students are enrolling in programs preparing them for STEM or professional service careers.

Too many students lack the information and motivation to enroll in career-education programs designed to meet the staffing needs of local employers. At the same time, employers complain they cannot find local entry-level talent. Instead of investing in meaningful local career-development systems, businesses cast their nets around the world looking to import qualified talent.[31]

According to the Conference Board of Canada, the nation still has several advantages. In comparison to other industrial nations, Canada has the highest percentage of labor-force participants with postsecondary degrees and thus far has attracted a large pool of talented immigrants. But the comparative amount that business invests in systematic job-related training and career education to prepare students is relatively low and has remained flat for the past decade.

For Canadian business, the reason may be a culture focused on pursuing publicly funded solutions. Historically, this largely has been the Canadian approach to its economy. In the nation's early beginnings as a very sparsely settled frontier society, Canadians often had little choice other than for government to provide essential infrastructure and support for commerce. Canada was also part of the British colonial system that continued well into the twentieth century. Old traditions die hard.

Unfortunately for Canada as a capitalist country in the twenty-first century, this tradition has resulted in a large, multilayered education-to-employment bureaucracy that chokes innovation and change. This has contributed to poorer returns on investment in training and education by public and private entities. Reform is urgently needed in both student career education and workforce training to address the specific societal and business needs across Canada.

The new foundation of Canada's economy between 2010 and 2020 will rest largely on how well it further develops its talent. Many plans with the common theme of partnership between local businesses, education institutions, unions, government, and community leaders have been put forward. Investing in human capital is what a knowledge economy is all about. Those Canadian businesses that make this investment will survive and thrive. Those that do not may fail to find the talent to compete successfully in the world marketplace.[32]

LATIN AMERICA

In recent years Latin America's 550 million people have begun real-
izing some of the economic benefits of durable mass democracies.
Except for a few notable exceptions, most have begun developing
viable market economies. Between 2002 and 2006, some 15 million
households rose out of poverty across the region. According to calculations by Banco Santandar, a Spanish bank, this new middle class
may become the majority in much of Latin America if this trend
continues to 2010.

Demographically, like much of the developing world, the population bulge in Latin American nations is in the cohort under the
age of fifteen. In the nations we will profile, this age group constitutes a significant proportion of the total population (Mexico, 29.6
percent; Costa Rica, 27.2 percent; Brazil, 27 percent; and Chile,
23.6 percent).[33] Thus the quality of their education systems and the
extent to which they prepare students for STEM careers will have
a crucial role in the economic prospects of these nations.

In his 2007 book *Forgotten Continent: The Battle for Latin
America's Soul*, Michael Reid points to several important factors.
Child labor has plummeted by almost 66 percent for children ages
five to fourteen. An International Labor Organization study indicates that this will produce $340 billion in economic benefits over
the next two decades for this region. This return is more than three
times the investment of $105 billion to achieve this expansion.[34] Not
a bad return on investment (ROI) for a human capital investment.

Increased funding has been largely in education. For the first
time, the new middle class has many more schools than their parents' generation, and poor families are able to keep their children in
school.

With Latin American economies growing, government aid programs in Mexico, Brazil, and elsewhere help parents keep their children in school. In Chile, the Solidario Program helps even the

poorest families support themselves. Its small monthly stipends enable parents to keep their children learning, rather than working. Before, because of deep poverty, a family's survival often rested on a child's income, no matter how tiny. In both Mexico and Brazil, one family in five is now enrolled in such a program.

The industrial structure of Latin America is rapidly changing. In São Paulo, Brazil, small service companies in computing and biotechnology have replaced the sprawling car factories that have shrunk or moved away. Business needs more talented workers in a variety of skilled technological fields where once only the semi-skilled worker held sway.

But many challenges remain. Progress toward building a robust talent pool is uneven across Latin America. The biggest problem is the way education is organized. In the mid-1990s, the richest 10 percent of Latin American adults had received eleven years of education. The poorest 30 percent had only six years.[35]

Globalization has seen foreign firms shop the world looking for low-cost havens, but more importantly for talented people who can use new technology. They have invested in Latin America, boosting demand for more skilled talent by often paying 10 to 20 percent more than domestic firms. This in turn motivates local businesses to find talent who can also handle newer technology and shed workers who are unskilled or refuse training. The key to this global talent scenario that we will see played out again and again on our global talent journey is the essential role played by local access to education at all levels. Few developing nations have the ability to enlarge their pool of talent fast enough to match growing global demands.[36]

Only 1 percent of the world's investment in research and development happens in Latin America. Mainly this is due to the region's talent shortage in top-notch engineers, scientists, and technical support personnel. Let us take a closer look at how four countries in the region are handling global talent issues like these.

Brazil

Luiz Inácio Lula da Silva, Brazil's second-term president, likes to boast, "Never in the economic history of Brazil have we had the solid fundamentals we have now."

Lula's approach of slow but steady economic reform has raised the average family's income to $8,600 per year (versus the $43,500 U.S. average in 2007). The future of Brazil, he says, "will be built on strong investment in education and training, with tax relief to encourage new investment, notably in science and technology." Poverty among the population has fallen from 43 percent in 1993 to 30.7 percent in 2005.[37]

Globalization Brazil has quietly adapted to the opportunities of globalization. Since privatization began in the 1990s, the government sold off Brazil's steel industry to six separate companies between 1991 and 1993. Productivity has jumped. Production increased from 22.6 million tons in 1990 to 25.2 million tons by 1996, with a workforce of 65,000 (a 44 percent reduction in head count). Another example of adaptation is Companhia Vale do Rio Doce, an iron ore and transport company. Since 1997 sales have risen 250 percent and profits by 1,300 percent. It is today the world's second-largest multinational mining company, employing 39,000 workers (up 279 percent).

As protectionism has waned, the economy has shifted. Take, for instance, São Paulo's transformation.

São Paulo is the largest industrial center in the Southern Hemisphere. After Brazil's economic opening in the 1990s, when some traditional industrial firms were unable to compete, São Paulo reinvented itself. It has become the only truly global financial and service center in Latin America.

The Education-to-Employment System Part of this current strong economic growth can be credited to Lula's predecessor, Fernando Henrique Cardoso. He ended ruinous decades of inflation that at times exceeded 70 percent for one month. Cardoso also universalized primary education, which helped reduce poverty and is now helping the middle class grow. According to UNESCO (2005), 10.9 percent of government spending now goes to education, and more than 88 percent of adults and 97 percent of youth are literate, with about 70 percent of students completing high school.[38]

However these statistics can be deceiving. A prior UNESCO report showed that at least a quarter of Brazilians age fifteen or older remain functionally illiterate.

Though the government invests the majority of its education funds in higher education, the quality of instruction is substandard. Technology and STEM-related curricula are insufficient to support a modern tech-based economy. Institutions of higher education are poorly distributed across Brazil. Collaboration between businesses and universities is insufficient to better prepare more new talent to support a modern tech economy.

Chile

The Geneva-based World Economic Forum identified Chile as South America's most successful economy in 2006. Over the past two decades, Chile has achieved and sustained rapid economic growth, with the economy growing at an average annual rate of 6 percent. Poverty among the population has fallen from 45 percent in the mid-1980s to 13.7 percent in 2006.

Globalization Chile's prosperity is tied to globalization. Free-trade agreements with the United States, the EU, and Korea have raised exports from 12 percent of the gross domestic product (GDP) in 1970 to 41 percent in 2005. Prudent and increasingly sophisticated government finances have allowed Chile to break free from its past boom-and-bust cycles. This has encouraged private infrastructure investments. The result has given Chile the most modern network of airports, roads, and port facilities in Latin America.

Chile's positive market-driven economy has spawned a new

dynamic business class. Foreign direct investment is encouraged. Chile has a large number of domestic businesses helped by its own deep capital markets. These companies are now investing throughout the region.

A unique institution, Fundación Chile is an incubator that spurs business research and development. This public-private technology agency has helped develop the salmon, wine, and flower industries by attracting foreign consultants, encouraging technology investment, and establishing quality-control laboratories. The current focus is to act as a start-up incubator, concentrating on research and development, and then turning over a business to private partners once it becomes viable.

The Education-to-Employment System   Chile likes to compare itself to other small, open economies like Finland, Ireland, or New Zealand. But there are a few hitches in its talent-creation system. Overall Chile has been ranked as the world's twenty-seventh most competitive economy, but in the general quality of its education it has been ranked seventy-sixth. And in the quality of its math and science education, Chile dropped to one hundredth.

Other international education studies show Chile is worse than some countries (Costa Rica) and better than others (Brazil). Chile is below other nations with similar national income levels and investment in education.[39] But money may not be the main problem.

Radical education reform measures began more than twenty-five years ago, in 1981, under the military dictatorship of General Augusto Pinochet (1973–1990). Control of the schools was handed over to the country's municipalities, and a quasi-voucher system was initiated under which private and public schools compete for students and state grants. Though more than 18 percent of all government spending goes to education, inequality between schools in funding and quality remains the system's Achilles heel. This might prevent Chile from becoming a fully developed economy.

Maria de los Angeles Santander of Freedom and Development, a nongovernment organization, believes that "The government has done everything with the best of intentions but the reforms have been poorly implemented." Besides funding issues, the national core curriculum is overloaded, preventing sufficient time to innovate. Many teachers are poorly trained. Incompetent people are difficult to sack. "They are the main obstacle to achieving better results," says Sergio Bitar, Chile's education minister.[40]

International studies show that fewer than 10 percent of Chile's poverty-level students go from high school to college.

Even in private schools, textbooks are too few and the physical plants are often substandard: graffiti-covered desks, peeling paint, filthy bathrooms. Agreement on broad reform centered on improving overall academic quality in both public and private schools seems to have been hammered out by politicians and business. This will provide further economic stimulus for more innovation and research and development. If Chile's economic success story as South America's most successful free-market economy is to continue, the pipeline of talent must be broadened from the bottom to the top (elementary school to college or university).[41]

Mexico

Mexico has many economic advantages, including plentiful natural resources. Mexico has far more oil than fast-growing Dubai, and almost as much as Qatar. Blessed with thousands of miles of beautiful coastline and spectacular ancient pre-Columbian ruins, the country is a tourist haven. Mexico abuts the United States, its largest trading partner, whose companies often employ workers in Mexico. Though Mexico's economy has not grown as spectacularly as that of China, since 2000 the percentage of people living in extreme poverty has fallen below 20 percent for the first time in the nation's history.

Since signing the North American Free Trade Agreement (NAFTA) with the United States and Canada in 1992, the highland state of Tlaxcala, east of Mexico City, has become studded with new factories. Some supply Volkswagen's giant plant, Mexico's main production center for North America.

Though NAFTA alone cannot deliver instant prosperity for all Mexicans, it has raised exports by 50 percent and boosted foreign direct investment by about 40 percent. Mexico has been able to diversify its economy, which is now much more in sync with industrial production in the United States.[42]

Since the beginning of the twenty-first century, Mexico has enjoyed more economic stability and greater political freedom than perhaps at any other time in its history. Lower interest rates have triggered a house-building boom. A tangible benefit from this stability is a growing middle class. Why, then, do 400,000 to 700,000 Mexicans each year abandon their country and flee northward across the border to the United States? In one word—jobs.

A few big Mexican companies control most of the economy. They do not create many jobs. A handful of families own the bulk of Mexico's wealth. Incredibly, nearly half of it seems to be controlled by one person, billionaire Carlos Slim.

This economic concentration has severely limited competition for whole sectors of the economy: petroleum, telecommunications, real estate, and tourism. As a result, job creation is limited, and so is the support for more talent through a better-educated workforce.[43]

Globalization   Over a decade ago wealthy nations used globalization to shed millions of low-wage jobs in apparel, electronics, and auto parts. Millions of low-wage workers in Mexico and elsewhere benefited from the great demand for low-skill people at rock-bottom wages.

Then super-cheap Indian and Chinese labor came along. By 2001 many people thought that Mexico's *"maquiladora* sector" was finished. (The name refers to the model of assembly plants utilizing cheap labor set up just south of the border for re-export to the United States.)

On the contrary, more than 150,000 of the 270,000 jobs lost between 2000 and 2007 have been recovered. One company that has taken part in this resurgence is Kyocera, a Japanese electronics manufacturer. On its production room floor, men and women in white lab coats and face-masks carry out precision work on mobile telephone computer chips. Others in dust-free operating rooms prepare chips for a thin, gold conductive layer.

Saul Garcia, Kyocera's Tijuana plant manager, says part of the reason for the sector's resurgence is Mexico's proximity to the United States, which facilitates both a quick turnaround on orders and the clustering of manufacturing in specific products, such as flat-screen televisions in Tijuana or car parts in Ciudad Juarez just to the east. Such concentration of scale helps attract supporting infrastructure and service companies, thereby also cutting costs and delivery times.

But Garcia, who is also the president of Tijuana's maquiladora association, says by far the biggest piece of this success story is that all these operations have moved light years up the value chain. Before, workers did only simple assembly of parts or stitching together of ready-cut clothing fabric. Today workers can carry out much more skilled and complex tasks.

Garcia explains how. "We have made a big bet on increasing the technological input, and the level of training and skill of our employees is much greater than it was."[44]

The Education-to-Employment System   Over the next decade the most successful nations by far will be those that use education to ramp up their workers' skills to take advantage of new technologies and to improve quality. The income of skilled workers in Mexico will rise much faster than that of low-skill workers.

However, though elementary school attendance is near universal, less than 70 percent of children enroll in high school. Only 25 percent of those who graduate from high school enroll in college.[45]

Ricardo Haneine, an A.T. Kearney consultant in Mexico City,

advises the Mexican government and the auto parts industry on future strategies. He believes that Mexico must pump more money into both "technological development and the training of skills." Unless the education-to-employment system in Mexico continues to improve, business leaders will be unable to continue along the higher road of technology. More of Mexico's children need to graduate from high school. More will need a specialized postsecondary career education. More companies will then be able to use higher technology by training workers to use it. More talent creation will advance Mexico's economy throughout the next decade.[46]

Costa Rica

Costa Rica is the region's oldest functioning democracy. An oasis of peace while many neighbors have been torn by wars, Costa Rica scrapped its army in 1949. The resources were reallocated so successfully to human development that the country boasts the region's highest per capita income ($10,180 in 2005) and a literacy rate on par with that of the United States.

Globalization Like Singapore and Ireland before it, Costa Rica has quietly attracted technology investment. Intel, Hewlett-Packard, Microsoft, and many others have invested hundreds of millions of dollars, catapulting this small nation's (4.3 million people) agrarian economy into the Cyber-Mental Age. By leveraging its native talent and this investment in technology, Costa Rica is using its "near-sourcing" strategy to lure U.S. firms to establish outposts closer to home rather than in Asia or Europe. What is behind this success story?

The Education-to-Employment System The real roots of Costa Rica's transformation from a farm-based to tech economy (8.7 percent vs. 28.9 percent, 2006) began in the nineteenth century. Since 1870, primary education has been compulsory and free. Almost all students complete the first nine grades of school. About 70 percent attend the upper grades, and 25 percent attend college.

The country's universities are producing top-notch technology workers, and this strong talent base helped persuade Intel to open an assembly and testing plant there in 1998. Intel has grown: more than 2,900 employees now provide circuit designs, software development, procurement, and financial services.

The economy has flourished beyond the technology software sector. Medical device makers such as Baxter International, Boston Scientific, Procter & Gamble, and GlaxoSmithKline have been lured here by the talent pool, lower costs, political stability, and tax incentives.

According to the BTM Institute in 2005, Costa Rica ranked third, behind giants India and China, as the most competitive offshore destination. However, the country's small size and small population is not producing enough talent to keep up with potential overseas capital investments.

An obvious solution is to move toward a compulsory, quality high school education program between 2010 and 2020. Expansions of Costa Rica's postsecondary colleges and technical schools are also in order.[47]

CONCLUSION

Though the overall economies of Latin America were growing by 5.6 percent (as measured in GDP) in 2007, this is actually rather anemic. A 2007 United Nations comparison of GDP growth reveals that many other nations and regions are outperforming Latin America, including China, India, the rest of Asia, former Soviet Eastern Europe, and even Africa.[48]

Still, progress has come in spite of uneven results. In the past, political instability and a lack of economic continuity have discouraged domestic and foreign investments in Latin America. Now, durable mass democracies have begun to alter the environment.

Much of this has been powered by members of a new middle class who have emerged almost overnight across much of Latin America. They are the main beneficiaries of the region's hard-won economic stability and recent economic growth. Having left poverty behind, tens of millions of people are now charting further progress, and the years 2010 through 2020 remain a decade of opportunity for Latin America and the rest of the Western Hemisphere.[49]

We will next turn to examine how China, India, Japan, Korea, Singapore, and other Far East nations are responding to the incessant worldwide demand for more talented people.

CHAPTER 2

ASIA

The tigers and dragons must make haste.

—Surin Pitsuwan, Secretary General, Association of
Southeast Asian Nations (ASEAN)

Asia today contains more than half the world's population. The IT revolution's collapse of communication and information costs, low sea and air transportation costs, and ongoing economic liberalization have again given Asia's nations significant power in the world economy.

In the 1980s, "Japan, Inc." was seemingly on the road to taking over the world's economy. Faltering U.S. businesses enviously studied Japanese companies. (Remember the rage for Quality Circles?) Rockefeller Center in New York, Pebble Beach in California, and large chunks of Hawaii were purchased by titanic Japan. Land values in Japan soared, at one point reaching such a height that the acreage of Tokyo's Imperial Palace was more valuable than the entire GDP of Canada. Then, in the early 1990s, Japan's bubble burst, producing a dismal economy for the next decade. Now it is suddenly China and India's turn to soar. Countless pundits predict that China's ability to manufacture almost anything cheaply and India's IT revolution will eclipse the U.S. economy. Distinguished economic historian Angus Maddison predicts that China's economy will pass the United States by 2030, with India becoming the third-largest economy. But just as the Japanese bubble burst, there today are serious social, political, and economic challenges ahead in the future paths of China, India, and the other nations of Asia.[1]

Over the past decade this region has seemed to be on a path to becoming the technology and manufacturing workshop of the twenty-first century. Multinational companies have expanded operations across Asia, hoping to find the smart STEM workers who are in short supply in America and Europe. More than one hundred Western and Japanese companies have established research and development centers in India and perhaps as many in China. General Electric, Motorola, Nokia, Microsoft, IBM, and Accenture—to mention only a few—are expanding the absorption of local talent and building a base to penetrate a growing Chinese middle-class market.[2]

Yet despite all the hype about booming economies and a huge number of people, Asia is beginning to suffer from a major talent shortage. As we will see, the shortage is about to get much worse.

This seems odd. How can India and China, countries that together produce about 7 million college students each year, be running out of talent?

The answer lies in the region's rapid economic transformation that has already drained the immediately available pool of talent. Add to this a major push by Asian businesses to move up the value chain by designing and producing their own advanced technologies. A rapid transformation is under way in the type of talent business needs, from low-skill jobs in labor-intensive industries to knowledge workers in STEM areas for high-tech-based manufacturing and service industries. The overall result is that suddenly most of Asia's education-to-employment systems are becoming obsolete.

A new exodus is now occurring. Asian STEM specialized workers—scientists, engineers, and technicians—who had settled in the United States, United Kingdom, France, and Canada are returning in growing numbers to their home countries. Taiwan and South Korea also have been very successful in absorbing these talented people from abroad. China and India now are following the same path as rapidly as possible.[3]

The combination of socioeconomic forces that have triggered talent shortages elsewhere is now apparent across Asia as well. These factors include unprecedented economic growth, corporate and national ambitions, generally weak education systems, inadequate physical infrastructure, and widespread corruption in both government and many business sectors. These are important issues that now plague many Asian economies. From Chinese tech manufacturers to Singapore's financial and biotech industries, a major battle for talent is now under way for more technicians, engineers, and scientists. Those Asian nations that succeed in meeting the challenges of the global talent showdown will be poised for economic prosperity in the next decade.[4] In this chapter we will look at India, China, Japan, South Korea, and Singapore.

INDIA

More than sixty years after it ceased being a British colony and became the world's largest democracy, twenty-first-century India has emerged as one of the world's most dynamic economies. Though China has a far larger economic footprint thanks to globalization, the Indian tiger's roar can be heard around the world. The Indian economy's annual rate of expansion—9.2 percent as of 2006—compares favorably with China's 10.4 percent. What is behind this sudden economic transformation?

Decisive changes began in the early 1990s when Manmohan Singh, then India's finance minister, initiated sweeping economic reforms. He led the charge to consolidate a competitive, vibrant democratic economy. Famine is gone. The absolute poverty rate declined by 50 percent. Literacy levels climbed. Major improvements were made to the health system. India suddenly became globally competitive in information technology, business process outsourcing, pharmaceuticals, and telecommunications. Since the 1990s India has created more billionaires than any other Asian country. The country now ranks as the world's fourth-largest in purchasing-power parity.[5]

A major economic shift occurred in the early 1990s when India, China, and the former Soviet Union (Russia) all began to embrace some form of market capitalism. The sheer size of these giants' labor force suddenly doubled the world supply of workers from 1.5 billion to 3 billion. In almost one stroke, these low-wage countries reduced the global price of labor. Foreign capital investment (particularly in China and India) flowed in, taking full advantage of the huge supply of low-wage and low-skill labor. But as these economies have grown, both China and India have invested heavily in education to give them the talent to move up the value chain through the production of more sophisticated products and services.[6]

Workforce Demographics

India's economic boom is set to continue, supported by the demographic fact that nearly half of its 1.2 billion people are under the age of twenty-five. This promises an enormous future labor supply that, if properly educated, could morph into a potentially huge consumer middle class.

In the view of many outsiders, India is flush with English-speaking workers ready to fill advanced tech or service jobs. That perception is incorrect, says T. V. Mohandas Pai, director of human resources at Bangalore-based Infosys Technologies, Ltd., India's second-largest software services company. "The demographic dividend theory in India is bogus," Pai states. "They are not trained people."[7]

Globalization

By 2030 India is projected to overtake China as the most populous nation on earth, when India's population will surpass 1.5 billion people.[8] But India's population will be far younger, giving it the world's largest workforce—986 million people—and a gigantic potential national marketplace.[9]

Global business executives understand this dynamism. IBM has invested more than $2 billion in India. Local staff has increased from 9,000 to 43,000, spurred upward by the local acquisition of the back-office outsourcing firm Daksh eServices.[10]

However, what Western executives are just beginning to learn is that India has a finite pool of well-trained talent with relevant skills for IT and other service industries. These labor shortages are beginning to encourage global executives to invest more in training and development and to place greater emphasis on performance-related pay to retain and motivate staff.[11]

About 170 biotech companies and 1.3 million Indians work in the IT industries. But that represents only one quarter of 1 percent of the nation's labor force of more than 400 million. According to Scott R. Bayman, president and CEO of General Electric, India, the country's economic growth "has been largely jobless." Three hundred million people still live on less than one dollar per day. They are still waiting for their piece of the economic action (better jobs, schools, roads). In the final analysis, "India is still more of a bet about the future," says Bayman.[12]

As the IT outsourcing boom continued to gather steam from 2000 onward, Indian-based companies began encountering severe skill shortages. By 2005 business was growing so fast that India's National Association of Software and Service Companies predicted that the country's IT and BPO (Businesses Process Offshoring) sectors faced a shortfall of 500,000 professionals by 2010. This will threaten India's dominance of global offshore IT services. Even G.E. Capital has posted signs in its Indian office saying, "Trespassers will be recruited."[13]

The Education-to-Employment System

Compulsory, free, primary education was introduced across India only in 2001. India's workforce is 35 percent illiterate. Just 15 percent of students reach high school and only 7 percent graduate. About half of India's girls remain illiterate.[14]

Though total Indian higher-education enrollment increased dramatically to 10.5 million as of 2005, only 10 percent of Indians ages eighteen to twenty-four attend, as opposed to 24 percent in developed countries. But even these graduates are of dubious quality. Over 17 percent are unemployed—a higher level than the country's overall jobless rate. As a result, India's Supreme Court closed nearly one hundred private universities because of their low quality.

"Scientific research has reached an all-time low point," says Bikash Sinha, director of the Saha Institute of Nuclear Physics in Calcutta, after the first flight of India's Agni II long-range missile ended with an ignominious splash in the Bay of Bengal. "Even 10 years ago, India held a pioneering position. Now the situation is radically altered."[15]

Yes, India still produces about 400,000 engineering graduates each year. But a recent NASSCOM-McKinsey study found only one in four engineering graduates to be employable. The rest lacked required technical skills, ability to work on a team, English fluency, or ability to make basic verbal presentations. About 7,000 Indians receive a Ph.D. each year. But only fifty of these degrees are earned in India, the rest at overseas universities. Most of these Ph.D. earners fail to return to their country. India's dozen or so top business, technology schools, and universities are on par with U.S. Ivy League schools. But they represent a rarified sliver of excellence. Overall India's higher-education system is undermined by below-par teachers, a stifling bureaucracy, and outdated curricula.

The same is true of its primary and secondary schools. "Many, if not most, children finish government primary schools incapable of simple arithmetic," concludes a 2006 World Bank study on India's education system.[16]

For the majority of students, education in the new India is just plain lousy. Teachers are absent in droves, and masses of unidentified pupils crowd decrepit schoolhouses that are often devoid of basic instructional materials or even drinkable water.

This is the picture presented in the "Annual Status of Education Report 2007" facilitated by the Indian education organization Pratham. On the plus side, more children are in school than ever before. But the contrast between public and private schools is stark indeed. Among the poorest 20 percent of Indians, 50 percent are illiterate. The bottom-line message: India's inadequate universities are supported by a foundation of primary and secondary schools largely built on sand. Something has to give.[17]

"Inshoring" Replaces Offshoring

The Indian talent shortage is now becoming acute. Fierce competition for talent has led to wage inflation. The result is that expatriate software engineers are returning home from Silicon Valley, attracted by high salary packages and senior positions. Doctors, professors, and professionals of all stripes are now part of a reverse brain drain from the United States, the United Kingdom, and elsewhere. Between 30,000 and 40,000 Indians have returned to Bangalore alone.[18]

The Ministry of Overseas Indian Affairs has created a major incentive for these returnees by offering them the right to hold dual citizenship. About 50,000 overseas Indians have applied for this new "overseas citizen of India" status.

Here is one example of the Indian talent squeeze. In 2005 the California start-up Riya, Inc. opened an office in Bangalore. The twenty software developers earned just a quarter of what experienced Silicon Valley computer engineers earned. Then the talent shortage took hold. Indian salaries have soared. In 2006 Riya paid its Indian engineers 50 percent of Silicon Valley wages. By early 2007 it had soared to 75 percent. Taking into account considerable remote management costs from the United States, Munjal Shah, Riya's president, decided, "We weren't saving any money by being there anymore." By April 2007 Shah pulled the plug on Bangalore and offered to move half of its engineers to San Mateo, California, with work visas.[19]

Riya, Inc. is far from an isolated incident. In fact, this movement of jobs back to the United States has become so common that the term "inshoring" has been coined to describe it.

The future of India's tech industry rests not on providing the lowest costs, but on producing enough talent to provide quality work. However, India's talent shortage is not limited to the tech industry. India is building thousands of new offices, malls, homes, roads, ports, airports, industrial parks, and power plants. But not fast enough. The number of bricklayers, welders, painters, and other skilled construction workers is totally inadequate to build the infrastructure India desperately needs.[20]

As India approaches the next decade, its economy will find its own way—not collapsing, but falling short of the spectacular success some aspire to. India will emerge slowly from behind its highly bureaucratic, socialist economic culture. Its relatively small middle class will continue to grow in numbers and create more demand for the world's consumer goods. This will put increasing pressure on the government to reduce many high protectionist tariffs.

For India to emerge as a major economic power, it will need a massive infusion of capital into its physical and human infrastructures.

"Unless India invests in educating all its people," says Jo Johnson, the *Financial Times*' South Asia bureau chief, "and equipping them for employment, it is hard to see how the country will enjoy a demographic dividend on the scale that some are predicting." More poor people must begin to tangibly benefit from the country's growth. Otherwise, says Johnson, "India's economic model could prove politically unsustainable."[21]

CHINA

Two Chinas exist. There is the "virtual China"—the gleaming future promise of what the People's Republic might become. Then there is China today—a very uneven economy, where the lack of real social and material progress outside the major cities is often astonishing.

China's onrushing market capitalism is now colliding with an inadequate talent-creation system. There is simply not enough talent to go around. Given China's enormous social and structural problems, past performance may be a weak predictor of its future trajectory over the next decade. As we have seen in other countries, workforce demographics, globalization, and the education-to-employment system are major roadblocks to talent creation.[22]

Workforce Demographics

Demographic changes in the next decade will be exacerbated by China's "one-child policy." Across China, plant owners are looking for younger (under age twenty-five), more highly skilled people. Yet the twenty-to-twenty-four-year-old cadre is shrinking because of the demographic reality of China's one-child policy. Also, more Chinese in this age group are going to postsecondary technical schools and universities.[23] China's working-age population is set to begin shrinking by 2015. The government is anxious to avoid any sudden changes in the overall demographic structure. On one hand, China is having great difficulty in creating enough new jobs for its current population. By 2025, at least 200 million people will have reached age sixty-five. Yet China also lacks any comprehensive government pension system. People are driven to save prodigious amounts of money for their old age. This is beginning to cause great economic problems for China. The country urgently needs to begin a major shift from being an export- and low-price-driven economy. China's next economic phase envisions going up the value chain with products that will be bought internally by a growing Chinese middle class in a market-driven economy. Arguments that China's domestic spending has increased are certainly true. But as a percentage of China's overall growth, such spending has actually decreased in the last decade and a half.[24]

Keep in mind that there are longstanding doubts about the quality of China's official statistics. Anomalies abound. The sum of the GDP reported by each province regularly exceeds the national total reported by Beijing. Only 3 percent of the National Bureau of Statistics' 90,000-person staff has a university degree. Other ministries collect their own data, each using a different method. It is no small wonder that, measured by expenditure, China's growth accelerated in 2005. But when measured by production, it was unchanged![25]

In 2007, in a move to make China's economic data more transparent, the International Monetary Fund, the World Bank, and the Asian Development Bank recalculated China's GDP using purchasing power parities. This was done through a survey of prices for more than 1,000 goods and services in 146 countries and was the first time that China's economy was evaluated using a more rigorous method. The findings were that China's GPD was 40 percent smaller than previously thought. Its 2005 GDP was $5.3 trillion, not $8.9. The number of people living below the dollar-a-day poverty line was 300 million, not 100 million. These are important calculations. "China is just not that big now," says Albert Keidel at the Carnegie Endowment and acting director of the U.S. Treasury Department's Asia Office, "and will not get that big any time soon."

This revision does not reduce China's growth rate—the fastest over thirty years of any large country in history. It just adds some realism to the picture.[26]

China's transformation has major talent implications. One difficulty is over the sustainability of both China's human capital and physical infrastructure as a super-size developing country. China in a short time has achieved a significant position in the world economy. However, without major policy changes to improve the quality of its talent-creation system, a nasty collision with reality may be just over the horizon.[27]

Globalization

China is now the world's largest exporter of technology goods—laptop computers, mobile phones, and DVD players. Typically only assembled in China by foreign companies, their high-value components come from elsewhere. As China has moved up the value chain, this is creating talent problems.[28]

Ask senior Chinese executives what is their main problem? "The shortage of talent!" will be at the top of their list. Much of this talent bust is due to a Chinese education infrastructure that has not evolved fast enough to keep up with the ever more rapid evolution of the economy. Talent may be the weakest link in China's economy over the next decade.

In 2002, China's Ministry of Labor and Social Security found that just 3.5 percent of China's 70 million technical workers possessed advanced skills. China continues to push its people out of rural areas into its industrializing cities, including Beijing and Tianjing. But in 2006 the city of Shenzhen saw about 400,000 manufacturing jobs unfilled, and in the city of Longnan, Larry Ho, a manager at Top Form, complained, "It's hard to find skilled workers here. That hurts our efficiency." Yet millions of unskilled workers still depend on southern China's low-cost factories for their jobs. Where will they find employment?[29]

The transition from a low-cost to a high-value product economy can be difficult, as attested by the rusting plants throughout the Western world. The Chinese business economy must be very careful not to lose its competitive advantage—which can be hard, if not impossible, to regain—before the necessary talent resources for the future are developed.[30]

In the early 1990s, China entered the global marketplace with a gigantic pool of low-cost unskilled workers for labor-intensive manufacturing. Such cost advantages caused U.S. companies and those of many other nations to set up factories in China. This Chinese "discount" is now beginning to wane.

China has moved higher up the global manufacturing chain toward more advanced exports that require skilled labor, such as small electronics and now automobiles. The price of these exports is starting to rise partly because of wage inflation in export-oriented industries suffering from increased talent shortages.

Factory owners across China are being forced to give double-digit raises to find and keep young workers at all skill levels. "Factories are coming back and asking for 30, 40, 50 percent price increases," says Nate Herman, director of international trade at the American Apparel and Footwear Association in Arlington, Virginia. In 2007, one in six Chinese textile companies lost money, crunched by rising labor costs.[31]

China is now going through what Korea and Taiwan experienced two decades ago—a burst of job opportunities and galloping salary increases across the economy. Turnover from poaching crosses industry lines as well as job and pay classifications. For high-skill jobs, some companies are beginning to offer the same carrots as the West: stock options, housing allowances, retention bonuses, and training programs.

The downside is that businesses are losing staff about as quickly as they are trained. Indranil Sen, a vice president for strategic intelligence at DHL, observes that, "Multinational operations in China must contend with a 20 to 30 percent annual staff turnover rate and recruit 1,000-plus employees annually."[32] Rampant wage inflation has become a major pitfall of operating plants in China. Over the past twenty years many foreign companies have invested in China simply for the cheap labor. Often local government provided the land and even the buildings. In many ways it was easy to invest in China. China now faces the real threat that companies will pick up and move to other low-wage havens in Asia.[33]

The Returning "Sea Turtles"

The Chinese call them *hai gui* or "sea turtles," a play on the Chinese word for turtle, which is pronounced just like the word for "coming home." The Chinese diaspora is estimated at 35 million around the world. Many Chinese people arrived in America or other Western countries as international students. At least 200,000 Chinese immigrants from overseas have returned home for job opportunities, as China desperately needs them to grow its high-tech and service industries.[34]

There are indeed many attractions to return. Competition is so intense that expatriates in the West are being lured home by what some call "crazy" salaries. Wage inflation has been running so hot because of the growing talent shortage that analysts now it describe as "acute." Steve Mullinjer, head of the Heidrick & Struggles China practice, explains that China needs 75,000 quality people (2007) to fill senior vacancies at both multinational and expanding domestic companies. But the available talent pool can supply only about 5,000 candidates with suitable credentials and experience.[35]

At the same time, the overall quality of life has improved spectacularly, at least in China's major cities. The government has also established a program to woo back the diaspora. They have introduced mind-boggling enticements for expatriates: bigger apartments, access to the best universities and fellowships, chauffeur-driven cars, even fancy titles and shiny new office buildings.

China's recent technological renaissance owes much to this group. Microsoft, Intel, and Motorola all run Beijing research labs headed by Chinese returnees.

However, some Chinese remain afraid to return home. Repressive social and political factors influence many individuals. "I cannot say anything because I am on the authorities' watch list and I still have family in China," warns an IT researcher living in the United States. From a nation's talent springs innovation and creativity. A country's political climate affects the talent-creation climate. If personal freedom is denied, much top Chinese talent may never return from its education overseas.[36]

The Education-to-Employment System

Though expatriates may ease some of China's immediate talent needs, the long-term solutions must come from within China's own talent-creation infrastructure—the education establishment. How are they responding to this talent challenge?

On the surface, China seems almost unbeatable. Sean Cavanagh, an *Education Week* reporter, visited a dozen schools in China during three weeks in 2007, studying the country's approach to teaching math and science. He found that math instructors are required to take upward of twenty advanced math courses to teach at the middle or high school levels. This is far more than most U.S. teachers will complete.[37]

However, China's rote-learning and Confucian tradition of unquestioning acceptance of what is taught limits the initiative and practical, applied skills of graduates in engineering, finance, the life sciences, and management.[38]

As of 2004, China graduated more than 600,000 engineers annually from its postsecondary institutions. Surely such numbers will more than provide an adequate technical STEM workforce? But numbers do not tell the whole story. Unfortunately a great quantity does not equate to high quality. The McKinsey Global Institute estimates that only 10 percent of Chinese engineering graduates meet the global professional standards of major American and European firms. Talent constraints include limited language proficiency, poor general or STEM education quality, personal cultural work issues, and job accessibility.[39]

However, this does not belittle China's considerable achievement over a very short period. What we are really looking at is a Chinese talent-creation system that is only thirty years old.

"When you look at what they have accomplished in thirty years . . . it's a rather amazing system for what they are doing for a very small slice of Chinese young people," says John Dornan, executive director of the North Carolina Public School Forum, after taking a delegation to China. It was only in 1986 that China enacted its free, compulsory education law mandating education for all.[40]

Across China, almost every child attends primary school. But their schools are very uneven. About 70 percent of Chinese youth begin high school. Only 24 percent then enroll at universities or technical schools. Though China has mandated education, it is only to the ninth grade. The law is poorly enforced, particularly in the countryside.

In April 2007, Gao Xue-qui, a top education official, was quoted by the state-run *China Daily* about the "worrying" increase in illiterate Chinese. He said the number had grown by more than 30 million people from 2000 to 2005. Because of inadequate public funding. the free, public schools now charge parents fees. Poor parents are forced to choose between educating a son or daughter. In 2003, a United Nations report estimated that about 80 percent of illiterate Chinese were women.[41]

Statistics from China's ministry of science and technology show the rapid expansion of the country's higher-education system. Total undergraduate enrollment rose from 7.2 million in 2001 to 9 million in 2002. Yet government spending on education has failed to match the pace of education expansion at the elementary, secondary, and university levels. Moreover, for a country with over a billion people, China's graduates numbered only 8.5 million in 2007, with 2.3 million in STEM areas. As a proportion of GDP, government funding hardly grew at all in the 1990s.

To make up the difference, colleges have been permitted to increase fees and other charges. Over the past decade, prestigious state schools have opened 249 satellite campuses across the country. In effect private colleges, they now enroll more than 680,000 students. However, too many of these schools are of dubious quality. China's employers often see these graduates as inferior to those of the parent university. This helps explain the increasing numbers of unemployable STEM college graduates in China.[42]

Many of these higher-education institutions are situated in more rural areas of China, where 60 percent of the country's 1.4 billion people live. Highly publicized measures by the central government to improve rural life have been disappointing. Outlays on education and health care have actually fallen as a portion of government spending from a decade ago.

China needs to create 15 million jobs a year, since it is estimated that 70 million to 100 million rural workers will abandon agriculture between 2000 and 2010. The capacity of businesses in smaller cities to absorb them is doubtful. This is causing significant unrest among the rural population, who feel they have been left behind while wealth is increasing enormously in China's cities.

If China does not invest more in education to expand this potential vast pool of rural talent, "it may lose its competitive edge over India, Korea, Japan," says Yasheng Huang, associate professor of International Management at the MIT Sloan School of Management.

Without broader cultural changes, more investment alone will not help China attain its academic ambitions. Plagiarism is rife among academics. The Communist Party often distributes research money based on political favoritism. Scientists suppress information if it contradicts the official line. How can a university become world-class without academic freedom?[43]

Chinese private companies could create demand for talent expansion with new high-skill, high-wage jobs, replacing the labor-intensive, low-wage enterprises owned by the government. However, rampant corruption across China continues to stifle the development of a true market economy driven by local creative businesses that can rely on the rule of law and on secure intellectual property rights.[44]

Child Labor

Officially the Chinese government prohibits children younger than sixteen from working. Yet increasing evidence shows it does too little to enforce the law. As many as 10 million children are now at work doing their part to turn China into a low-cost sweatshop. "We know enough about the problem to know child labor is extremely wide-spread," said Robin Munro, research director of the China Labor Bulletin, a Hong Kong based labor-rights organization focused on mainland China, in 2005.[45]

Only two years later the Chinese government was forced to admit that hundreds of children, some as young as age eight, as well as adults had been systematically abducted and forced to work as slave labor under brutal conditions in brick factories and mines across central China.

Investigators rescued 350 people, including sixty-five who were mentally challenged and twelve children. After trying to suppress coverage of these abuses, the Communist party legislature enacted a clause punishing state officials who overlook or tolerate these labor rights violations. Though the Communist Party responded with tougher labor-law regulations in 2007, foreign chambers of commerce and labor activists were skeptical regarding the efficacy of these measures.

Almost a year later, in 2008, factories in the prime export manufacturing zones of southern Guangdong Province, near Hong Kong, flouted labor laws by luring and even kidnapping hundreds, perhaps thousands, of poor children of the Yi ethnic minority group. They live inland in remote, mountainous Sichuan Province. These coastal export factories are increasingly desperate for cheap labor. They now struggle to adjust to soaring wages, a fast-rising currency, and a talent shortage. Even if these children are paid, they earn only twenty-five cents per hour, far below the official sixty-five-cent minimum wage.

These labor scandals are a serious blow to a Communist vision of a society sharing equally in an economic boom. They once again clearly demonstrate an underlying cultural problem: that economic growth is no antidote to party graft and repression.[46]

The Future

Today China is divided into three worlds: traditional, communist, and modern. At this moment Communist China is gradually being squeezed out by the other two. What will emerge is still unclear. We can only hope that the mandarins who are now running China will avoid an implosion and continue to evolve into a fully modern economy sometime in the 21st century. It is certainly in the world's best interests, and that of the United States, that we carefully partner with this waking Asian dragon and use our open markets to benefit both Chinese workers and those of the free world.[47]

Though China and India's large populations and notable economic strides have captured the lion's share of current headlines, three other Asian nations—Japan, South Korea, and Singapore—also are major players on the world's economic and talent stage. Let us now complete our tour of Asia by examining these dynamic nations.

JAPAN

Following the utter devastation of World War II, Japan's postwar economic rebirth amazed the world. Japan became the world's largest exporter and the premier manufacturing economy. Japan peaked in the late 1980s buying trophy real estate like Pebble Beach in California and New York City's Rockefeller Center. Then its real estate and speculative stock market bubbles popped. Japan's economy has clawed its way back. It is the world's largest foreign investor in China's explosive growth.[48]

Workforce Demographics

Now Japan's population of 127 million is forecast to plummet to about 95 million by 2050. Its workforce of 66.5 million will shrink to 42 million. In 2007, about 20 percent of Japanese were over age sixty-five. This contingent will rise to 25 percent in 2015 and 33 percent by 2050. Less than half of all Japanese then will be of working age (fifteen to sixty-four years of age). If any country's work force declines and higher production per worker does not compensate, its economy will shrink. This is Japan's talent nightmare.

In the spring of 2008, the Bank of Japan reported that the unemployment rate had fallen to 4.1 percent, the lowest in eight years.[49] Once the world recession that began later in that year abates, workforce demographic declines will again grip Japan with a vengeance.

Japan has few immigrants (1.57 percent vs. 12 percent in the United States). Homogeneous Japan will accept educated foreigners: engineers, health care professionals, and educators. But they prefer immigrants who arrive with Japanese-language skills and who fit in well culturally. To cut medical costs, the government has welcomed Filipino nurses. Beyond nursing, no one expects a big rise in immigration.[50]

Many Japanese companies have a mandatory retirement age of just sixty. If the retirement age were raised to seventy, it would reduce the rate of decline in the Japanese workforce by half.[51] Because most companies have pay scales that reward seniority over merit, raising the retirement age will be expensive. Thus far, only smaller businesses have been eager to hire senior workers.

Another longer-term strategy is to encourage a higher birthrate. In 2005, the government established a new Ministry of State for Gender Equality and Social Affairs. New legislation now allows one parent to take a year's maternity leave at up to two-thirds pay.

The government is considering earmarking $15 billion to $23 billion to encourage women to resume working after giving birth. The funds would help improve child-care centers and make maternity leave more flexible.

A more unusual Japanese approach to talent needs is the robot. Most Japanese have a positive attitude toward humanoid robot servants. For them, robots are benign, friendly, and even lovable. Tests show that robotic servants work particularly well with older Japanese, improving their mood and vigor. "The scenario we are working on is that everyone who has a car might have a robot in thirty to fifty years' time," says William De Braekeleer of Honda.

Robots have played a major role in Japan's automated factories. More than 370,000 robots (about 40 percent of the world total) were working in manufacturing as of 2005. The Trade Ministry now is calling for 1 million robots throughout industry by 2025.

The long-term Japanese strategy is that robots will replace people in a wide range of essentially menial activities for which human workers are unavailable or for work they are unwilling to perform. Today robots already make sushi, plant rice, and tend paddies. Other robots serve as receptionists, vacuum offices, serve tea, and spoon-feed the elderly. At a hospital north of Tokyo a child-size white and blue robot wheeled patients to and from outpatient surgery. It remains to be seen if Japan's future million-robot army can supply the talent to replace 10 million people.[52]

Globalization

One of Japanese businesses' key talent strategies for the next decade and possibly beyond is to develop offshore talent where it can be found. Kazunori Yagi, executive vice president of Yokogawa Electric Corporation, makers of industrial control systems, says of its strategy, "We aim to leave our core development skills in Japan, but we expect more and more overseas production in the future." To stay one step ahead of competitors, many companies, such as Toyota, keep secret proprietary equipment at home to thwart industrial piracy. They move only low-value-added production and assembly operations overseas. They retain more research and engineering at home to better focus on making innovative high-value-added goods.[53]

With plants in twenty-seven countries, and more under construction, Toyota is testing this talent management strategy to its limits. They are trying to replicate the company's outstanding success while modifying operations to adjust to a foreign country's work culture.

The key to Toyota's success has been its training centers in Toyota City, Japan, and another in Georgetown, Kentucky. Toyota has learned it could not simply impose Japanese practices on workers in other countries. "This is about a greater maturity about globalizing and transferring knowledge," says John Paul MacDuffie, a professor at the Wharton School of Management. Such training maintains quality and reduces recalls.[54]

Toyota owns 580 different companies around the world, with fifty-one factories outside Japan, and sells cars in over 170 countries. Creation of the talent that holds all these operations together is embodied in a Toyota culture that continuously invests in its human capital. This is at the core of what I have called "the Sixth Discipline": balancing the immediate needs of the present for profits, while ensuring the long-term vitality of the enterprise.[55]

Other Japanese companies have followed this talent-creation strategy. Nissan, for example, is investing $2.6 billion in its Global Training Center in Yokosuka. Nissan has been training overseas workers for years. Japan's future role in the world economy will be determined to a large extent by how well it can implement this near and far talent strategy.[56]

The Education-to-Employment System

Japan's talent-creation system features near universal literacy, high school graduation, and over half of students attending universities and colleges. Students in Japan attend school 240 days per year (the U.S. average is 180 days).

As school-age populations have shrunk because of the declining fertility rate, Japanese schools have struggled to reinvent themselves. Many have moved away from an emphasis on rote learning to programs designed to foster high-level thinking skills. Faced with competition for a dwindling student population, Japanese colleges and universities are being forced to improve instruction and programs or else perish.[57]

Japan, the land that symbolized high tech, is running out of engineers. Business is fretting over coming STEM shortages as fewer young people enter technology-related fields. The universities call it *rikei banare*, or "flight from science." Japanese young people are behaving more like Americans. They see little value in slaving over plans and numbers when they could make more money and have contact with more people in fields like finance or the arts. Since 1999, undergraduate science and engineering majors have declined by 10 percent. There are 4.4 job openings for each engineering or electronics major.

"Japan is sitting on a demographic time bomb," states Kazuhiro Asakawa, a professor of business at Keio University. "An explosion is going to take place. They see it coming, but no one is doing enough about it."[58]

SOUTH KOREA

South Korea's astonishingly fast rise as a successful modern economy is one of the world's greatest economic success stories. From being a Japanese colony that was one of the world's poorest agrarian countries, South Korea has been transformed fifty years later into a middle-income industrial economy, the world's tenth-largest. South Korea boasts many world-class companies in telecommunications, electronics, shipbuilding, cars, and steel.[59]

However, South Korea is experiencing a rapidly aging population. In 2005, more than 9 percent of the population was over the age of sixty-five while the fertility rate (the number of children born per woman) stood at 1.08, one of the world's lowest. As a result, businesses are facing skills shortages due to the decline in the economically active population.[60]

Globalization

Yet for all its vaunted talent, foreign investment in Asia's third-largest economy has been slowing markedly. Sandwiched between a well-developed and up-market Japan and an emerging, red-hot China, foreign direct investment declined to only 7 percent of GDP as opposed to 35 percent in China.

The South Korean government is pushing for reforms to liberalize its markets and make the country more attractive to foreign direct investment. The power of the *chaebol*, Korea's conglomerates, remains a significant issue. The arrest of Chung Mong-koo, the chief executive of Hyundai Motors, on charges of embezzlement has added more momentum to move Korea to the next stage in its remarkable development.

"This is not to say that the *chaebol* don't have a role to play, but that the business sector must be expanded," says Myron Brilliant, president of the U.S.–Korea Business Council. "If South Korea wants job creation, innovation, and technology, it must seek a way to diversify its industrial structure."[61]

South Koreans are both well-educated and hard workers, a pool of talent that obviously appeals to foreign investors. But Korea will need a new generation of companies that are not relying on the government or the *chaebol* to drive future growth.[62]

Lee Myung-bak, South Korea's president, has set a course to bring back high growth rates by reducing the role of government and through the "opening of the market to the foreign sector . . . through free-trade regimes." This will not be easy because of Korea's traditional suspicion of foreign control, a legacy of its long occupation by Japan.

Yet many South Koreans see in Lee a personification of why their country rose to prosperity. He has their goodwill. Brought up in poverty, Lee worked his way through college and became chief executive of a large corporation at age thirty-six. "The Republic of Korea," says Lee, "is a country where we can dream our dreams and bring those dreams to reality."[63]

The Education-to-Employment System

South Korea's culture and talent creation are synonymous. Illiteracy is virtually unknown. Almost all students complete elementary and high school. About 90 percent attend a postsecondary university, college, or technical school. Over 16 percent of government spending goes to education. South Korean business culture, like that of Japan, places strong emphasis on the extensive training of its workforce to improve personnel performance and organizational competitiveness.[64]

In South Korea, graduating from one of the top three

universities—Korea University, Seoul National University, or Yonsei University—can mean higher status and better jobs. This is similar to attending Harvard, Princeton, or Yale in the United States or Oxford and Cambridge in the United Kingdom. But because South Korea is a small country (population 47.8 million, according to the United Nations in 2005), a degree from one of these top three institutions carries even greater social and business standing.

Competition begins even in elementary school. Parents seek admission to elite private institutions renowned for English-language programs not equaled in the public schools. In 1971, the South Korean government ordered the nation's seventy-six private schools to admit students by lottery. University admission is based on a college entrance exam, grades, and activities. Parents often enroll their children in after-school academies, *hagwon*, which are cram programs that prepare a child to attend a top university.

South Korea's education system has been accused of producing good bureaucrats but not innovators. Yet in international comparisons of students from thirty nations, South Korea placed first in problem-solving, second in reading, and third in science.[65]

Parents who are dissatisfied with the country's rigid education system and the stress it places on students have followed a unique migration solution. More than 40,000 South Korean schoolchildren are living abroad with their mothers in the United States, Canada, Australia, and New Zealand. The parents seek better English instruction and critical thinking to give their children skills crucial in an era of globalization. These "wild geese children" hope that their years overseas will get them into top South Korean colleges, where courses or entire programs are in English, or admission to higher-education institutions in the United States or other English-speaking countries.[66]

Also, concern is growing that a lack of engineers and scientists may create a serious problem for the country. Why is this happening?

During the transformational decades, South Korea's President Park Chung-hee promoted economic development through chemical and heavy industries. In the late 1990s, when the Asian financial crisis hit, Korean companies shed engineers and scientists to improve their balance sheets.

In the past decade, admissions to science and engineering schools have plummeted across the country. South Korea's Ministry of Science and Technology projects a shortage of 4,500 holders of doctorates in science and engineering by 2014. To create more critical talent, the national government has begun offering more scholarships in these fields at both the undergraduate and postgraduate levels.[67]

SINGAPORE

Perhaps the most impressive economic performer in Southeast Asia is Singapore. Singapore's achievement of sustained economic growth seems largely attributable to its uncorrupt and efficient government and an education system ranked as one of the world's best. In 2005, the World Economic Forum ranked Singapore as the world's most successful economy in exploiting new information and communications technologies. In large part, this is due to consistent government efforts to boost information and communications technologies penetration, as well as to Singapore's lead in math and science education.[68]

Workforce Demographics

But Singapore's talent pool is not bottomless. Its birthrate is flagging. Also, young, educated Singaporeans are emigrating elsewhere to seek better-paying jobs. A 2006 Manpower survey of twenty-six countries showed that talent shortages in Singapore's red-hot economy were driving up some wages as high as 55 percent. To offset this wage inflation, the government has liberalized its immigration policy to help the population grow from 4.7 million to 6.5 million over the next decades.

The main talent focus is attracting well-educated workers from India and China. They are impressed by Singapore's order, prosperous free-market economy, and straight-laced politics. Also, earlier immigrants from those countries helped turn the country from a nineteenth-century swamp into the financial center it is now. They now make up more than 25 percent of the population and a third of the workforce.[69]

The government is hoping to attract educated workers needed particularly to fill jobs in four thriving areas: a financial sector that has cornered the regional market in private banking for the wealthy; marine engineering and biomedical firms, both of which are growing at about 40 percent annually; and manufacturing, which still accounts for about 25 percent of Singapore's GDP.[70]

Singapore anticipated the competitive threat from China and has moved up the value chain away from low-end electronics to lucrative new niches. Its latest talent efforts have centered on inviting graduate business schools from other nations to set up in Singapore to serve the future business talent needs of the entire Southeast Asian region. Add to this the world-class IT and biotechnology parks that have begun to draw researchers from around the world.

The Education-to-Employment System

Singapore's more long-term talent-creation strategy is based on its maintaining a rigorous elementary, secondary, and university education system. Literacy is almost universal across the country. All students complete elementary school and about 75 percent finish high school. About 80 percent of class time in elementary schools is devoted to math, science, English, and one of Singapore's three ethnic languages: Chinese, Malay, and Tamil. Students attend year-round schools for 280 days per year.

A quarter of Singapore's students attend one of the nation's three excellent universities, admission to which is based on examination results. Other students enroll in U.S. colleges. Often they are admitted as juniors because of their prior knowledge obtained in Singapore's rigorous K–12 school system.

To reduce rote learning, Singapore has introduced a learning strategy known as "Teach Less, Learn More" to promote critical thinking by fostering more class discussions and student self-expression.

The next decade for Singapore looks bright, thanks to its continued efforts to build a knowledge economy.[71]

CONCLUSION

China and India offer immense economic opportunities over the next decade. But they are not the only tigers and dragons in Asia who are booming. As we have seen above, Japan, South Korea, Singapore, and other members of ASEAN are moving up fast. They have increased their global share of manufacturing from under 7 percent to over 9 percent. Investments have been diverted away from China and India to Vietnam, Thailand, Taiwan, and the Philippines. This has been in response to some of the socioeconomic issues we have reviewed in China and India's economies. Other major talent trends will be emerging from 2010 to 2020.[72]

For more than two decades, low-wage manufacturing and service jobs have been migrating to Asia from the developed world. However, in 2006 this began to reverse when U.S. companies began to use in-shoring to return manufacturing and IT jobs to the United States.

This is occurring for two reasons. First, wage inflation has begun across Asia, as too little talent has begun chasing a burgeoning demand for more STEM-educated people. Second, U.S. business continues to upgrade technology and management processes. As a result, productivity has risen. Using fewer talented people with the latest technologies lowers costs, improves quality, and raises profits.

As China and India lose their low wage advantage, they must upgrade the quality of their workforce. This will take time since they need to upgrade their education-to-employment systems that are comparatively far weaker than those in the United States or Europe.[73] The next decade will require broad cultural shifts to expand and upgrade the talent-creation systems of these nations.

From Asia we turn now to the final stop on our tour: the EU and other nations in Europe.

CHAPTER 3

EUROPE AND RUSSIA

What we need to do on skills, productivity and enterprise is fairly obvious. We just need to get on and do it.

—Tony Blair, Former British Prime Minister

March 2007 was the fiftieth anniversary of the EU success story. Founded as an economic pact by six Western European nations, the EU has grown to twenty-seven member states, 500 million people, and an economy equal in size—though not in strength—to that of the United States.

Today millions of Europeans cross their national borders without showing a passport. A single currency, the Euro, unites these economies as never before. Yet each nation is struggling to keep its cultural identity while pledging support to something bigger.

During the next decade, a talent crisis will add to the dilemma at the core of the EU, which is itself part success story, part unfinished grand vision. Skill gaps have already appeared.[1] Nearly four in ten European youths are unemployed, often as a result of a lack of basic skills or unwillingness or inability to relocate for labor market opportunities across Europe, a separate EU study concluded.[2]

As we will see, the whole EU needs to better mobilize a twenty-first-century workforce that can meet the growing talent demands of its high-value member economies. Addressing the skilled worker gap will be critical if the EU is to avoid constraining job creation and new economic growth.

Population decline is a crucial issue in Europe and especially in Russia. Births have been in a long, steep decline. Demographers tell us every population needs a fertility rate of 2.1 babies per woman to sustain itself. Left unchanged, Europe's figures foretell a forthcoming demographic catastrophe: Germany, 1.37; Italy, 1.23; Spain, 1.15; and France, 1.9. The lowest rate is Ukraine's 1.12. Italy, France, Poland, Portugal and others are now offering incentives to families of newborns. Iceland and Eastern Europe, on the other hand, have populations that are young and growing.[3]

MEETING FUTURE SKILL NEEDS IN EUROPE

In 2007 the EU issued its first forecast of future talent needs from 2006 to 2015. In 2008, 80 million out of 210 million European workers were in high-skill jobs. This proportion is set to rapidly rise.

Between 2006 and 2015, Europe is set to add 12.5 million high-skill jobs and 9.5 million medium-skill jobs. It will shed 8.5 million low-skill jobs. But even unskilled manual workers will need more education to do their work.[4]

Sixty-four million jobs will need to be filled across Europe at all skill levels. Replacing retired workers will be the dominant theme. These impending retirees represented almost 25 percent of the entire 2006 workforce. Of the 64 million jobs to be filled between 2006 and 2015, 51 million (or 80 percent) will be jobs that are due to baby-boomer retirements. (In the United States it is 65 percent.)[5]

The challenges for the EU are at two levels. First, the declining population, and consequently shrinking workforce, will require mobilizing a larger proportion of Europeans to enter the workforce than are currently participating. The other alternative is to encourage immigration of mainly high-skill talent. According to a 2008 study by the Ifo Institute, a leading German economic think-tank, the EU will need to attract 190 million talented immigrants between 2008 and 2035 to keep their economies afloat. Immigration on this scale will be very difficult if not impossible.[6]

Second, the EU talent-creation system has become an eroding pool of knowledge. According to Jean Pisani-Ferry, director of Brueghel, a Brussels economic think-tank, comparative data show, "that the average EU adult is significantly less educated than adults in other industrialized countries" (two years less schooling than in the United States, one year less than in Japan). Also, only 15 percent of all EU students currently enroll in postsecondary education institutions. Finally, few EU countries have successfully devised immigration policies to attract high-skill foreign talent.[7]

Shortages of talent have become acute across the EU in such occupational areas as engineering and IT. Vacancies are rising as a result. According to the OECD, France and Germany in 2006 reached the highest level of vacant positions since at least 1990.[8] The EU's rising labor shortages are symptomatic of the breakdown of its education-to-employment system on several fronts. At the high end, universities are producing graduates in subjects with limited job opportunities. At the low end, there are just too many techno-peasants who possess a weak general education background and also lack specialized career preparation, particularly for STEM-related occupations.

Technology and globalization enable work to be digitalized and moved anywhere on the planet. The EU and the rest of the world have become increasingly reliant on the quality of their workers' knowledge to compete.

At one end of the education spectrum, many EU countries have taken great pride in their high student rankings in OECD international test comparisons. But over the past decade this phenomenon has begun to change. Lower native birthrates have combined with a rising immigrant population of students. This combination has, in some instances, dramatically lowered national education rankings. The OECD has found that in nearly all the EU countries analyzed, numerous immigrant children are falling behind in math, reading, and problem-solving skills. It warned that in many nations, "the odds are weighted against students from immigrant families right from the start." Factors include attending underperforming schools, low parent or student motivation, and a disruptive classroom environment.[9]

EU government investment in elementary and secondary education was "far from maximized," according to the OECD, which also concluded that, unlike other professions, "education had not reinvented itself." Teachers tend to be rewarded according to length of service and academic qualifications, not individual classroom performance.[10]

At the other end of the education spectrum, Europe still boasts some of the world's best universities. But America currently has 17 of the world's top 20 universities according to a widely used global ranking system. Also the United States invests twice as much of its GDP in higher education than Europe does.

Though Americans have to pay for their postsecondary schooling, unlike Europeans, for whom it is basically free, a third of U.S. undergraduates are from racial minorities, and almost 25 percent are from families whose incomes are below the poverty line.

The world looks to U.S. universities rather than those in the EU for many reasons. Seventy percent of the world's Nobel prize-winners teach in the United States. They produce 30 percent of all published science and engineering articles, and 44 percent of those are the most frequently cited. From bottom to top, the EU needs to do more in improving the quality of its talent-creation system.[11] However, there is another alternative that has been successfully used by American business: the importation of talent.

This has proved more difficult for the EU. Every year tens of thousands of desperate Asians and Africans brave the Atlantic or the Mediterranean hoping to find a low-skill job in Europe. However, only about 70,000 highly skilled foreigners are in the EU workforce. Why so few? Some potential talent fear social unrest if they are seen as foreigners taking jobs from natives. Also, EU economies lack dynamism and the long experience of the United States in absorbing and acculturating immigrants.

In 2007 the EU launched a plan to provide a "blue card" (for the color of the EU flag) to help attract more high-skill talent. EU Justice and Home Affairs Commissioner Franco Frattini explained that this plan will offer its holders the ability to change jobs, cross borders inside Europe freely, and go to and from the EU with ease. "We are trying to make Europe a bit more competitive," says Frattini. He hopes to raise up the number of highly skilled foreign workers modestly to 100,000 or more. Europe actually has already surpassed this number in the total immigrant population.[12]

The EU has begun to experience another labor phenomenon that has long existed in the United States—talent relocation. With the EU's open borders, Danes move to Germany for jobs. German doctors live in northern Norway (though, at present, Norway remains outside the EU). Polish carpenters have moved to the United Kingdom. EU migration is sending the right signals. If education and training are working correctly, people from across Europe will be able to go where the skill gaps need to be filled. Over time the EU economy will harmonize wage differences from Western to newer Eastern European member countries as well as from Northern to Southern Europe.[13]

In 1999 the EU began the Bologna Process to harmonize the widely different higher-education programs found in forty-five European nations. The Bologna Process calls for a three-tier higher-education system: undergraduate, master, and doctorate. Almost all the EU countries are on course to achieve this goal by 2010. In addition, the EU has funded a number of talent-creation programs within Europe that enhance education for students and increase the transnational mobility of talent.[14]

In a journey across Europe, we will examine the talent strengths and weaknesses of several nations. Many are EU members, but even they differ greatly in their demographic situations, responses to globalization, and their education-to-employment systems.

GERMANY

Germany's unemployment rate improved between 2004 and 2008, falling from 9.1 percent to 8.4 percent. Unfortunately, economists have noted a number of negative contributing factors: a lower birthrate, workforce shrinkage due to retirements, and a diminishing talent pool of skilled people. These forces have now combined to lower the unemployment rate, but make it far more difficult for German business to fill job vacancies going forward. Businesses have begun to poach workers from each other across the entire country.[15]

Workforce Demographics

Among the EU's major industrialized countries, Germany will be the most affected by a major demographic change. Its baby-boomer generation, born between 1955 and 1965, is large and compact. Between 2010 and 2035 most will exit the workforce, which will shrink by 25 percent.

A 2006 survey conducted by the German federation of chambers of commerce predicted an era of bitter competition for the country's shrinking pool of qualified hands and heads. Already, managers in many economic sectors name a lack of qualified personnel as their biggest challenge. In 2006, 16 percent of German firms were unable to fill about 110,000 jobs because of a lack of qualified candidates. This cost the economy about $27 billion, or one percentage point of GDP, according to a survey for Germany's Economics Ministry.[16]

Globalization

Among all the EU member states, Germany has been the biggest beneficiary of globalization. It is one of the few mature industrial economies that has taken full advantage of its trade opportunities. China, India, Russia, and other fast-growing economies want the industrial goods in which Germany specializes. Machine tools are a good example, and orders for them are at the highest level in thirty years. Germany has achieved comparative advantage by combining high quality with lower unit-labor costs. Off-shoring has integrated Germany into the world economy. Almost half the added value of German exports is now produced abroad.[17]

The Education-to-Employment System

A large number of Germany's unemployed are unskilled. Almost 27 percent of all unemployed people have no career qualifications, and about a quarter are over age fifty. These talent issues mainly reflect the inadequacies of Germany's current education-to-employment system, which is struggling to keep pace with the changing needs of fast-growing export-oriented companies for all kinds of STEM workers. Unless Germany's education system is fundamentally restructured to reach all of Germany's residents, it could inflict long-term damage to Europe's most technically driven economy, according to Michael Glos, a German economics minister.[18]

Germany, for many decades, had one of modern Europe's finest education systems. Then in 2001 came the "PISA shock." The Program for International Student Assessment (PISA) is the OECD's comparison of student achievement in thirty-two countries. The

2001 results ranked Germany only twenty-first in reading skills and twentieth in math skills. The overall performance of fifteen-year-olds was ranked only twenty-fifth. What happened?

The simple answer is that 7.3 million people in Germany are legal foreigners (about 12.5 percent of Germany's 83 million citizens in 2003). Over 2 million are Turkish citizens. About 575,000 Turks have become German citizens since 1975. PISA shined an unflattering light on the poor academic performance of many immigrant and low-income children. Turkish students placed more than two years behind their German contemporaries. Germany seems to be raising a generation of immigrant children who are far below the culturally accepted achievement curve. And Germany will need these immigrant students' future brainpower. Let us briefly look at both the education system and the roots of this cultural problem.[19]

In the German Dual System, schools and industry partner with the government to prepare about 70 percent of high-school-age youth for the world of work. There are more than 370 specific careers with accredited training programs and internationally recognized diplomas (the so-called Journeyman's Certificate). This is a true collaborative process. The government provides a portion of the funding, industry takes care of the practical training, and the schools are in charge of the theoretical and education aspects. All three agencies are involved in the accreditation process, with the major responsibility staying with the specific business trade associations.

The German educational system encourages businesses to take a long-term view of training. Employers share with the government the cost of worker training. The business pays apprentices a small stipend, and the government funds classroom instruction.

The Dual System has for the past fifty years worked very well for modern Germany. The result has been a technical-industrial economy that is extremely productive largely because of one outstanding factor: a highly talented workforce.[20]

Educating the Children of Immigrants   If the Dual System has worked so well, why has it broken down now? One reason is immigration. Since World War II Germany has witnessed a huge influx of foreigners from Eastern Europe. In the immediate postwar years when there was a worker shortage, people with German ancestry were particularly welcomed. Immigrants without German roots were invited as "guest workers," but they were expected to go home when no longer needed. It did not work out that way. Many of these 14 million "guests," particularly the 2.6 million Turks, stayed on in Germany.

Only recently has German immigration policy begun to accept this new reality. For the first time, many German-born children of foreigners have the automatic right of citizenship. Also, the government has relaxed restrictions on high-skill immigration to enlarge the talent pool in the engineering, IT, and other tech-related sectors.

Germany, like the rest of Europe, is torn culturally between the economic necessity of using immigration to help enlarge a critical pool of talent and the historic idea of the traditional, European, ethnically homogeneous nation-state.[21]

There are many well-educated and integrated immigrant families all across Germany. But frequently there are significant challenges in educating immigrants. Too often, educators encounter families in which the parents are unemployed, poorly educated, and speak very little German. Many live in Turkish ghettos and have little contact with Germans. Also, most Turkish men in Germany marry wives who are from Turkey. Therefore, their children are raised the traditional way, and they do not learn enough German to integrate properly, starting in the schools.

Germany is starting to try to address these problems through an "openness offensive" by providing language classes in elementary schools to more than 6,000 immigrant mothers. Also, a pilot program for parents now combines language instruction with information about how the German school system operates. This is an important program that needs to be embraced throughout the country. "They don't know German schools, how the system works, what teachers expect from parents," says Ulrike Glassau, who oversees immigrant programs in the Berlin education ministry. So far, about 250,000 immigrants have taken federally financed language and civics classes.[22]

Some of the individual German states are moving faster on those education updates than others. Baden-Württemberg is often seen as a model in German education. Its schools have done an exemplary job providing for upward mobility for many. Also, even before the PISA Shock, they had started to address immigrant and other talent-related issues.

The core reforms have been to give each school a fair amount of autonomy over what to teach. Now the curriculum is centered on building student competencies. School days have been lengthened. Lesson periods have grown to ninety minutes. Most importantly, schools have shrunk. A smaller school and smaller classes (maximum twenty-five children) provide more individual attention, which all children, and most often immigrant children, desperately need.

Also, Baden-Württemberg and nearby Bavaria enjoy local economies based on clusters of small and medium-size STEM-related businesses of up to 200 employees. They have low unemployment (4.8 percent, 2008) compared to the rest of Germany (over 8.0 percent, 2008). This has provided excellent job opportunities that make the Dual System's apprenticeships more attractive to students. These states' economies are based on cutting-edge talent spanning microelectronics, aerospace, car-making, and financial services. Here are located a panoply of advanced engineering companies and clusters of their suppliers and service providers. All of them need a broad pipeline of talent to compete in the global marketplace.[23]

German immigration policy must become part of Germany's strategy to address the global talent showdown. The nation's future prosperity will hinge on how well it can prepare everyone for these high-skill occupations whether in business, the professions, or tech-related careers. Germany must attract and educate a large enough pool of talent, whether ethnic Germans or recent immigrants, to maintain its economic competitiveness.

THE UNITED KINGDOM

The United Kingdom is a nation that is now seeking to deepen its bonds with continental Europe though its participation in the EU while maintaining its strong ties with the United States and its former colonies. Its demographic profile is mixed. In 2007, 20 percent of its population was under age sixteen. But for the first time, the percent of the population of pensionable age (sixty-five for men, sixty for women) was larger. However, in recent years the fertility rate has been rising. In 2007 it was 1.9 children per woman.[24]

Closing the talent gap has been a major focus of the British government since 1997. Tony Blair, then prime minister, announced that the top priorities for his government were "education, education, and education." Since then the United Kingdom has pumped a great deal of new funds into a largely unchanged education-to-employment system, with very mixed results. What has happened? What needs to be done?[25]

Results across the United Kingdom have been very uneven. Some regions—such as the Thames Valley, Yorkshire, parts of Scotland, and Wales—have benefited from business-government-education collaboration, whereas other regions have continued to languish. Some areas have developed a high-quality workforce that attracts foreign investment, whereas other areas still lack the depth of talent to deliver new high-wage jobs.

Globalization

In 2004, foreign direct investment in Britain reached $78 billion. The wider Thames Valley, sometimes nicknamed "Europe's Silicon Valley," attracted a host of tech companies, including Siemens, Dell, Vodafone, Oracle, Microsoft, and Cisco. Fifty percent of new regional investment in the Thames Valley comes from U.S. West Coast technology companies. They look to expand in the United Kingdom and the rest of Europe.

Thames Valley productivity is high; its workforce is highly skilled. But the talent well is running dry. A large part of the region's population lacks basic skills or the software or technical communication knowledge required by technology industries.[26]

In Scotland, recent job growth has come from financial services, oil and gas, manufacturing, biotechnology, and whiskey. "What attracts us to Edinburgh is the people," explains Aladair Reid, northern Europe head for State Street, a U.S. custody bank. "Our clients tell us the quality of staff they deal with in Edinburgh is fantastic." Talent does show. Thirteen percent (13.4 percent) of the Scottish financial services workforce has advanced education, as opposed to only 6.3 percent across the rest of the United Kingdom.[27]

In Wales, the biotech sector employs more than 15,000 people and is valued at over $2 billion in annual sales. The local Welsh government has encouraged cooperation between academia and business—for example, between Cardiff University and the Institute of Life Sciences. G.E. Healthcare, AstraZeneca, and local companies such as Phytovation, SteriTouch, and Magstim are growing fast, relying on the local STEM talent pool.[28]

These regions have profited from the U.K. economic evolution through globalization. Most other areas of the United Kingdom lag behind. With the exception of GlaxoSmithKline in pharmaceuticals, aerospace leader Rolls-Royce, or Vodafone, most companies in growth industries are foreign owned. The United Kingdom still lacks the talent to profit from introducing or exploiting its own nationally based innovations. This must change soon.[29]

The Education-to-Employment System

Between 2005 and 2008 20 percent of all job vacancies were attributed to a talent shortage. A 2007 survey by the Chartered Institute of Personnel and Development found that 32.4 percent of employers identified a skills shortage as their greatest concern. U.K. managers reported annual wage inflation of more than 5 percent because of this tight labor market.[30] The world recession that began in late 2008 may temporarily alleviate these problems, but it may also drive more low-skill jobs from the U.K. Once the recession ends, the demand for more high-skilled people will only increase.

There are two main reasons for these talent shortages. Britain's universities are unable to supply enough first-rate graduates. Secondly, there is a huge glut of students graduating without basic literacy and numeracy skills. This does not even touch upon Britain's continuing large number of school leavers (dropouts).

A significant drive to "upskill" the workforce has focused on a two-prong talent-creation initiative:

- Motivate more students to stay in school by offering them more relevant career studies for twenty-first-century occupations.
- Retraining the existing workforce for the high-performance workplace. The current U.K. workforce will continue to fill two out of three jobs between 2010 and 2020.[31]

Other government talent-creation efforts include raising the age of compulsory education from sixteen to eighteen and overhauling Britain's technical education programs. The United Kingdom has never offered organized technical education. A new diploma initiative will now give fourteen-to-nineteen-year-old students the opportunity to enroll in a career-related academic program with a core of academic subject instruction.

How well will all these reforms work to create a larger U.K. pool? Over the next decade the United Kingdom will be able to judge from the ongoing results of all these different reform models. One important determination will be how enthusiastic British teenagers become about higher education. At present the United Kingdom is near the bottom on international comparisons of the fifteen-year-olds who plan to attend a university.[32]

Oxford and Cambridge remain two of the world's top ten universities. U.K. higher education has expanded to include polytechnics and colleges as well as universities. Postsecondary education has moved from being totally free to requiring a maximum annual fee of about $6,000 per year. Loans and scholarships are available for poorer students. Though higher education has expanded, not all institutions or degrees are equal. However, the top-performing students seem mainly attracted to STEM- and business-related programs.

Scotland has a separate university system long known for its rigor and research. These universities hold 11 percent of the scientific patents awarded. Scotland also has an excellent system of technical-scientific secondary schools that feed into their university system. Scotland has a higher proportion of STEM graduates than the U.K. average, which gives it an important innovation advantage because of a local, better-educated pool of talent.

All twenty-nine of Scotland's higher-education and research institutions are now collaborating to help forge links between academics and businesses. They seek to increase the amount of "product innovation" by helping an organization develop new products or services. This has paid off handsomely in the invention of the CAT scan, MRIs, the discovery of the p53 cancer suppressor, and stem cell research. These efforts currently contribute $10 billion to the Scottish economy, employing 100,000 people, or 5 percent of Scotland's workforce.[33]

In short, Scotland clearly illustrates how an excellent collaborative education-to-employment system can produce long-term benefits across an economy.

The continued rebirth of the U.K. economy hinges on the quality of available talent. But several decades of well-intentioned efforts to improve the overall talent pool seem to have led only to a permanent state of systemic upheaval. There have been too many plans at once, without allowing enough time to see what specific program works best. One thing is evident. Both the business community and government will have to invest more in the nation's human capital if they expect a new talent creation system to make the United Kingdom more competitive in the world economy.

"What we need to do on skills, productivity, and enterprise is fairly obvious," says former Prime Minister Tony Blair, "We just need to get on and do it!" Of the three, skills creation is by far the most important.

Gordon Brown, the current Prime Minister agrees. Enlarging the British pool of talent will have a major positive impact on the other two issues. A coherent, high quality talent system is not the only way for a modern nation to grow its economy. But it certainly remains the best current alternative for Britain.[34]

IRELAND

Globalization has brought Ireland on an astonishing journey caused by a decade of heavy investments by multinational companies attracted by a low tax rate, as well as a young well-educated and English-speaking workforce.[35]

By 2008 Ireland had experienced a 7 percent annual growth in GDP for fifteen years and a twenty-fold increase in exports between 1970 and 2000. In the 1990s, Irish personal disposable income doubled.[36]

Some experts trace the true beginnings of the Celtic Tiger's success back to the education reforms of the 1960s. Free high school education was introduced only in the mid-1960s, with compulsory attendance to age fifteen. This was followed by the rapid inauguration of technical career high schools, regional technical colleges, and two new universities. The results were that secondary-school enrollment rose from 96,000 to over 116,000 between 1958 and 1968, university attendance doubled between 1961 and 1971, and at the same time technical college enrollment quadrupled. This helped create the education-to-employment system that today furnishes the talent for the Irish economy to burn so brightly.[37]

At the beginning of 2008 Ireland had a very low unemployment rate—4.9 percent. A booming economy attracted large numbers of skilled immigrants, particularly from Poland, Lithuania, and Nigeria. In 2007 immigrants represented 10.4 percent of the population.

Ireland's native-born population is also booming. Ireland has the youngest population in the EU, with a median age of about thirty-three. Demographers say it will remain young for decades, with the population rising to over 5 million by 2020. Thus, Ireland will escape the graying meltdown of the rest of Europe. These favorable demographics, plus education reform, should enable Ireland to make a strong recovery once the global economic downturn of late 2008 shifts to an upward course.[38]

SCANDINAVIA

In recent years, Europe's socialist model of capitalism has started to bend under the weight of the global talent showdown. Yet its defenders have taken to praising Scandinavian nations to the skies. The "Nordic Model" is said to deliver strong growth and low unemployment, making Norway, Sweden, Denmark, and Finland among the world's most competitive economies.

In reality there is no single economic "Nordic Model" to follow.

Finland and Denmark have the two most effective education-to-employment systems in the region. A more accurate overall picture shows that there are chronic talent shortages across the region, triggered by forces we have already discussed—economic growth, aging populations, and labor-market inflexibility. All the Nordic countries have a hard time attracting and keeping talented workers. Dismal weather, difficult languages, perceived hostility to outsiders—all contribute to the problem of attracting foreign talent.

Workforce Demographics

Finland is a small nation of 5.2 million people, and its demographic problems appeared earliest in the EU. It has already attracted 47,000 Russian-speaking immigrants to fill vacant jobs. A Finnish labor ministry's foreign-worker promotion video (in English, Polish, and Romanian) seeks to brand the country as "the cool attic of Europe." Among Finland's attractions are "managers who treat workers almost like friends." This seems to have a ring of desperation.

By 2010, Finland's working-age population will begin a sharp decline. Retirees will increase from 17 percent to 27 percent of the population between 2010 and 2035. The greatest challenge to Finland's businesses is not insufficient demand but lack of qualified talent. To remain globally competitive, Finland's government has made education and research a top priority in order to create a larger talent pool. This focus on a knowledge economy has played a major role in the emergence of Nokia, Finland's largest exporter and the world's biggest mobile phone manufacturer. Nokia and Finland's economic success would have never happened without the government's consistent focus on providing the very best possible education to every Finnish student. Finland's fifteen-year-olds have repeatedly attained top scores in OECD PISA rankings.

Nokia has clearly benefited from the Finnish talent system. But it has also pursued other talent strategies in outsourcing production first to Germany and now Romania.[39]

Globalization

Norway has a population of less than 5 million people. But as a major North Sea oil producer, it has a booming $230 billion gross domestic product, and its citizens enjoy a world-leading $53,000 per capita income. At one time Norway was Sweden's poorer brother. The economic situation has now reversed. "For the first time in modern history," states Morris Beschloss, an international economist, "the flow of excess labor is coming into Norway from Sweden, rather than vice versa."

Norway has admitted 120,000 foreign workers to cope with a chronic labor shortage, but only a minority are highly skilled. Norway has drawn some 20,000 workers from other Nordic countries. Seven percent of Norway's population is now foreign born.

But because of high living costs and taxes, the Nordic region is not the first choice for most EU migrant workers. Talent shortages are showing up throughout these economies, especially in health care for rapidly aging populations. Sweden's migration minister says hospitals in southern Sweden would have to close over the summer if it were not for migrant workers.[40]

The Education-to-Employment System

Denmark has allowed highly qualified people from outside the EU to seek work. But 20 percent leave after one year and 40 percent after two years. Denmark restricts workers from the new EU states. The country's "flexicurity" talent-creation system feeds a booming economy (2.0 GDP growth in 2008).

About 20 percent of Danes lose their job each year, but because of an extremely low unemployment rate most find a new job quickly. However, if a Dane who has lost a job lacks skills to qualify for a new one, the state pays for courses at a local technical college. Often these costs are shared with the new employer, and even sometimes the old employer. This talent system is not cheap. But it has kept the economy growing and made the pool of talent very adaptable to the changing needs of business.[41]

Across the Nordic countries there is less fear of immigrants and more concern that the far-north region and its high costs and taxes will divert foreigners elsewhere. According to Kim Graugaard, deputy director general of Dansk Industri, the Danish industry confederation, "It's one thing to open your borders, and another thing to attract people to cross them."[42]

EASTERN EUROPE

Since the expansion of the EU in 2004 loosened borders and increased job opportunities, millions of Eastern Europeans have left home for better opportunities elsewhere. The region's high unemployment rate and low wages have caused the most motivated and best-educated to look abroad. Between 600,000 and 2 million Poles have resettled, mainly in Britain, Ireland, and Sweden. More than 500,000 Romanians are working in Italy.

About 30 percent of people leaving Poland have college degrees. This has caused a brain drain and a talent shortage. For example, Wroclaw, a city of 640,000 people near the German border, has attracted Phillips, Siemens, Volvo, and 3M, but it needs workers. Pawl Romaszkan, a Wroclow official whose job is to bring talented Poles back to that city from places like London or Dublin, says, "I talked to one computer specialist who's been offered a job in London that pays twice what the mayor of Wroclaw earns. This guy told me, 'I'm not coming back.'"[43]

Though Poland's economy is expanding and wages are rising rapidly, it will take time for wages to harmonize between Eastern and

Western Europe. In the meantime, Poland is experiencing major talent shortages for engineers, as well as for construction workers, welders, and even seamstresses. Poland employs 400,000 iron workers, but another 300,000 are needed.[44]

Workforce Demographics

Poland demographically has the opposite problem of other EU countries. It has a large workforce of 17 million people. A bulge of young people are coming into the job market. Emigration has acted as a safety value for Poland. But too many talented Poles have left who may never return. Also, a steep decline in STEM-related technical studies has added to this talent crunch.

Labor shortages can produce unlikely partnerships. For example, Romania has become Italy's talent life preserver. More than 11,000 Italian companies with full-fledged operations were in Romania as of 2007. They employ more than 600,000 people. As noted earlier, 556,000 Romanians have immigrated to Italy for jobs. Many nurses in Italian hospitals are from Romania. Italy also employs large numbers of Romanians in the IT, construction, and restaurant business sectors. "I am convinced that this phenomenon of immigration is not temporary. The demography is so clear," said Romano Prodi, Italy's recent prime minister.

Italy desperately needs talent. With one of the world's lowest birthrates (1.23)—slightly more than one baby per woman—Italy's population will shrink 33 percent by 2050. Only Italy's use of foreign direct investment and immigration has kept the economy afloat thus far.

In another talent strategy, the Italian government began giving a $1,300 one-time payment for couples to have a second child. Across Italy towns are dying. The tiny village of Laviano in the Campania region began its own program of giving money to parents over the first five years of a child's life. Since 2003 about twenty couples have used the child bonus plan. "We have no people," says Mayor Rocco Falivena. "You can't create industry or jobs."

Romania and Italy are now embraced in a delicate talent dance. But for how long will they maintain this balance of talent supply and demand? Over the next decade both Romania and Italy will be challenged to grow more of their own local talent by creating new education-to-employment systems.[45]

Hungary is also in the midst of a talent pool transition. The country suffers from a serious shortage of skilled workers, particularly among those over age forty-five. Half of the workforce has few career qualifications. Also, Hungary must deal with huge numbers of nonworkers. Of a 6.4 million workforce, only 3.6 million are employed. Many retired before age fifty-five. This is a huge drag on the economy and helps produce Hungary's 8.1 percent (2008) unemployment rate.[46]

Since 2004 many foreign businesses have moved to Hungary. IBM's International Shared Service Centre was attracted by younger workers' high levels of education and language skills. KPMG's Mark Bownas, a Budapest-based partner, cites the fact that 90 percent of his staff (average age twenty-seven) are college graduates. He compares this very favorably to their Manchester, England service center, where only 5 percent to 10 percent are graduates and the average age is forty. "You have a more flexible, thoughtful workforce in Hungary than you might have at home," says Bownas.[47]

The difficulty for all Hungarian businesses is that sudden economic growth has exposed a significant STEM talent shortage that plagues more specialized companies. It is hard to get good technicians, especially electrical engineers. Hungary is in a good position to catch up to these talent demands over the next decade because of the country's "excellent and appropriate graduate education," says Nick Flint, a director of Hewitt, Europe.[48]

Over the next ten years, Hungary's great challenge will be to aggressively offer quality retraining to older workers. The country needs to enlarge its talent pool, or Hungary may lose new economic investments to other developing EU workforces.[49]

The Education-to-Employment System

Poland's talent strategy for the next decade is to attract new high-skill industries into the country that offer better wages, while continuing to build up the quality of its talent pool. A good case study of this approach is offered by Wroclaw's mayor Rafat Dutkiewicz. He envisions this city establishing a European Institute of Technology. Wroclaw has twenty-three colleges and universities with 134,000 students. They can be part of a collaborative program with firms such as Hewlett Packard, LG Philips LCD Company, and Whirlpool Corporation. His goal is to create 100,000 new jobs over the next five years. But none of this offers an instant talent solution for Poland. As Zbigniew Bachman, director of the construction industry's chamber of commerce states, "This labor shortage affects the whole of Europe."[50]

Wroclaw's plans are not just some wishful thinking. Nokia, the Finnish cell-phone giant, decided to move a major production plant to the tiny village of Jucu in northwestern Romania. Though the country is missing hundreds of thousands of workers who have migrated, Nokia found a pocket of talent. Nearby is Cluj, a Transylvanian university town. "We have a big university center and have a hundred thousand qualified students," says Nicolae Beuran from the Cluj Chamber of Commerce. Residents hope that Nokia's decision will act as a magnet to attract further foreign investment and well-paying jobs. Already Dutch, French, German, and U.S. businesses such as KPMG, General Electric, IBM, Kraft Foods, Renault-Dacia, and Porsche have invested in Romanian operations.[51]

RUSSIA

Though Russia is not a member of the European Union, it has major socioeconomic ties to Western Europe. Since its emergence from the former Soviet empire, Russia has undergone a major economic transformation that presents a set of unique talent-related issues.

Russia has complex talent issues. Because of an unprecedented demographic decline and political interference that clouds the economic picture, its socioeconomic numbers just do not add up.

Workforce Demographics

On the plus side, since the collapse of the Soviet Union, the GDP has jumped from less than $90 billion in 1992 to more than $1.3 trillion in 2008. On the debit side, despite a large migration of ethnic Russians returning from abroad, the population has fallen by 6 million to less than 143 million.[52] Since the 1960s, the country's death rate has leapt and the fertility rate has crashed. Russia's population is projected to continue falling by about 700,000 each year until 2050, when there will be fewer than 100 million Russians left across this gigantic country. As the population goes, so does the workforce. Russia's pool of talent is set to also dramatically shrink from 140 million in 2010 to 77 million by 2020.

In the United States people talk about age forty being the new thirty, or even eighty being the new sixty. But in today's Russia, thirty is becoming the new forty. A Russian male has only about 50 percent chance of making it to age sixty-five. In other developed nations, people in their eighties make up the fastest-growing population segment. What is happening in Russia?

In fact, Russia leads the world in a long list of social and medical ills: the highest heart-disease rate anywhere ever, a suicide rate five times that of Britain, a murder rate twenty times that of Western Europe, plus high rates of smoking and alcoholism.

Smoking, drinking, a poor diet, sedentary lifestyles, and obesity can be added to excessive pollution, including radioactivity, and a dilapidated, corrupt national health system. AIDS is also a major problem to which the central government and public awareness have been slow to respond. The HIV infection rate is the highest of any country outside Africa. AIDS-related deaths are hard to measure because of Russia's astronomical level of tuberculosis. Karl Kulessa, the United Nations Population Fund's chief in Russia, summarized the demographic decline in this way: "There is no reason to assume that Russia can recover from the crisis and stabilize its population."[53]

All of these issues warp Russia's future talent pool. Until the end of 2008, the booming construction industry could not find skilled labor. Employers across Russia also reported shortages of technicians, engineers, and commercial managers.

At the beginning of 2008 Russia's unemployment rate had plummeted from a peak of 13 percent to less than 6 percent. In Moscow, St. Petersburg, and other large cities, the effective rate was close to zero. However, worker productivity is very low—only 12 to 15 percent of that in developed countries. The world recession of 2008 will only temporarily relieve some of these talent shortages.

Even the Russian army is struggling to find enough healthy young recruits. As the population ages and sickens, the headline death rates underline a major plague on talent. The workforce is rapidly shrinking. Wages have risen by 15 percent between 2007 and 2008. The Hay Group found that managers at the big industrial companies saw their pay jump 60 percent during the same period, to an average of about $160,000.[54]

Globalization

The surge in oil prices has been a boon for the Russian economy, but the nationalization of the oil industry has made it less productive. Corruption is pervasive across the country. Bribing officials is often the only way businesses can operate. Corruption now emanates directly from the Kremlin and benefits officials and their friends who help run a few giant companies forged from Soviet-era assets.

Competition is being reduced, as Russian businesses are no longer protected by an impartial legal system. This has deterred most foreign investors. Of the $27.8 billion in foreign direct investment (2007), half went into mineral resources, very little into private enterprise.[55]

The Education-to-Employment System

Talent availability is a major issue. The old Soviet school system had high standards in the past, but it did not prepare talented workers for the Cyber-Mental Age. Out of 15 million industrial workers, only 3 million have specialist industrial qualifications.

The quality of the current education system is declining. Russia spends less on its schools than any other major industrialized nation. Growing numbers of students drop out by age fifteen, and the populations of "street children" and orphans who do not attend school are increasing. Incredibly, 50 percent to 80 percent of school-age children are now classified as being physically or mentally challenged.

According to Harley Balzer, director of the Center for Eurasian, Russian, and East European Studies at Georgetown University, Russian education is becoming stratified. The top 10 percent to 20 percent, students from elite families, are well educated; the bottom 10 percent to 20 percent face a future of illiteracy. The vast majority of Russian students are sorely lacking in the skills that can give Russia an adequate talent pool to support a twenty-first-century economy.[56]

Russia's technical education system has collapsed. As a result, businesses often use illegal immigrants and pay off the police. Many of the goods now produced are of poor quality.

However, there are positive workforce developments. One example is Novosibirsk, Siberia, a turbocharged research town founded by the Soviets in the late 1950s. Today more than one hundred computer and software companies and at least a dozen universities have transformed it into a burgeoning high-tech hub. Intel, Microsoft, and Hewlett-Packard are all there because of its low labor costs.

Russian government officials envision high-tech hubs like this in Moscow, St. Petersburg, and elsewhere. But for now, Russia's technological progress pales in comparison to that of the United States or the EU. The Russian talent pipeline is broken, and repairing it does not seem to be a major goal of the current government.[57]

CONCLUSION

Europe made great economic strides forward after the end of World War II in 1945. Since the end of the Cold War in 1991, the European Union has undertaken a very ambitious program to harmonize twenty-seven diverse national economies into one cohesive social and economic union.

Finding high-skill talent for improved competitiveness must become a major EU goal during the next decade. Even in the short run, one EU state poaching talent from another is not sound economic policy for Europe. Wage and labor harmonization across EU borders will gradually end the low-wage chase from west to east.

The pool of talent across Europe and the world is not finite. It can be expanded. Current business inaction on creating more talent is both faulty and self-defeating. It delays what must now be done in the EU and other developed and developing economies: building new talent-creation systems for a global tech-based world economy. This is clearly in the long-term interests of business and local and national communities.

In summary, what might an improved model EU education-to-employment system look like? Some of the components already exist across Europe:

1. *Finland:* A very high-quality elementary and secondary school system
2. *Germany:* The Dual System offering exemplary technical education, particularly as practiced in the German states of Baden-Württemberg and Bavaria
3. *Scotland:* A collaboration between high-quality technical high schools and the universities and business community

4. *Denmark*: A Flexicurity System of lifelong learning to teach workers new skills that help keep both individuals and businesses more competitive
5. *Ireland*: A business tax system that encourages both foreign and domestic investment, thereby creating new jobs and new industries

From 2010 to 2020, the EU's talent challenge will be to help its nation-based economies learn from each other's talent strengths. From what we have seen, Europe already has strong existing traditions of business-government partnerships for education and technical training excellence. Today the EU is in a much stronger position to ramp up a talent-creation process that adapts these best existing education-to-employment practices. It is urgent for more businesses to take action now if Europe is to remain at the economic cutting edge of the coming Cyber-Mental Age.

Russia has the same challenges but a different cultural reality. Political checks and balances are badly needed to help buttress any serious new talent-creation solutions across its economy. The current government has done little to diversify Russia's economy, now largely dependent on oil and gas sales. The nation must also vigorously address its most pressing issues, including corruption, a plummeting population, a collapsed education system, brittle Soviet-era infrastructure, and an ailing health care system. Russia is a vast country inhabited by a vigorous, intelligent people. Its long-suffering population deserves a more effective representative government.[58]

This completes our journey reviewing the interlocking challenges behind the need for a worldwide talent revolution. Now that we have a better understanding of the talent gap, we will focus more on solutions in the second half of *Winning the Global Talent Showdown*. How have businesses and communities begun to increase their pool of talent across the United States and around the world? We will explore pragmatic strategies and tactics to mobilize businesses into action. Finally, we will review potential policies for unleashing the potential untapped talent pool needed by every nation.

PART 2

HARNESSING THE POWER OF PUBLIC-PRIVATE PARTNERSHIPS

E nough about talent shortages—let us look at how to increase the pool of talented people. In the second half of *Winning the Global Talent Showdown*, we will examine what works in growing new talent and why. We will also look at ways businesses can attract and keep talent that is already in the pipeline.

As we demonstrated in part 1, the global talent shortage is a product of three major economic and cultural forces: globalization, demographics, and the education-to-employment system.

We have seen a few examples of attempts to tackle the talent shortage from the globalization angle, such as the EU blue card that attempts to attract more high-skill talent and make Europe more competitive. However, most successful solutions focus on demographics and, particularly, education. Tackling the grim math of demographics requires finding talent that might be hidden in unexpected places. Growing new talent requires fixing the broken education-to-employment pipeline and equipping workers with the skills that businesses need through partnership programs such as Denmark's Flexicurity System or Germany's Dual System.

The innovative solutions we will look at in part 2 are the work of NGOs (nongovernment organizations) and CBOs (community-based organizations) with both public and private components. This makes sense. The global talent shortage is too big a job for individual businesses to tackle alone.

CHAPTER 4

EXPANDING THE TALENT POOL

Who says all those young graduates are going to be feckless, ill-disciplined and unwilling to work? Why do we presume older people have less to offer and that they have to be written off once the wrinkles and grey hair start to predominate? In a world of limited and diminishing natural resources, the waste of human talent we see today based on such prejudice is worse than a crime—it is a blunder.

—Stefan Stern, Management Guru

As we have seen, the worldwide supply of talent is drying up. Much of the world faces a grim labor-economic future caused by declining birthrates and the retirement of the enormous boomer generation with their STEM skills. In addition, generational work-life differences frequently disrupt the workplace. How employers address these differences will be crucial for recruiting younger workers and holding on to them.

Slower workforce growth is increasing pressure for all labor-force segments to more fully participate in workforce recruitment. Technological advances will enable an increase in nontraditional work arrangements. As the competition for high-skill talent heats up over the next decade, these various accommodations will increase the level of workforce participation by older people, women with children, individuals with disabilities, former prisoners, and others. In this chapter, we will see how employers are working to attract and keep skilled talent of all kinds.

GENERATIONAL VARIATIONS

As we have seen, 79 million baby boomers will retire between 2010 and 2025. According to 2007 U.S. Census Bureau data, only 40 million members of Generations X and Y are set to replace them. But there are major cultural lifestyle differences between these generations. For one, the very structure of the American family has undergone revolutionary change.

On one side of the age ledger, the baby-boomer population will rise by 73 percent for those ages fifty-five to sixty-four, and 54 percent for those ages sixty-five and older. Some Human Resources directors are strongly biased in favor of retiring workers over the age of fifty, claiming that older workers are expensive to maintain, adapt poorly to change, are hard to mesh with younger workers, and have a poor ROI for training. Many firms now understand that making the workplace more appealing to aging workers may be a critical key to averting the demographic challenge at the 2010 crossroad and beyond. Organizations are introducing flexible work schedules, retraining, health-and-wellness seminars, part-time positions, job sharing, and other strategies in a bid to retain and recruit older workers.[1]

Today's workforce is awash with many conflicting points of view. The typical workplace is far more age diverse than ever before and is liable to stay that way for the foreseeable future. All these generations working together are not just defined by their birth dates, but by the historical, cultural, and technical environment of their daily lives. Understanding different generational viewpoints is essential for business leaders who expect to recruit, engage, and retain talent.

LIFE WORK VS. WORK LIFE

A major contrast in attitudes for employers to consider is that Generations X and Y are less focused on advancing in the workplace than were their predecessors. A 2004 study commissioned by the American Business Collaboration found that the next generation of workers is less interested in putting work above all else. The survey reported that both men and women who are university educated are less focused on career advancement and increased work responsibilities than their predecessors a decade earlier. These younger employees consider work "as secondary to their lives outside the office."[2]

This translates into some real generation gaps. According to an Adecco Workplace Insight Survey (2007), 20 percent of Generation X and 19 percent of Generation Y members say that work-life balance is a main career concern, whereas only 13 percent of baby boomers have the same viewpoint.[3]

Bernadette Kenny, chief career officer at Adecco, believes that "Any flexible work arrangement must meet specific business needs first, as some jobs are simply not open to much flexibility due to their inherent nature. Taking a holistic look at how an organization structures programs and communicates them to employees is a great first step to creating a happy and productive workforce." Kenny anticipates a major shift in work-life balance arrangements over the next decade.[4]

Generation X members hold work-life balance expectations far higher than the boomers. For many work is secondary to their lives outside the office. To hold on to these mobile workers, more businesses now offer flextime, job-sharing, on-site child care, and telecommuting. The Employment Policy Foundation advises that time off is the most valued benefit a company can offer Generation X members. Today 27 percent of employers lump sick, vacation, and personal days together as a unit. People can use them for any reason, with their supervisor's approval.[5]

The 70 million members of Generation Y, also known as Millennials, are often the children of baby boomers and so are also known as echo boomers. This youngest workforce group was born into a high-tech world and is very comfortable with it. They are individualistic yet fond of networking. Millennials seem to have a sense of community "pay-back" often lacking with the Xers. The Millennials are the most demographically diverse generation in America's history. Though many enter jobs with what employers find a disturbing lack of basic skills, the Millennials want the higher-paying, meaningful jobs immediately. They also are more inclined to move anywhere in search of opportunity. Of the 50 million people relocating in 2006, 57 percent were Millennials.[6]

The good news for business is that these generational differences can be bridged. In reality these generations are more alike than different. They can profitably learn from each other in mixed teams. Here are some generational best-practice solutions:

- Offer a "lattice," not a "ladder." People can step up, move laterally, or down as their lives change.
- Provide mentors.
- Offer timely and constructive feedback.
- Tell people the truth.
- Give workers projects that tap their talents and grow their skills.
- Let younger workers thrive by letting them take risks.

- Encourage younger people to lead.
- Offer benefits that fit all workers' life phases.
- Give older workers structure.
- Offer younger employees more access to management.[7]

Besides better addressing these generational differences, what other groups can businesses potentially tap to help win their talent showdown? Several large underrepresented groups of Americans include the following:

- Sequencing mothers, or women who drop out of the workforce to have children and then return (27 million)
- Boomers (26 million)
- People who are physically or mentally challenged (20 million)
- People in the criminal justice system (3 million)

The above represents a potential talent pool of about 76 million Americans. Let us examine these groups and how they can be mobilized by community businesses.

Retaining Mothers in the Workforce

The growing stampede of talented women out the office door is set to get much worse. More mothers are staying at home, even when it causes financial pain. This is setting off alarm bells, particularly in small to mid-size companies. The first national study by the U.S. Bureau of Labor Statistics (2006) showed that more women at all income and education levels are leaving the work force to nurture their babies in the first years of life. A new mother's work hiatus tends to be one to three years. Reducing female attrition by 25 percent could add 220,000 qualified people to the U.S. science, engineering, and technology talent pool.[8]

What family-friendly perks are employers adopting to lure more mothers back into the workplace? Work and family expert Sue Shellenbarger says they now include

- Increasing maternity-leave pay
- Keeping in touch throughout the maternity leave
- Communicating benefits and support proactively
- Offering meaningful jobs with reduced travel and hours
- Giving mothers fair access to bonuses and incentives
- Facilitating longer leaves
- Offering part-time jobs, flextime, and job-sharing
- Letting mothers work largely from home[9]

Many nations in Europe have already adopted policies favoring sequencing mothers. Corporations in Japan are also instituting family-friendly policies for their employees: Toshiba now offers up to three years' leave for child care. Matsushita, the parent of electronics giant Panasonic, has enlarged its yearly child allowance. Nippon Telegraph & Telephone is allowing both fathers and mothers of children under nine to work shorter hours. Canon will pay for fertility treatment for its employees and their spouses.[10]

Retaining Boomers

When 79 million baby boomers retire, the U.S. labor-force growth will hit near zero by 2010 and remain low for the next decade and beyond. With a global talent shortage, astute employers will seek to fill vacant key positions by tapping underused groups such as retirees, whether they are boomers or older "veterans." However, according to a 2006 Manpower, Inc. survey, only 18 percent of U.S. employers are recruiting older workers, and only 28 percent plan to retain them. Separate studies by Ernst and Young (2007) and Buck Consultants (2007) confirm this same shortsighted business culture.[11]

Why? Employers fear that older workers cost too much, are less open to change, lack current skills, and will not stick around long. However, a 2005 Towers Perrin report, "The Business Case for Workers Age 50+," shows that doubling the retention of older workers boosts costs only from 1 to 3 percent. But replacing them with younger workers results in high one-time turnover costs, up to 39 percent of their total compensation.[12]

Some managers and Generation X or Y members think that boomers are less flexible and open to change. Not true, says Angelo Kinicki, professor at Arizona State University's W.P. Carey School of Business Management. He states, "Research shows that resistance to change exists across the board. It's not tethered to age."[13]

Other boomer research shows that older works will retain their math and verbal skills well into their seventies. When Microsoft offered older workers a Skills 2000 training program, it was rapidly oversubscribed. Also, consider that more than 350,000 Americans between the ages of fifty and sixty-four were pursuing degrees in 2006. Older workers beat younger workers at resolving conflicts, setting priorities, and handling ambiguity, and they have better interpersonal skills.

It also is patently false that older workers are not worth retraining because they will not be around for long. If anything, research shows that younger workers move from job to job far more quickly. They have little loyalty to employers. Older workers tend to remain at a job longer, if only because they are more concerned about finding a new job in the current business environment.[14]

Modern retirement is simply not working for either business or most boomers. Repeated surveys show that the majority of Americans would rather be working, at least part-time. Many need the money (61 percent). Others want to stay mentally active (54 percent) or physically active (49 percent). Others desire to do something useful or enjoyable, help others, and learn new things.[15]

Tamara Erickson, in her 2008 book *Retire Retirement: Career Strategies for the Boomer Generation*, predicts that because of increased life expectancy many people will begin new careers between the ages of fifty-five and eighty-five. Changing careers is not as difficult as it sounds. Many boomers already are doing it.[16] Here are some examples of people who have either changed careers or altered their working conditions.

- Hendrika de Korte, 82, worked twenty years in the operating suite of a Dallas hospital. Now she works half-time. "I know what the doctors need before they ask," she says.
- Art Nied, 51, was a data analyst. He went back to school and now has his dream job—repairing private aircraft in Irvine, California. "I love turning a wrench and make something work," he explains.
- John Sayles, 69, six months after his retirement party was recruited by his former employer to join a team of engineers on a reconstruction project in Baghdad, Iraq. "It's the best of all worlds," says Sayles, who at 71 still does occasional consulting.
- Bob Phillips, 58, a computer engineer, had lost several jobs to downsizing. He did not want another office job or to study for a new degree. So he started a new career as a truck driver. The industry was short 20,000 drivers in 2006—a number that will balloon to 111,000 in 2014.
- Jack Geisen, 64, is a retired software specialist from Lockheed Martin, Corp. He now works part-time from home for Tibico Software, Inc.[17]

Silicon Valley is becoming friendlier to experienced workers over fifty as the talent showdown bites. Valerie Frederickson, a Silicon Valley recruiter says that now, "if anything, our clients want older rather than younger." Eighteen of her past twenty-five placements were for people over age fifty. As of 2006, her older applicant placements had doubled over the past year.[18]

Boomer Help Wanted Businesses small to large have established programs to retain and attract skilled boomer talent. They offer flextime, health insurance, and flexible leave, as well as other benefits. An annual update on what U.S. business is doing to retain and attract boomer talent is available from the "AARP Best Employers for Workers over 50" yearly report.[19]

What talent strategies are the Japanese pursuing to avert a grim demographic destiny? Kato Manufacturing Company faces a problem shared by much of Japanese business: a dearth of working-age people. So Kato placed ads in local papers urging "keen people over 60" to apply. One hundred did apply, including eighty-two-year-old Toshiko Masutani. He commutes to Kato by motorbike three days a week. "I enjoy having something I'm responsible for . . . and if I stayed at home, I'd just be waiting to die." In the next decade Japan will need many more Toshikos as its workforce drastically shrinks.[20]

However, one large corporation, Kawaski Heavy Industries, has begun a new approach. In 2009, to entice more baby-boomer workers to stay on, it will raise its mandatory retirement age to sixty-three while reducing pay. This is a significant step toward ending the self-defeating seniority-based pay system.[21]

Many other businesses also are pursuing hiring highly experienced boomer talent as consultants or as temporary executive placements. All the big employment players—Manpower, Kelly, Adecco, and Spherion—now give their clients the options of rehiring their retired employees as "consultants," thus providing vital knowledge on an "as needed" basis.

Numerous boomer employment networks are springing up. For example, in 2003 Jerry Tooner retired after working at Dow Chemical for twenty-five years. Three years later he had a consulting job designed specifically for boomers through an employment network, YourEncore.com. Founded in 2003 by Eli Lilly and Procter & Gamble, YourEncore is an online recruitment firm for boomer jobs at the aforementioned companies as well as at Boeing, National Starch and Chemical Co., 3M Co., and Ethicon. These are mostly contract jobs, but some are salaried positions.[22]

With no signs of the talent crisis abating, boomers with the right blend of knowledge can realistically plan to continue working throughout the next decade and beyond. Phased retirement, part-time and flextime work, and "rehirements" will become the standard options for boomers. Many economic benefits will result from these boomer jobs, including increased household savings, higher tax collections, and a reduction of the fiscal strain on unfunded Social Security and Medicare liabilities (estimated at $54 trillion).[23]

Granted, society's attitudes toward retirement will not change overnight. But the current talent showdown offers businesses an opportunity to show some leadership. More people are going to have the opportunity for a flexible boomer job, combining paid income with some pension income. People will be able to phase in and out of work and change careers and roles, becoming advisers rather than top managers.

Hiring People With Disabilities

Businesses worldwide are beginning to embrace the profitability of hiring people with disabilities to help them address the growing, critical talent shortage. About 20 percent of the U.S. workforce is in some way challenged. (About 45 percent of U.S. college graduates with disabilities are unemployed or underemployed.)

The goal of one Walgreen distribution center, for example, is to employ two hundred disabled workers. The value of government benefits it will then receive will total about $3.5 million. Its disabled employees include people who are autistic, legally blind, have cerebral palsy or other ambulatory issues, or are mentally challenged. All received company job training.

The Walgreen distribution center is 20 percent more efficient than the company's older facilities. On some days the disabled employees, who are 40 percent of the staff, are its most productive workers.[24]

Though some negative hiring attitudes persist, research shows that job training for the disabled worker is very effective. A report from the W.E. Upjohn Institute for Employment Research shows that education and skills training for disabled and nondisabled workers can yield equal results for a business.[25]

"American employers often indicate that while they want to include people with disabilities in their recruitment efforts, they do not know where to find qualified candidates," says W. Roy Grizzard, assistant U.S. secretary of labor for disability employment policy.[26] (For a list of organizations that offer both private business and government access to qualified disabled job candidates, see the Resource A section.)

Those days are now over. Microsoft, Hewlett-Packard, Procter & Gamble, Xerox, Motorola, and Sears are among the companies that employ challenged workers profitably and also support these job sites. Also, about 5,000 nonprofit organizations across the United States are currently employing the disabled.[27]

Since 2002, the American Association of People with Disabilities (AAPD), with Microsoft's help, has sponsored a paid college student internship program with federal agencies in Washington, D.C. In the 1980s the AAPD also pioneered a national business mentoring and apprenticeship program. More than 16,000 students have gained real-world work experiences from sponsoring businesses across the United States.[28]

Surveys have shown that employing challenged workers reduces absenteeism and increases worker loyalty, with additional dollars going to a company's bottom line through government subsidies. As a part of winning the talent challenge, the time is overdue for companies to tap into this labor pool and increase the employment of skilled disabled people.[29]

Hiring Former Prisoners

Back in 1994, a national get-tough-on-crime climate cut nearly all federal funding of inmate education. Since then, the U.S. prison population has gown by 50 percent to over 2.3 million—that is, one in every one hundred adults. The annual cost, $49 billion, is likely to rise to $74 billon by 2011, according to the Pew Center on the States. In 2005, the average prisoner cost taxpayers $23,876 per year. Though crime rates have been in a decline for a decade, the U.S.

prison population continues to grow largely because of drug and property offenders. As of 2008, the United States ranks as the world's number one incarcerator.[30]

Each year, more than 600,000 people are released from prison. What happens to them? Sixty-six percent of California's ex-inmates are back in prison within three years. In Illinois the recidivism rate is 50 percent.[31] Why does this happen?

One big problem is getting a job. Terrence Johnson of Memphis, Tennessee, explains. After serving eight months in a halfway house for a felony wire-fraud conviction, and then serving home confinement, he was back in the job market. Unlike most offenders, he had graduated from high school and even had some college education.

"At every job interview, it was the same thing," Terrence explains. "We'd go through all the usual questions. And I'm thinking that people are interested in me. . . . The question about my conviction always comes up. . . . And then there's the inevitable letdown."

The problem is that "a felony conviction is a life sentence," says Yolanda McFadgon, executive director at Second Chance, a program founded to help ex-prisoners near Memphis. "You've paid your debt to society, but you're marked, and no one will give you a job."[32]

To help any employer overcome this risk issue, the U.S. Department of Labor created the Federal Bonding Program. As of 2006, more than 44,000 people had been bonded and placed in jobs, with a 99 percent success rate in regard to claims filed. The Federal Bonding Program provides low-cost individual fidelity bonds for at-risk job seekers. The bonds cost employers and job-seekers nothing. There is no paperwork for the employer. This fidelity bond, offered by the Travelers Property Casualty Insurance, protects the employer in case of any loss of money or property due to employee dishonesty. Businesses also receive a federal tax credit for each such hire.[33]

A second major problem is lack of education and specific career skills. As of 2003, 41 percent of all prisoners had less than a high school education. Nineteen percent of inmates do earn a high school equivalency certificate during their incarceration.[34]

Some training takes place in prisons, but its quality and magnitude is uneven and varies with each state. "Though many offenders are in great need of employment assistance, few prisoners receive employment-related training," says Robert I. Lerman at the Urban Institute.[35] This may be about to change, as many states cannot build prisons fast enough to house their ever-rising inmate populations.

While some may say "nothing works" when it comes to released prisoner rehabilitation, that is simply not true. "Some programs appear to be modestly successful," states Dan Bloom at the University of Michigan, whose research on prisoner reentry shows "there are hints of success for older offenders, for programs that provide integrated services both before and after release."[36]

Darrell Hayes was sent to an Illinois prison four times in eleven years. At age forty he left prison for what would be the last time because Chicago's Safer Foundation found him a job. About 20,000 men and women return each year to Chicago from Illinois prisons.

Founded by two former Catholic priests, for over thirty years the Safer Foundation has fulfilled each of its missions of "connecting people coming back from prison [to their communities], and focusing on work and the skills needed for work," says Jodina Hicks, Safer's vice president for public policy and community partnerships. Almost 2,000 ex-offenders are placed in jobs each year. Employers are more willing to hire people with a record for warehousing and distribution and other "back-room," relatively well-paying jobs. Safer provides its clients with specialized assessments, education programs, employment services, and intensive case management.[37]

Research by both U.S. and international organizations has confirmed that the aforementioned best practices can yield a new stream of local, qualified talent for a community. Many other local programs exist that provide ex-offenders these job-training services. But local communities also need to organize an extensive network of employers who have the need for talent and demonstrate their willingness to hire ex-offenders. One example of such a network is in Greater Des Moines, Iowa, which faces a shortfall of 60,000 workers in the next decade. Forty local employers participated in a job fair for about three hundred inmates, held at the downtown convention center in 2008. Here is where the role of a local CBO or NGO can prove critical by helping to establish these essential connections and making them sustainable.[38]

CONCLUSION

In this chapter, we have offered some best-practice ideas to better mobilize more talent from the different generations in the workplace, including sequencing mothers, boomers, challenged workers, and qualified ex-offenders. But this is only half of the equation in terms of finding the people. In chapter 5 we will look at how public-private partnerships can help rebuild the education pipeline and connect more quality student talent to future employment. We will also explore how businesses and other organizations can contribute to their sustainability and long-term growth through education and training that updates their employees' knowledge and skills.

CHAPTER 5

FIXING THE EDUCATION-TO-EMPLOYMENT SYSTEM

Every enterprise is a learning and teaching institution. Training and development must be built into it on all levels—training and development that never stops.

—Peter Drucker

A cross the United States a wide spectrum of secondary-education career initiatives is now under way. These are local community collaborations with business, foundations, public entities, and nonprofit organizations. They represent an essential component in rebuilding the local education-to-employment talent pipeline. Let us look at a cross-section of these schools.

PHILADELPHIA'S TALENT PIPELINE

For more than forty years, Philadelphia Academies, Inc. has provided the talent to hundreds of city and regional businesses through the United States' oldest career-academy program. Philadelphia Academies, Inc. is a nonprofit organization funded by the local business community to provide career-focused programming that prepares students for employment and postsecondary education.

In 1968 Philadelphia experienced some of the worst riots in the city's history. Economic stagnation, poverty, and soaring unemployment had planted the seeds of growing discontent. In tackling this crisis, community, business, education, labor, and government leaders forged a new coalition. They decided to focus on the soaring high school dropout rate.

What was born from that collaboration was the so-called Academy Model for a schooling revolution. The first modern U.S. career academy was born the following year—the Electrical Academy at Edison High School, supported by the Philadelphia Electric Company. Thirty students were enrolled; they were promised employment upon graduation.

Philadelphia Academies, Inc., a CBO, gradually organized programs in thirteen fields, including automotive and mechanical science, aviation and aerospace, environmental technology, health, and information technology. Today the academy model is flourishing in Philadelphia, with an enrollment of approximately 6,500 students in thirteen high schools and at twenty-four academy program sites.

Today more than three hundred businesses participate in the academies while providing a management structure to interface with the public schools. These academies are financed by corporate contributions (33 percent), foundation grants (30 percent), and public funding (35 percent). About 90 percent of graduates continue in postsecondary education or go to work. Academy students outperform their peers in attendance, promotion rates, and senior graduation rates.

This career academy model has been adopted in many parts of the United States. Today more than 1,000 career academies are preparing students by incorporating career information into a liberal arts curriculum. "Business is demanding skills that the general high school populations are not getting," says Connie Majka, a Philadelphia Academies, Inc. manager. "Academy students receive the best education and career components expertly blended together."[1]

CAREER CHOICE: WHAT COLOR IS YOUR COLLAR?

Throughout the past century there has been a sharp class distinction between white-collar and blue-collar jobs. This division existed in terms of both social status and income expectations. For the decade between 2010 and 2020, instead of blue collar or white collar, think "gold" collar. As we have seen, STEM-related careers are destined to become increasingly popular as the world's economy clearly moves into the Cyber-Mental Age. With the projected shortages in many STEM-related areas, wage inflation is almost a certainty. These jobs will indeed literally become gold-collar occupations for many, while new education-to-employment systems will help rebalance the U.S. and world labor markets.[2]

This is one reason why career academies are a growing phenomenon in high schools nationwide. According to the National Career Academy Coalition and other experts, their basic formula for success includes strong public-private funding, small learning communities, the blending of liberal arts and specific career curricula, teachers who are credentialed for their field, and continuous professional development for teachers provided by experts from both inside and outside the academy. Broad and active business collaboration ensures that careers fit the local economy, and businesses provide student internships and other work-based learning experiences.[3]

Business people are worried that popular culture and local education institutions will not support more STEM education or the advanced skills more students will need for jobs in the twenty-first-century economy. To that end, many leaders in business and academe are arguing for combining a traditional quality liberal arts education with specific hands-on knowledge and skills. They recognize "that decent paying jobs with opportunities for career advancement will require at least some education beyond high school, as well as lifelong learning to adjust to a fluid labor market," says Lynn Olson, editor of *Education Week*.[4]

These career academies offer a blending of learning that develops in students the capacities often listed by employers as the very qualities now sought in the workplace, including

- Analytical, communication, and integrative capacities
- Problem-solving, intercultural, and collaborative abilities
- Scientific, technological, and quantitative competence
- Cross-cultural, aesthetic, and historical knowledge
- Ethical and civic engagement and responsibility
- Preparation for work in a dynamic and global economy

For example, employers tell students preparing for engineering careers that they will need a strong background in science, technology, and mathematics. But to function effectively in a modern global economy, these STEM-related career majors also need the aforementioned liberal arts education components. Combining the best of both academic areas provides students with a strong foundation for many career opportunities, as well as a strong grounding in core career concepts and related scientific methods. The concept behind the success of these liberal arts career academies is not offering the students an either/or choice of studies, but a stronger hybrid program of both. This means a longer school day and a longer school year.

This hybrid model also seems popular with students. A 2006 survey by the James Irvine Foundation found that 90 percent of struggling at-risk ninth- and tenth-graders wanted career-related courses. The focus of career academies is to ensure an overall academically rigorous program leading most students into a postsecondary certificate and either two- or four-year degrees (or both) and that include the formation of the capacities listed previously.[5]

Surprisingly, studies show that many adolescents who are at risk of dropping out are getting good grades. But they feel disinterested in traditional high school programs. These students say they would be more motivated to stay in school if at least some of what they learned was relevant to potential career opportunities.

Proving this, the 2008 Lemelson-MIT Invention Survey found that more than 50 percent of teens think their high school is not properly preparing them for STEM careers. Furthermore, 79 percent of U.S. teens see value in "hands-on, project-based science, technology, engineering and math (STEM) education and learning in high school." They want these programs expanded. Almost three out of four U.S. teens think technology can solve some of the world's most pressing problems. Nearly two-thirds believe they could invent some of these solutions.

But parents remain skeptical. Most Americans believe that we must improve math and science education. However, a 2006 Business Roundtable and Compete America survey found that only 5 percent of parents would encourage their children to pursue a STEM-related career in a standard high school or career academy program.[6]

Most parents' education and career development took place during twentieth-century economic and technological conditions that are rapidly changing. But as today's students are finding, it is not their parents' workforce anymore. STEM-related careers will clearly dominate a larger proportion of twenty-first-century job opportunities. No matter what an individual's personal interests or aptitudes, career academies will help more students successfully pursue productive and financially rewarding lives in a diversity of careers over their lifetime.

Before we turn to international examples, let us examine a few more U.S. career academies.

The Biotechnology Academy and the Biomanufacturing-Technology Academy are part of the Minuteman Regional High School in Lexington, Massachusetts. The Biotechnology Academy's four-year program balances a liberal arts education with courses in bioethics and genetics and honors courses in math, chemistry, physics, and extensive lab experience. Course work alternates, with each week of liberal arts subjects followed by one week of biotechnology courses. Students also are educated in related career skills. Almost all biotechnology students enter college, as opposed to 60 percent of all Minuteman Regional High School students. The sister program, the Biomanufacturing-Technology Academy, though less rigorous, prepares students for laboratory careers as laboratory technicians, quality control lab inspectors, manufacturing technicians, and other medical areas. Students in both academies can get college credit at local postsecondary institutions. Both programs also offer internships and job shadowing with local biotechnology companies such as Biogen and Genzyme Corp. Other biotechnology academies can be found in San Diego, Seattle, Silicon Valley, North Carolina's Research Triangle, Miami, and Baltimore.[7]

The Center for Advanced Research and Technology (CART) is a public charter high school in San Joaquin, California's Central Valley. Founded in 2000, it combines a liberal arts curriculum with careers in the professional sciences, advanced communications, global business, and engineering. Currently 1,350 eleventh- and twelfth-grade students from eighteen nearby high schools are bused to CART, where they attend half-day classes in state-of-the art labs. This center is funded by many companies, including PG&E, DeVry Universities, Grundfof Pump, AT&T, Wells Fargo, Kaiser Permanente, and

Community Medical. Employees from these companies partner with teachers in class instruction. At CART, students team up to work on socially relevant projects such as investigating mock homicides, presenting research on local social issues, and engineering new products for the disabled. Physics, chemistry, English, or history are combined to provide comprehensive information for these projects. CART is designed mainly for average or below-average students. They are at higher risk of dropping out, and are not prime candidates for college or technology-based careers. Ninety-five percent of CART's students enroll in postsecondary institutions. CART offers systemic culture change through business-education collaboration that expands the future career opportunities for San Joaquin Valley students.[8]

The Met in Providence, Rhode Island is a public high school composed of six separate buildings, each with a principal and about 120 students from diverse cultural, ethnic, and socioeconomic backgrounds. Its Learning through Internships Curriculum philosophy is to educate one student at a time within a diverse community of learners, using many kinds of learning experiences. Each student has an internship site mentor, who also collaborates with the student's teacher on progress and learning. Through readings, meetings, and conference attendance, the student experiences the workplace as a community of learners. Students take credit courses at the Community College of Rhode Island. Seniors travel internationally to broaden their personal perspectives and interests. Parents sign an agreement supporting the teacher in understanding and educating their child. They participate in all formal curriculum-building activities for their child, developing quarterly learning plans and serving as panel members at quarterly student exhibitions. The nonprofit Big Picture Company founded The Met, which also received support from the Bill and Melinda Gates Foundation. The Big Picture Network sponsors seventy other liberal arts and career academies across America.[9]

San Clemente High School Auto Tech Academy in California is one of the relatively few high school programs offering realistic preparation for high-tech auto repair careers. An important feature is that the program gives another chance to many students who have struggled in traditional classrooms and might have dropped out. Students at the auto academy do take a full program of liberal arts courses in math, science, English, and history. They also take increasingly complex auto technology classes four times a week. Dozens of local dealers and repair shops provide internships. With entry-level jobs beginning at $30,000 a year (rising to $60,000 after five years), these high-tech students are not grease monkeys anymore. According to the U.S. Bureau of Labor Statistics, the number of these tech jobs nationwide is projected to grow from 773,000 in 2006 to 883,000 in 2016.[10]

The California Academy of Mathematics and Science (CAMS) is a collaborative program between California State University (CSU), eleven Los Angeles area school districts, and high-tech or aerospace industries. The academy features an accelerated curriculum preparing students for postsecondary education and STEM-related careers. Two-thirds of the six hundred CAMS students are drawn from the top 30 percent of inner-city school classes. The academy's curriculum features a student "cohort" support structure, the blending of intensive liberal arts with math and science courses, and an advanced college-credit program on the CSU campus. Seventy percent of academy graduates enroll in college STEM-related majors. Corporate sponsors include Boeing, Honeywell, Hughes, Northrop-Grumman, and Honda.[11]

The DeVry University Advantage Academy High School in Chicago, Illinois, and the Bard High School Early College, New York, New York are examples of a hybrid form of career academy, called "early college" high schools that accelerate the high school experience to move motivated students into more rigorous college content. Students simultaneously earn a high school diploma and an Associates degree, or two years of college credit toward a Bachelor's degree. These schools are designed to support underrepresented minority and other students who have not had access to academic programs needed to meet college and career readiness standards. Students in the Bard program take college classes in finite math, neuroscience, geotechnical engineering, and Italian Renaissance art. In the DeVry Program, students graduate with a computer science degree. One hundred seventy schools across the United States are participating in these early college high schools, supported by funding from the Bill & Melinda Gates Foundation, Carnegie Foundation, and the W. K. Kellogg Foundation.[12]

The Austin Polytechnical Academy in Chicago, Illinois is the only career academy in Chicago dedicated to careers in high-skill manufacturing. Austin Polytech opened with a freshman class of 145 students. Another grade will be added over the next three years until five hundred students are enrolled. Thirty-five manufacturing companies are collaborating with the school and are providing internship learning opportunities. Students are taught in extended class periods that blend liberal arts instruction with a pre-engineering curriculum, Project Lead the Way. Classes continue to 4:30 p.m. each day. Austin Polytech is one of one hundred new schools that are part of Chicago Renaissance 2010 initiative to reinvent public education through opening career academies, charter schools, and other experimental school models. Three more tech academies are planned for Chicago.[13]

At the Cristo Rey Jesuit High School in Chicago, the concept is to allow at-risk kids with the right attitude to use internships to work their way through a liberal arts college-preparation education. The reality since 1995 is that 109 Chicago firms provide 129 jobs shared by 535 students every year. They earn about $6,250, with parents contributing $2,700 a year. Cristo Rey High School is located in Chicago's Pilsen neighborhood, an urban area that struggles daily with poverty and gang violence. Students are bused from there once a week to internship jobs they share at Sidley & Austin, Madison Dearborn Partners, Loyola Medical Center, McKinsey & Co., Deloitte & Touche, museums, and other businesses. Cristo Rey combines challenging college-preparation courses, a personalized, supportive setting, and motivating programs that include internships. "It's bringing to America's poorest communities the three 'Rs': rigor, relationship, and relevance," says Marie Groark of the Bill and Melinda Gates Foundation, which supports the program. Ninety-three percent of the students in this program begin college; in the twelve years since its inception, 82 percent have graduated from college or are still attending a postsecondary institution. There are Cristo Rey High Schools in twenty-one other U.S. cities, and plans are under way for more.[14]

CAREER ACADEMIES AROUND THE WORLD

More than 60 percent of England's secondary schools are now "Specialist Schools" with an emphasis on engineering, art, math, or science (somewhat similar to a U.S. career academy). They still have a national curriculum, but it allows for some specialization.

England's "Academy Program" was launched in 2000. In 2006, about twenty-seven academies were in existence, with at least two hundred planned by 2010. Each one has specialties in business, arts, science, technology, or other areas. They are part of the strategy to raise standards in the most disadvantaged areas of the country. They will be publicly and privately financed, but free from most local government control (similar to U.S. charter schools).[15]

German Education 101

In a Hamburg classroom, a group of eighteen-year-olds sit reviewing the concepts of double-entry bookkeeping. In the next room, their classmates monitor bubbling chemistry experiments in a well-equipped science lab. These are scenes from a secondary school in Western Europe. However, these students are not in a school building, but in classrooms at a company, Beiersdorf (producer of Nivea face cream). Their instructors are Beiersdorf employees. When the classes change, the accounting students will attend chemistry class (among other subjects) at Beiersdorf, and the chemistry students will study accounting.[16]

The Mercedes technical training center in Sindelfingen, Germany has a high-quality apprenticeship program as an integral part of its Dual System that pays students about $600 per month during training. This program is a fast track to a high-tech adult job. Academic studies are demanding, and they dovetail with the high-tech job training of the Mercedes-Benz apprenticeship. Because Mercedes takes the viewpoint that its training center is an investment in its next generation of employees, it has the most advanced technology in order to maximize what students can be taught.

The company's estimate of the full cost for an apprenticeship is over $60,000. Can Mercedes believe it is getting its money's worth from this investment in human capital? "If you accept that this is an investment into possibly a lifetime's work, then it's an excellent investment. When they are through with their apprenticeship, you have really first-class specialists," asserts Helmut Werner, Mercedes' chairman.[17]

ENCOURAGING STUDENTS' INTEREST IN STEM CAREERS

With each passing year, fewer employers are passively waiting for more high-quality talent to emerge from their countries' schools. In addition to becoming engaged in career academies, businesses, particularly technology businesses, are encouraging students interested in STEM areas with a variety of incentives. Here are some examples of companies who are working to encourage youth participation in STEM career areas.

In 2008 between 75,000 and 95,000 engineering positions in

Germany were estimated to be vacant due to a lack of suitable candidates. Such vacancies may grow to 140,000 by 2014.

As a result some German companies have launched programs that may yield more long-term results. Siemens, ThyssenKrupp, and Bosch, some of Germany's largest manufacturers, are trying to get children interested in science from an early age—kindergarten. Siemens's "discovery box" contains experiments in electricity, the environment, and water, designed for three- to six-year-olds. One uses simple batteries, lights, and wires for young children to make a basic electric circuit. "We want them to learn in a playful, not a pedagogic, way, and they can learn so much more at that age than they can later," states Maria Schumm-Tschauder, the project's coordinator.[18]

These companies and others invite teachers and professors to see how a twenty-first-century high-tech plant operates. "They are normally totally shocked at how different it is from their preconceptions," muses Thomas Kaeser, chief executive of Kaeser Kompressoren, a compressed air provider.

ThyssenKrupp steel company holds an Ideas Park, a biennial event in Stuttgart, that fills vast halls with hands-on experiments for children and adults. Nearly 300,000 people attend. "It is a great success," says ThyssenKrupp's chief executive, Ekkehard Schulz.

In another strategy, Lenze, a maker of mechanical drives, established three businesses inside different technical colleges. They are attempting to both commercialize their innovations more rapidly and attract new engineers to these projects.

Hewlett-Packard supports about seventy U.S. school districts with an enhanced math and science Scholar Program. This is part of a larger career initiative called Diversity in Education, wherein HP offers jobs to students right after their freshman year of college. Says HP's Cathy Lipe, "The summer internships and working with HP mentors are the key to their retention in their major."[19]

The Higher Education and Advanced Technology Center

(HEAT) in Denver, Colorado is a collaborative career effort between local community colleges and corporations, including Cisco Systems, Intel, Lucent Technologies, Miller Electric, Haas Automation, and Parametric Technology. These companies provide state-of-the-art facilities for the new technologies they use every day to educate future gold-collar workers in such technologies as electronics manufacturing, laser troubleshooting, precision joining, electron optics and fiber optics, vacuum systems, biotech manufacturing, and digital film and video production. HEAT also trains K–12 teachers on how to offer their students classroom instruction in these new technologies.[20]

Cisco Networking Academy, established ten years ago, offers curriculum designed to augment technical education. It partners with a broad range of organizations worldwide to create e-learning that reaches 700,000 learners in more than 160 countries. CCNA Discovery and CCNA Exploration are curricula that give learners a firm grounding in networking technology. Cisco Discovery features interactive tools, easy-to-follows labs, and quick application exercises for students with basic computer skills. Exploration offers students in postsecondary schools and working professionals more technical depth by engaging the learners' advanced analytical skills. The Networking Academy offers its courses in collaboration with secondary and postsecondary schools, universities, technical-vocational schools, even prisons and homeless shelters.[21]

The Technology Student Association (TSA), founded in 1978, has helped more than 2 million middle and high school students explore STEM-related topics through cooperative teams, curricular activities, competitive events, and related programs at the local, state, and national levels. I was able to participate when the national TSA competitions were held in Chicago. It was amazing to see 4,000 very enthusiastic, smartly dressed teens—boys in suits and girls in skirts— willingly participate in contests in areas such as robotics, computer applications, automotive technologies, and architecture, as well as in other STEM-related group projects. Currently 150,000 middle and high school students are participating in forty-eight states at 1,800 TSA school chapters. Many corporate sponsors, including Raytheon, DuPont, Applied Technologies, Alphabyte Technologies, InfoComm, and Pitsco, support TSA programs.[22]

The Academies Creating Teacher Scientist Program was launched in 2004. Federal scientists from twelve U.S. Department of Energy labs, including Argonne, Fermi, Lawrence Livermore, and Oak Ridge, are paired with middle and high school teachers. They craft activities and lessons for classroom use. So far, more than two hundred teachers have taken part, receiving $800 weekly stipends for four to eight weeks over three consecutive summers. Many live in housing at these federal labs. The goal is to produce lead science and math teachers who can, in turn, tutor their colleagues in local schools across America.[23]

The IBM Academic Initiative offers accredited postsecondary institutions around the world academic course materials, textbooks, software, tutorials, forums, webcasts, and newsletters. Faculty and students have access to all IBM software and IBM staff so that they may learn the latest IT technologies. Faculty can keep up on the latest skills, and students have increased access to placements and industry certifications. This program helps prepare students for computer science, IT, and STEM-related college majors. It increases potential partnerships with IBM customers and business partners.[24]

AT&T Aspire is a $100 million initiative whose aim is to help reduce the high number of high school dropouts through four programs: (1) Grants are offered to support "existing proven high school retention programs, or to build capacity to launch such programs"; (2) 100,000 high school students will be paired with AT&T workers for a first-hand look at work through job shadowing, in a program run by Junior Achievement Worldwide; (3) John M. Bridgeland, coauthor of *The Silent Epidemic: Perspectives of High School Dropouts* (2006), will conduct a new study on the issue by examining the perspectives of teachers and school administrators; and (4) America's Promise Alliance will organize one hundred state and community dropout prevention summits for community, business, and education leaders.[25]

The Kalamazoo Promise is "You go to college and I'll pay for it." Broadly speaking. that is what the community of Kalamazoo, Michigan has said to its public high school students. Though the fund's benefactors remain anonymous, I suspect they include the leading businesses of this region and several people with deep pockets. The motivation is clear: create more talented people and you will begin to enhance the Kalamazoo region's economy. They have made available unlimited college scholarship funds (including tuition and mandatory fees) over a long-term period to primarily help lower-income students stay in high school and attend a postsecondary institution. Since the program began in 2005, there was a 30 percent increase in female public high school graduates as of 2007. "This program has great long-term potential to enhance the region's human capital," says Michelle Miller-Adams, visiting scholar at the W.E. Upjohn Institute, a local research think-tank, that has published a book on this program. Already the Kalamazoo Promise has created a new optimism in much of this community and seems to be helping raise the motivation of at least some students who see additional education leading to a brighter future.

The Kalamazoo Promise has had a powerful positive effect on other communities. Since its announcement on November 2005, more than a dozen other U.S. cities have announced their intention to implement similar programs.

The Kalamazoo Promise and similar community programs all have the potential to add a major new piece to reinventing local education-to-employment talent systems.[26]

CREATING TALENT IN THE HEALTH CARE SECTOR

Few people will dispute that over the next decade health care will remain a major growth industry. But to what extent will the health care sector drive an entire community's local economy? Several American communities may provide us with answers as they seek to grow and prosper.

Both the Mayo Clinic in Rochester, Minnesota and the Cleveland Clinic in Cleveland, Ohio are clearly reshaping their region's economies and future workforces. These are both huge hospitals with revenues in the billions.

Both hospitals devote a great deal of attention to talent creation because they will both experience significant increased demand for patient services over the next decade. Mayo and Cleveland are hard at work to find the potential talent to fill thousands of additional nursing, technician, and institutional support jobs. How are they doing this?

The Cleveland Clinic offers a "School at Work" program to upgrade the skills of current workers. Through the Tri-State Community College, the hospital provides tuition-free, on-site nursing and radiology-technology education programs to longer-term employees.

The Cleveland Clinic Lerner College of Medicine of Case Western University began offering tuition-free education to encourage top students to enter academic medicine. The school's goal is to prepare physician investigators who can both conduct research and teach. Lerner is the first U.S. medical school to forgo tuition for every student. This greatly enhances the Cleveland Clinic's career-preparation role at the level of higher education.

Both hospitals are also committed to extensive career-education programs in the city's schools so that parents and students alike have information and first-hand exposure to future opportunities in health care careers. The future success or failure of Mayo and the Cleveland Clinic will be directly linked to how well they can help rebuild their local education-to-employment systems.[27]

Other American small towns are beginning to see the impact of health care as an economic driver. In *Boom Town USA*, Jack Schultz identified several other cities that have the potential to become regional health care hubs and growing high-tech employers. Those include Lebanon, New Hampshire; Traverse City, Michigan; Columbia, Tennessee; Bend, Oregon; and Yankton, South Dakota. In each case the limits of their future success will be largely determined by how well they can foster community collaboration to expand their local health care and technology talent-creation systems.[28]

THE LIBERAL ARTS COLLEGE PREP CAREER ACADEMY

The dropout epidemic, particularly in America's urban high schools, must be brought to an end. This is one of the weakest links in the current U.S. talent system. A major 2006 study by Peter D. Hart Research Associates, "The Silent Epidemic: Perspectives of High School Dropouts," gave some surprising insights and answers to this problem. The top reason dropouts gave for leaving school was "Classes were not interesting" (47 percent). "Failing in school" was cited by about one-third of the students.

To keep students in school, these dropouts suggested three basic reforms: real-world learning opportunities, better teachers, and more individualized instruction.

Do these ideas sound familiar? The study recommended a school that combines academic and more hands-on preparation for college and future careers. This seems to appeal to most students.

Both liberal arts and career courses will offer credit to meet postsecondary enrollment requirements. This will help broaden the talent pipeline and improve the quality of high school courses. This is one of the chief goals of the Liberal Arts College Prep Career Academy.[29]

The Liberal Arts College Prep Career Academy will help adjust career expectations to society's current talent needs. It seeks to combine the best of the liberal arts with a broad array of career skills, emphasizing contextualized learning, while mobilizing close business linkages and financial support. The Liberal Arts Career College Prep Academy will help shut down America's "dropout factories."

In *Raising the Grade—How High School Reform Can Save Our Youth and Our Nation*, Bob Wise, a former governor of West Virginia and member of the U.S. Congress and now president of the Alliance for Excellent Education, states his belief that "A critical lack of investment in secondary school education is contributing to the social, political, and economic breakdown of generations of young Americans while at the same time undermining United States global competitiveness."[30]

At the heart of the new education-to-employment system, the Liberal Arts College Prep Career Academy will revitalize public and private financial support of highly effective strategies that offer more students open career opportunities. "Isn't it better to find out [your interests] in high school than when you're a junior in college, where you're paying for your credits and you've invested three years of your life?" asks Cheri Pierson Yecke, Florida's chancellor of K–12 education. "As adults we do students a disservice if we allow them to wander aimlessly through thirteen years of school."[31]

The goal of the Liberal Arts College Prep Career Academy is to ensure that every student graduates with a meaningful high school education.

The key to all these programs is that *all* students will graduate from high school and then move on to a variety of postsecondary options for a better-paying job. To keep everyone satisfied, let us call all these options simply "college."

Seventy percent of the thirty fastest-growing jobs require career education beyond high school. Yet data from the U.S. Bureau of Labor Statistics and the Educational Testing Service show that over the next decade only 40 percent of higher-skilled jobs will require a four-year degree or more. However, the other 60 percent of middle-skill jobs call for two-year degrees, one- to two-year certificate programs, or two- to four-year technical apprenticeships. The problem is that talent projections indicate a serious slowdown in the growth of the number of people who will attain these education requirements.[32]

Research indicates that unprecedented technological change over the next decades will create many new jobs and career areas while rendering others obsolete. There is a clear need to broaden education preparation at all levels. It is encouraging to note that data from the U.S. Department of Education show an unprecedented 85 percent rise over the past decade in the number of college bachelor's degrees with double and, more rarely, triple majors.

"They are doing double majors to make sure they have all the skills they need to make themselves employable," says Cheryl Beil, assistant vice president of academic planning at George Washington University. Darby Walters, a recent graduate in molecular biology/English literature from Pomona College in southern California, offers this echo boomer insight: "The great thing about our generation is that we don't feel we are limited to have one profession in life. We feel we can change and start over." This is a goal that the Liberal Arts College Prep Career Academy can help more Americans achieve.[33]

Offering students this more powerful, blended, liberal arts plus career preparation will take more time. "It's not 'either-or'; its 'both' and 'more,'" says Jim Shelton, executive director of the Eastern division of the Seattle-based Bill and Melinda Gates Foundation.

In addition to supporting career education many businesses are also actively engaged in investing in their human capital through quality training-and-development programs for employees. They are practicing the "Sixth Discipline" to address current and long-term employee talent needs. Let us see how.

TRAINING—A NEW PERSPECTIVE

The 2010–2020 society will be a knowledge society. For the U.S. economy to thrive, this will mean concentrating on producing high-value services and products. This new knowledge economy relies heavily on many kinds of knowledge workers: teachers, doctors, lawyers, engineers.

But according to Peter Drucker, the most striking growth will be in the number of "knowledge technologists." These are software designers, industrial and manufacturing technicians, computer technicians, or medical technologists of all kinds.

In the twentieth century, semiskilled and unskilled workers in manufacturing were the backbone of the social and political forces that helped create the U.S. middle class. In the twenty-first-century Cyber-Mental Age, it will be the knowledge technologists in both services and industrial/manufacturing areas who are likely to become the dominant social and political force shaping U.S. culture and its high-tech economy.[34]

What is now beginning to emerge is that some global business leaders are investing more on training and development to grow this knowledge workforce. Since 1990, U.S. business investment rose almost 30 percent to over $56 billion in 2008.[35]

Employers embracing this new perspective undertake to provide their employees with lifelong learning opportunities. Employees commit to acquiring three sets of skills that underpin their effectiveness: technical career skills specific to a job, IT skills that use technology to create innovations and increase business advantage, and personal behavior and management skills for a high-performance work culture.

Of course, the range of skills and proficiency levels depends on the nature of each person's job and career expectations. But every individual will require a strong foundation of liberal arts and thinking skills to complement these special career and specific job skills.

What is the major goal of this business perspective shift? To unlock employees' potential for innovation by helping them learn "how to learn" more effectively throughout their careers rather than simply hoping that employees will take the initiative in improving their learning abilities and acquiring more knowledge throughout their working lives.[36]

"The skills gap affecting many industries . . . means companies are no longer simply paying lip service to the slogan 'People are our most important asset'," says Pat Galagan, an executive editor at the American Society for Training and Development.

Talent management has become an issue of strategic importance for most businesses. Talent creation will soon join it as a vital activity to ensure that companies can fill key positions to survive and thrive, which entails retraining and reeducating the current workforce to fill open positions. Seventy percent of the workers who will be on the job in 2020 are today's employees. Motivating more people to engage in high-quality, lifelong learning is not just a nice option; it is now a business operational necessity.

To that end, training-and-development culture is changing, says Martyn Sloman at the Chartered Institute of Personnel and Development. According to Sloman, "The way in which these skills are delivered is shifting from a traditional top-down instructional model (college classroom education) to a more decentralized approach that puts greater emphasis on learning at work." In the end, talent creation is all about changing people's perspective on what they do at work and how they do it.[37]

TALENT CREATION 101

How does U.S. business invest over $50 billion annually in employer-sponsored workforce training and development? Several annual surveys offer a snapshot of programs, trends, and issues.

Based on its survey results, the publication *Training*, in "Training Top 100" (2006) and "Training Top 125" (2008), profiled the best corporate learning and performance improvement programs. These are America's talent miracle workers. They spend over $5 billion and provide an average of fifty-two hours of training per employee. The top five organizations were Booz Allan Hamilton, IBM, Ernst and Young, the Ritz-Carlton, and KLA-Tencor. They have been in the top ten for at least four consecutive years. Some of the best were smaller companies: Protis Executive Innovations (thirty employees), American Power Conversion (two hundred fifty employees), and Washington State Employees Credit Union (five hundred employees).

Typical programs range from leadership development to first-line supervisory training, coaching, mentoring, sales training, or succession planning. Some companies offer more innovative training. Shaw Industries of Dalton, Georgia operates the Shaws Skills Center, which offers one-on-one tutoring in math, reading, and writing, as well as small-group and computer-based learning. It also provides a company-based general educational development (GED) program.

General Mills offers employees more than 1,000 courses, including cereal production and other technologies, quality, maintenance, and food chemistry. Allstate Insurance Company partnered with a local university to start an on-site MBA program as part of its succession planning effort. Cerner Corp., Kansas City, Missouri, developed an online process tool that trains and supports employees in the design, testing, and maintenance of its software.

Research shows that employer training and development is most effective when it occurs in a work environment. It generally can achieve high rates of financial return if enough time is used to achieve effective skills development that raises worker performance and productivity. This applies equally to learning programs for executives, first-line supervisors, production and office staff, and entry-level workers. Strategic public-private partnerships for low-income or various types of challenged workers are also most effective when they are workplace-based and offer the trainee immediate on-the-job application of what is being learned.

Training's survey revealed that ninety-nine of one hundred of these businesses offer tuition reimbursement. Many have no maximum dollar limit per year, and forty-one organizations do not require that the courses be tied to specific job development. Paying for employee courses is a great motivator and retention tool for all companies.

As more businesses are unable to find the talent to fill vital jobs, they are beginning to follow a more comprehensive training-and-education strategy by developing current staff who have the motivation to learn and advance. Furthermore, these organizations see talent development as a continuum process for keeping employees loyal by offering them career paths for advancement. Over the next decade, as the talent pool diminishes, more businesses will adopt this enlightened human capital strategy.[38]

GRADUATE STUDIES: THE CORPORATE UNIVERSITY

Peter Senge, in his book *The Fifth Discipline*, is widely credited with establishing the concept of a business as a "learning organization." His ideas helped spawn the corporate university movement across the United States, Europe, and Asia.[39]

What is a corporate university? Some are similar to traditional universities, offering a qualification described as a "degree," such as Allianz Management Institute near Munich, Germany. Others blend elaborate course offerings in classroom settings with professional development via e-learning. Among the major players are Disney, Mars, National Defense, Farmers Insurance, and General Electric (GE).

Every year hundreds of people attend the GE University John F. Welch Leadership Center in Crotonville, New York. Some call it a "business school boot camp," a mixture of classes and case-study preparation. In-house faculty are supplemented with guest professors from Harvard and Wharton. Top GE management drop by.

"When I come here, it's a big deal because I feel like the company is investing in me," says Anne Algapiedi from GE Capital Solutions. She has taken six classes at the University. "I get to meet people from all over the world and I get exposure to business leaders I wouldn't ordinarily get to see," she says. For multinational companies, such campuses are important means of preparing younger executives to fill the shoes of the experienced leaders who will be retiring over the next ten to fifteen years.[40]

Experts estimate there are more than 2,000 corporate universities in the United States alone. They often exist because many organizations see traditional university business schools as too theoretical and slow-paced. In addition, research from Corporate University Xchange in Pennsylvania suggests that investment in corporate universities improves the bottom line.

Overall training at these corporate universities, or within more traditional business training departments, uses a variety of methods to educate their employees. Surprisingly, classroom training remains the most used and the most popular with employees, according to a 2008 *Training* survey and the American Society for Training and Development.

E-learning has many positive applications. But many research studies continue to show that blended learning (classroom and e-learning) seems to yield the best learning outcomes for most training topics and audiences.[41]

CREATING VALUE—THE SIXTH DISCIPLINE

Q. If changing employee demographics are changing businesses learning and strategies, why do so few businesses (16 percent) still make workplace learning a top priority?

A. The business community accepts that making physical capital investments today, such as building a plant or purchasing equipment, may yield a good profit tomorrow. However, business does not yet accept the idea that making intangible "human capital" investments today may yield a good profit tomorrow.

This was confirmed by "Tomorrow's People, Managing Talent in a Diverse World," a 2007 study by the Hay Group and the Management Consultancies Association (United Kingdom). Line managers find it difficult to give people enough time to develop their talents. Sixty-one percent agree that talent development is essential for an organization's survival, but less than 25 percent think their companies' present training-and-development programs can deliver the future talent they need. This confirms the wisdom on the street that says managers will always turn away from creating more talent in order to hit their short-term targets. The irony is that better development of their team's talent will make it easier to achieve their targets.

There are four practical reasons given for a business-culture learning disconnect:

1. Training is an expense, not an investment.
2. Training cannot produce a decent financial metric.
3. Training reduces motivation.
4. Training provides results in the long term, whereas the business focus is on short-term profit.

First, business accounting standards are stacked against workplace learning. The U.S. accounting system classifies training and educating people as a business "expense," and purchasing equipment, machines, buildings as an "investment." Particularly for publicly traded companies, this means that learning programs are deducted from quarterly earnings, whereas capital investments can be depreciated over time (according to IRS regulations).

In the minds of most business people, this makes investing in human capital a very unattractive business expense. Business guru Stephen Covey explains, "That's a psychology that affects the training-and-development industry. If people are an expense and not an investment, imagine the psychology that spreads throughout an entire organization. It's like doing bloodletting when we understand germ theory. We can try to do bloodletting better, but the underlying paradigm is that people are an expense. And yet 80 percent of all value added comes from people."[42]

In a twenty-first-century knowledge economy, expensing training does not make any sense. Current U.S. accounting standards were basically written for a twentieth-century industrial-age economy. The result is a self-defeating management psychology and profound alienation within U.S. business culture. This needs immediate change through the development of accounting standards and IRS regulations that will allow businesses to begin depreciating training, development, and education investments. The IRS already allows some training costs to be capitalized.[43]

Second, business does not value training because its financial return cannot be proved. In other words, what is the ROI for a specific training program? The Sarbanes-Oxley Act of 2002 has put the financial people back in firm control of business investments. But can the training community provide them with a realistic training ROI? Today the answer is in the affirmative. Several financial measurement systems make it possible to accurately account for training transfer, eliminate other business variables, and depreciate the training effect in computing a more accurate ROI.[44]

Third, talent management and talent creation underpin a major shift in the last decade from "training" to "learning." For many business people, "training" is a bad word, a "demotivator." Training is for behavior change and is instructor led. But learning is more self-directed to increase a person's innovative job capacities. Though related, training and learning are different. You can put people in a training classroom or in front of a screen, but they cannot be made to learn.

What is the point of business learning? It is to enable people to reach a higher level of knowledge that produces new ideas and innovations inside a business. Learning takes resources and time.

The great majority of American businesses are underperforming because their internal culture continues to suppress adequate investment in their most important intangible assets—expanding the ideas, creativity, and innovative capacity of their knowledge workers. This has been the basic modus operandi of U.S. business throughout the twentieth century. These business-culture attitudes are at the heart of the United States' talent crisis.[45]

Fourth, "short-termism" is seriously undercutting long-term investment in serious talent-creation efforts. In a market economy, projecting future earnings and tracking quarterly performance is important. But when the pressure to impress Wall Street becomes too intense, companies are placed in a position that can actually damage their long-term profitability. With each passing year, the focus on quarterly earnings has increasingly overshadowed the rest of a company's job—that is, sustainability and innovation. This excessive focus on "short-termism" helped to produce the U.S. financial meltdown in the autumn of 2008.

As a result, a new consensus is growing among chief executives, regulators, and Wall Street analysts against "quarterly guidance," a practice that is illegal in most other countries. "It's all part of a growing trend," says David Chavern at the U.S. Chamber of Commerce. The Chamber and such economic leaders as Warren Buffett are cheering on CEOs and CFOs to approach their boards about stopping this destructive practice.[46]

Quarterly guidance often misses the mark, says an editorial in the *Financial Times*, because "Business simply does not go in a straight line. There are bound to be moments of volatility. Investors should accept this, while managements should get better at communicating their longer-term ambitions."[47]

Why is this issue so critical to the talent question? If your company's objective is to build up a more skilled and knowledgeable workforce, the answer can be expressed in one word: motivation. What motivates knowledge workers to learn and innovate in your business? They enjoy the process, feel it advances their status and capacity to do the job, and care about the organization.

Quality life-long learning provided by a business can help workers manage their knowledge and skill needs. The lines between management, staff, technicians, and professionals have become increasingly blurred because of technology and lean-management operations. Continuous professional development that was once provided only to executives is becoming an operational necessity for more and more of the workforce. Today, employee knowledge needs constant refreshing, as the pace of change and innovation is driving an information explosion.

Higher-quality training, development, and education for employees that is applied to solving specific business performance and productivity issues will yield a better ROI and result in a more talented staff. On the other hand, poorly designed, sporadic, flavor-of-the-month, scattershot training programs are often applied as a solution to bad management decisions.

How many of yesterday's bright ideas do you remember experiencing? Benchmarking, the Balanced Scorecard, quality circles, sixth sigma, theory X/Y? What impact did any of the above have on your performance? Commonly, these ideas often failed to become embedded in a business, as organizations moved on too quickly to the next new idea. Change fatigue and disillusionment set in, as new ideas never reach deep into all levels of an organization.

Globally each nation's business culture may be somewhat different. However, the Chartered Institute of Personnel and Development Talent Creation study in 2006 found no fundamental difference in these basic talent-creation issues. "The underlying model proved to be the same throughout the world," says the Institute's Martyn Sloman. The only caveat is the need for a business to offer talent programs in different ways, and at different levels, that match the prior education experiences of the adult learner.[48]

In *The Fifth Discipline*, Senge introduced a systems approach to create a so-called "learning organization." Senge's five disciplines provide the business system that can successfully adjust individual company talent programs to the prior learning experiences of each worker. These five disciplines will trigger a business culture of change. The organizations begin to see talent creation as another profit driver, rather than as something alien and outside of entrepreneurship.[49]

To reinforce this system, business also needs what I call a "Sixth Discipline for Talent Formation." This Sixth Discipline helps a business strike a balance between meeting short-term profit goals and investing in long-term sustainability. Organizations can use five basic strategies to achieve the goals of the Sixth Discipline:

1. Use continuous education, training, and development programs as a talent-creation means to achieve core business requirements.
2. Offer a blend of classroom and technology-based learning.
3. Collaborate with community partners to broaden the education-to-employment local pipeline.
4. Measure the ROI of both these internal and external learning programs.
5. Budget investments in human capital and physical capital to achieve the goals and objective of the business.[50]

The Sixth Discipline for Talent Formation (see Figure 2) aims at helping a business both recruit and develop more highly talented people and increase employee performance and innovation. People

Figure 2: The Sixth Discipline for Talent Formation

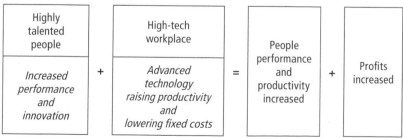

Source: Edward E. Gordon, 2009.

will make better use of advanced technologies that require fewer employees for the amount produced and level of quality. The Sixth Discipline's goal is to raise both people performance and organizational productivity that will increase profit and rebuild talent pipelines around the world.

INNOVATE TODAY OR PERISH TOMORROW

Until now there has been no real sense of urgency regarding the talent crisis. As we have already seen, numerous studies, surveys, and reports have already been issued, first on the "literacy crisis," then on a "skills crisis." But now the true effects of a global talent showdown have begun to ripple across the world business community. Between 2010 and 2020, companies will have few alternatives but to hire large numbers of people who do not have the required talent, and then try to fill in their knowledge gaps. There will not be enough available qualified talent to fill millions of essential vacant positions.

What we need now is an honest discussion about talent and globalization. What are the policy solutions to the challenges and opportunities that this cyber-mental world economy is thrusting on every nation?

Without an adequate supply of talented people, it will not matter if a business tries to use advanced technologies or hammers out better trade agreements.[51] A new mind-set is needed.

What does this new mind-set look like? Peter Drucker gave us two essential components. First, managers need to stop using workers "like cogs in a huge inhuman machine." Forget Frederick Taylor's stopwatch management. Start treating people like "brain workers." Second, community leaders need to realize that knowledge and talent creation are the two most important economic resources for any advanced society.[52]

This chapter has shown that many companies are doing some major rethinking about the basic role of business in expanding the talent pool for a twenty-first century workplace. But one company, no matter how large, cannot do it alone. Intensive community collaboration to rebuild the broken talent pipeline is now the name of the game for business sustainability.

As we will see in the next and final chapter, communities like Santa Ana, California; Fargo, North Dakota; Danville, Illinois; and Mansfield, Ohio; and many others, are making unified community efforts to rebuild their fractured education-to-employment systems. Such initiatives are making the talent system work better all over the globe.

CHAPTER 6

PRODUCING NEW TALENT

We can only see a short distance ahead, but we can see plenty that needs to be done.

—Alan Furing, father of modern computer science, 1950

Those nations that better manage their talent resources will become more productive and competitive. Future growth in most nations around the globe will hinge on businesses putting their people resources to more efficient use. The comparative advantage of the developed economies is the existence of high-value, knowledge-intensive activities. Future employment will have to shift toward an increase in higher-skill-based jobs if such nations are to maintain their economic growth. Nations whose cultures resist this talent shift risk being left behind.[1]

BUSINESS SUSTAINABILITY

The international business community has a huge stake in overcoming the education shortcomings in both developed and developing nations. Traditionally, U.S. business has treated the development of education and talent as a part-time charitable activity. But now the global talent crisis is forcing business leaders to think again about sustainability. Hau Lee, a professor at Stanford University, defines sustainability as "ensuring that we are using resources today that will not jeopardize the resources of tomorrow." Self-interest now compels businesses to better develop talent resources today, so there will be a tomorrow.[2]

In 1957 the S&P 500 Index of leading U.S. companies was created. Forty years on, just seventy-four of the original companies still appear on this list. Old complacent companies become victims of "creative destruction," frequently to satisfy the short-term whim of market investors looking for the true value of a stock. It is now becoming more difficult to recruit talented and committed workers than to find investors.[3]

Corporate social responsibility amounts to enlightened self-interest. The big talent challenges of the next decade, once seen as obstacles to companies, have become opportunities for innovation and business development. Companies with this philosophy are becoming the places where people want to work. How are they doing this? By partnering with their local communities to create CBOs and NGOs whose programs and initiatives are rebuilding the jobs pipeline all over the world.[4]

For companies, such CBO/NGO partnerships give all parties a way to share in the talent benefits. "I think businesses have tended to move away from philanthropy to become much more committed to partnerships . . . [that] have more depth to them these days," says Dax Lovegrove, a consultant in business and industry relations.[5]

Once established, these CBO or NGO community talent-creation systems will be used as potential education-to-employment system models for a state, region, across the United States, and across the entire world. They can help bridge the divide between employers, workers, and the future.[6]

WHAT ARE CBOs AND NGOs?

Community-based organizations (CBOs) and nongovernment organizations (NGOs) can be broadly defined as independent voluntary associations of people acting together on a continuous basis for some common purpose. NGOs include only private-sector partners. CBOs also encompass government entities. What they are now doing across the United States is bypassing the empty political rhetoric at the top to shape the debate, at the local level, about the goals and aspirations of the people. CBOs and NGOs worldwide have grown from 1,400 in 1975 to 30,000 today. Peter Drucker has referred to them as the "third sector of society." They are accomplishing what business and government acting alone have failed to do. Through their collaborative power, they have had a significant cultural impact on corporate and government strategy and decision making.

CBOs and NGOs do not duplicate services already available in a community, but rather leverage them into new combinations. They can do this because they offer a neutral civic space not owned by any single group. Every community has a variety of talent resources, but they usually are not all connected into a clear and coherent working network.

The principal function of CBOs and NGOs is to maximize all of the local available resources into a more powerful network of services. These networks usually include businesses; chambers of commerce; workforce boards; public and private elementary, secondary, and higher-education institutions; unions; parent groups; service clubs; and other local civic groups.

Each community's network is a living organism that consists of many relations that define the region's culture. CBO and NGO networks involve people learning, recognizing patterns of talent needs, and forging responses leading to stronger talent solutions.[7]

THE SECRETS OF CBOs AND NGOs

These bridges to the future are connecting human talent to the jobs and careers that businesses need filled.

Reviewing selected CBO and NGO case studies can help answer four basic questions behind these success stories: How to get started? Who takes the lead? What does it do? How to keep it moving forward?

How to Get Started?

In each case, CBOs and NGOs were started because key community leaders discerned that a deteriorating local economy might sink into a real long-term economic crisis. They realized that the local talent pool did not have the skills needed for current or future jobs.

Public town-hall-style meetings were held to explore these issues. These forums were held in a neutral civic space—a hotel, library, or public auditorium. Leaders listened as much as spoke. Effective engagement means understanding the points of view of other community activists who want to collaborate.

In every instance, these town-hall meetings took far more time than originally planned. This should come as no surprise. For the principal stakeholders: business people, educators, parents, union members, government representatives, it was a rare event to meet people outside their own silo.

The fact is we all live in silos. Cultural attitudes on jobs, careers, and education are all grounded in individual success stories from the current jobs system. As the system gradually waned in a community, members of each group usually blame others for personal financial pain, job loss, and a shrinking local economy.[8] (For an outline of the five steps in establishing a CBO or NGO, see the Resource B section at the end of the book.)

Who Takes the Lead?

As we will see, in some cases the local Chamber of Commerce began the workforce discussion. However, it was quickly joined by other community groups. In other cities or regions, the initial push may come from the workforce board, community college, economic development commission, foundation, or other civic group. The key is not so much who starts the process of civic engagement; the vital component is the quick broadening of the network that ultimately will support building a new local talent system.

What Does the CBO or NGO Do?

Most CBOs and NGOs select two to three initiatives on which they can focus. Two principal talent issues that have emerged are the re-development of the current workforce and K–16 career-education-information programs for students. They are also addressing many other socioeconomic issues that have broader tie-ins to talent creation.

Focusing on what to do is critical for any CBO or NGO, and it is the hardest task to accomplish. These organizations need to explore all the facets of a truly transformational initiative. Incremental change will not be enough. Partners need to get a clear understanding of what success will look like before a lack of focus starts dissipating their broader community support.

Once the CBO or NGO has defined an initiative, three steps are essential in its execution: aligning the resources, setting some milestones, and drafting an action plan to determine who does what by when. The organization also needs to establish an evaluation process to determine what is working and what changes to make as the initiative proceeds.[9]

At worst, CBOs and NGOs may face severe skepticism and sharp criticism when they choose the talent issues that will form their first focus. At best, they will still meet passive resistance because changing cultural biases takes time, as they are firmly rooted in the status quo.

Most CBOs and NGOs engage a reputable outside research firm to conduct an initial economic and talent development study. Data from this report can be used to strengthen the case for the choices of what to do first.

How to Keep the CBO or NGO Moving Forward?

As the CBO or NGO develops, it continuously needs to identify local quality resources for workers' lifelong learning. They improve the local-talent-creation system by delivering these education services through a centralized training center, at an education institution, at a business site, or all of the above.

K–16 career education and the raising of overall quality of education for every student are developed through a diversity of curriculum models prepared by public and private education institutions collaborating with local business.

To make the CBO or NGO sustainable, the process needs to be open, honest, and frank. It needs to build trust, emphasize speed, and even be fun. The basic rule should be: "We are going to expect behavior toward one another that will build trust and mutual respect."

Invisible fences can undercut this collaboration. Usually, 90 percent of a community's people are willing volunteers open to the CBO or NGO process. But 10 percent are "soreheads" who want no change. CBOs and NGOs need to concentrate on the 90 percent and ignore the rest.

Successful CBOs and NGOs are specifically organized around a strong mission. They find, focus, launch, and learn. CBOs and NGOs represent the leading community activists. They develop the financial and ethical power to implement their vision. CBOs and NGOs represent a stable force for long-term change.

They are scrappy and entrepreneurial in their efforts to cobble together breakthrough programs and effective funding. CBOs and NGOs represent any country's best chance to release forces of civic self-help to reinvent the education-to-employment system.[10]

In the coming years, we can expect local CBOs and NGOs to evolve from unofficial nonprofit associations to major culture-changing players in the restructuring of a new United States. Why? It is because of their collective leadership's greater conceptual capacity to digest the increasingly complex masses of information that top leaders must comprehend. CBOs and NGOs have greater ability than solo organizations to view, understand, and act instead of surrendering to gridlock, which only preserves the status quo.

This may be one of the reasons that, in recent years, traditional foundations have moved their charitable giving into more sustainable partnerships with CBOs and NGOs in support of a range of education and training initiatives. For example, the Bill and Melinda Gates Foundation, the Chicago Community Trust, and the Carnegie Corporation of New York are all supporting new, not-for-profit, grass-roots efforts in education and training. "If you're going to tackle education, you have to have a concerted approach," states Hugh Jagger, a strategic advisor to Cisco Systems. "The private sector doesn't have the resources to do the whole job, but it certainly has the capacity to help put the right models in place that the public sector can scale up."[11]

"WE ARE ALL IN THIS TOGETHER"

The world has entered a time of historic transformation—a Cyber-Mental Age. CBOs and NGOs will help us clearly rethink how we create talent in our communities. People need to be better prepared for a different cultural reality: jobs that are built on a knowledge economy.

"We are not presently succeeding in effectively educating a significant and growing segment of our student body," says Mark Dixon, a Springfield Missouri community activist. "I am curious if we are all ready to look more intently into the matter of the methods and resources that will result in success for all of our children? . . . It may well take all our ideas and support, both inside and outside of the 'system' to turn it around. But then, we are, after all, in this together, right?"[12]

CBOs and NGOs can help communities better answer this basic question. They are culturally bound together by something more than just self-interest: the pursuit of private economic advantage. "The greatest asset of public action is its ability to satisfy vaguely felt needs for higher purpose in the lives of men and women," says economist Albert O. Hirschman. This is the true secret behind CBO and NGO success stories. International businesses have come to the conclusion that combining their expertise with the broader influence of local CBOs and NGOs is the best way of addressing the talent sustainability challenge across the United States.[13]

Now let us take a close look at some successful collaborations.

Santa Ana—Crossing the Bridge to High School, Inc.

In the Los Angeles area, about 52 percent of the native-born adults have such low skills that they do not qualify for the Orange County jobs requiring advanced skill levels. Add to this issue the fact that over 150,000 of Santa Ana's 350,000 residents came from Latin America, according to the 2000 U.S. Census. This is not the talent formula for a high-end workforce.

Santa Ana is a sizable California city located near Disneyland. Nearly three quarters of its population speak Spanish at home. This is the largest proportion in the nation. Santa Ana has the second-largest concentration of small manufacturers in the United States. This includes high-tech companies such as Power Wave Technologies and Textron Aerospace Fasteners. By the late 1990s, its companies began to experience difficulties filling jobs. Some moved away. Twenty thousand jobs were lost during this time.

In 1998 the Santa Ana Chamber of Commerce convened a task force of business and education leaders. They reached three conclusions, stated Dale Ward, the chamber's executive vice president.

"First, Santa Ana had widening talent gaps between student/adult education and industry skill standards. Second, a talent solution had to be understood clearly, based on ever-changing business market requirements. Third, this initiative had to be business-led in close collaboration with educators."[14]

Thus was born the "Bridge to Careers" CBO, which over the next six years formed the initiatives for the development of an array of job readiness programs supported by several hundred local businesses.

In 2007 Santa Ana crossed that bridge by establishing High School, Inc., a liberal arts college preparatory career academy, the nation's first such public school, run jointly by a board of local business people and educators. Students take a broad range of liberal arts courses, including English, history, math, and science. In addition, six career academies located inside the high school provide courses based on the region's leading growth industries: engineering and construction, health care, automotive and transportation, global businesses, high-tech manufacturing, and new media. Courses are taught by a team of educators and business professionals.

"A lot of what students are learning here are things they can apply directly to current jobs," says computer graphics teacher Cynthia Holland. Her students draw 3-D building models, prepare Pixar-like computer animations, and learn other business software.

High School, Inc. also serves as an outreach program for small businesses, providing their workers with education and skills training programs.

The "English Works" program is the other principal initiative begun by the Santa Ana Chamber to address the needs of local businesses for employees with higher levels of English literacy. The chamber and the Rancho Santiago Community College District collaborated on a campaign to publicize this program.

To reach its goal of advancing English literacy skills for 50,000 Santa Ana residents, English Works holds classes in more than seventy locations across the region. This effort has increased community collaborations with local neighborhood associations. English Works also stimulates residents' participation in the civic process, while helping bring better employment opportunities and career advancement for many.

As a result of these programs, the Santa Ana Chamber of Commerce is evolving into more of a CBO model. It will still be a chamber, but it will be more responsive to changing business and community needs. It has become the Greater Santa Ana Business Alliance "to better mobilize partnerships across the public and private sectors," says Chamber president Michael Metzler. "We're receiving many inquiries about our innovative programs, and we think they will become models for many other urban areas."[15] If Santa Ana's past success is any indicator, they may be right.

North Dakota

Who would have thought of North Dakota as a model for rebuilding the U.S. talent pipeline? Yet that is what it seems to be. In addition to endless fields of wheat, this state is beginning to see something of an economic renaissance in technology and also is becoming a major source of oil. Beginning in Fargo, and spreading to Bismarck and other areas of North Dakota, the talent-creation machine is in high gear.

In slightly more than a decade, more than 1,700 companies have moved into the Fargo region. In 2007 *Forbes Magazine* ranked Fargo fourth on a list of the best Small Metro Areas for Business and Careers. This was the fifth consecutive year Fargo has made the top five in this category.

As a regional hub with a population over 300,000, the region encompassing Fargo, North Dakota and Moorhead, Minnesota boasts eleven postsecondary institutions. This includes a Skill and Technology Training Center that is a joint venture among the region's two- and four-year colleges. Businesses send their workers to the center for retraining. Also, high school and college students and unemployed workers use this fee-for-service technical-skills education center. The center draws people from a radius of one hundred to one hundred fifty miles, thereby creating new local talent.

But it is local community activists at the grassroots level—the Fargo-Moorhead (FM) Chamber of Commerce, the Greater Fargo-Cass County Economic Development Corporation, and many others—who have helped Fargo's economic rebirth with a new economy moving from agriculture into the technology-services industries.

"Cooperation makes us better," says David Martin, president of the FM Chamber of Commerce. He is illustrative of the overall community willingness to help each other and get things done by addressing the difficult twin issues of talent creation and related economic renewal.

More than 25,000 new jobs have been added during the past decade, and a 90,000-person workforce now staffs such businesses as Quest Corporation, Xcel Energy, Aggregate Industries, American Crystal Sugar, U.S. Bank Services, Innovis Heath, Microsoft, Pracs Institute, Ltd., and a host of others. Fargo is Microsoft's second-largest campus in the United States. Since coming to town in 2005, Microsoft's headcount has risen from more than 1,000 employees to 1,500 (2008). It is expected to rise to 1,900 by 2010 to 2011. Drawing on local Great Plains talent is important as Microsoft, like other high-tech organizations, is experiencing significant talent shortages. Such high-tech employment provides good careers to young North Dakotans and helps the state stem the flight of young people from the American Great Plains.

In other parts of the state, other companies like Bobcat, a division of Ingersoll-Rand Co. Ltd., also have found some of the same work culture advantages in sticking to its Gwinner, North Dakota roots. Also of major importance is the oil coming from a vast blanket of rock shale called the Bakkon Belt that may prove to be one of the largest recent oil finds in the United States. "North Dakota is producing oil at a rate not previously contemplated," says Morris Beschloss, an international economist. This surge in production will produce additional demands for specialized talent development at the state's higher-education institutions and job-training centers. The increasing world-wide demand for energy gives North Dakota additional incentives to literally fuel expansion of its talent-creation system.[16]

Fargo and other small towns in North Dakota are not the only ones working together through community activism to reinvent the local economy and rebuild the talent pool. Danville, Illinois is another community that has also followed this path.

The Talent Advantage

Danville in Vermilion County, Illinois is a city of about 34,000 people. As a blue-collar manufacturing town, it began struggling in the late 1980s when a General Motors plant closed and other employers soon shut up shop.

But Danville reached down deep into its community, organized a new CBO talent-and-economic development system, and changed its image. Between 1998 and 1999, the Vermilion Advantage was born through the merger of the local Chamber of Commerce, Economic Development Commission, and Workforce Development Board. The Vermilion Advantage has multiple programs providing career education, worker retraining, employment opportunities, scholarships, and lifelong learning. These Educational Workforce Programs are financially supported by sixty-six companies.

The member businesses in the Vermilion Advantage represent a broad range of organizations including Alcon, ConAgra, Fiberteq, MT Systems, Quaker Foods, Systrand, ThyssenKrupp, Blue Cross Blue Shield, First Midwest Bank, Walgreens, Hoopeston Regional Health Center, Provena United Samaritans Medical Center, and forty-eight other local enterprises. Thirty-nine elementary and secondary schools, both public and private, as well as five youth organizations participate in a wide range of career-building skills and informational programs covering such areas as character and ethics development, applied math and science experiential learning, the physical sciences and engineering professions, a career exploration laboratory, and a cutting-edge gateway to technology and project-based learning. Three career academies are operated as separate schools within Danville High School: Merit Career Academy, Aims Career Academy, and Project Lead the Way.

"FINISH FIRST!" is another component of the Vermilion Advantage's educational workforce programs. Its goal is to both improve school attendance and increase high school graduation rates. These are core cultural issues on which businesses must voice their support and take action. The sixty-six companies that support this student initiative are also encouraging adult residents to become lifelong learners. They are counseling their employers or job applicants to go back to school for skill updates or finish high school through the local GED program. Nearly 79 percent of Vermilion County residents over the age of twenty-five have a high school diploma or higher-education degree.

For the current workforce, the Vermilion Advantage educational workforce programs also offers "The Training System," which consists of postsecondary continuing education opportunities for workers in the technology, health care, and logistics business sectors. Programs include advanced metal work certification from the National Institute for Metalworking Skills, Engineers For Tomorrow, nursing, physical therapy, pharmacy, and computer network engineer logistics certificates.

Vermilion Advantage features the 442jobs.com Web site. It provides parents with information on career programs offered at local public or private schools. Also, every January Vermilion Advantage surveys its business members on their projected employment needs and the education, skills, and experience required for each position. The survey information is distributed to parents throughout the country and other interested parties.

"The purpose of the Vermilion Advantage," says Vicki Haugen, president and CEO, "is to bring the entire county together, interacting on the future of talent. Our aim is to create a sustainable community passionate about learning and focused on future economic growth."

The bottom line of the Vermilion Advantage has been the transformation of civic responsibility into active economic participation. For Danville, Illinois, that translates into a big talent advantage for a new decade of economic expansion.[17]

Mansfield Ohio's Shawshank Redemption

Mansfield, in Richland County, Ohio, is in an area that could have been the poster child for the rust-belt manufacturing of the 1980s and early 1990s. When I visited there in 2001, its real estate was labeled the cheapest in the nation by the nonprofit Center for Housing Policy. Mansfield was 15 percent below the state average per capita personal income.

Mansfield was also the site of the popular prison film, "The Shawshank Redemption," filmed at the now closed Ohio State Juvenile Reformatory. In this movie, Tim Robbins seeks to prove he was wrongly convicted of murder, while giving his fellow inmate (Morgan Freeman) and many others hope for their own future redemption.

I met two community leaders, Robert Zettler, then vice president of workforce and community development at North Central State College (NC State), a two-year technical school, and Douglas Theaker, then director of Richland County Job and Family Services. These two civic activists were determined to mobilize a community going down for the final count. They saw the potential to redevelop local industry and attract new businesses by reinventing the education-to-employment talent system. They then went out and did it.

To see their results, consider the story of Tim Toth, a Mansfield resident, who recently was unemployed. His counselor at the Job and Family Service One Stop suggested that he investigate the free training options offered through the Training Workers in Advanced Manufacturing Pilot Program at NC State. On January 3, 2006 Tim entered the Tool and Die program and later added classes in Computer Numerical Controls. In just a few weeks, he was hired by Tyco Electric Company, starting at $13.58 per hour. Because of his new knowledge and excellent work ethic, Tim has received several position upgrades and pay increases. In December 2006 Tim was elevated to Shift Lead Person on the third shift, and his hourly rate increased to $16.01 per hour. Tim's earnings have increased to over $33,000 in less than one year because of the excellent training provided by this unique pilot program.

The entire project was the product of twenty-three separate public and private collaborations in which the Richland County Commissioners provided $565,000 to construct a Tool and Die Training Facility at NC State, $270,900 in additional training dollars, and more than $90,000 to purchase up-to-the-minute training equipment. Also, private industry donated an estimated $1.5 million in equipment for the Tool and Die Training Facility.

These local collaborations were the basis for a $1,897,000 pilot training grant from the Ohio Governor's Discretionary Workforce Investment Act Fund. The pilot was designed to completely eliminate the bureaucratic red tape associated with government programs, while working in concert with those programs. It has an estimated training cost per student of $1,743.00 for 1,900 participants. The grant was expected to last for three years and was exhausted in less than fifteen months. "It was a demonstration of the incredible demand for this kind of training in our area," says Bethany Dentler, Norwalk economic development director.

The results of this locally driven Mansfield effort combined with state matching funds were amazing:

- More than 3,000 students have been served, at a cost of $713.00 per student.
- 2,411 certificates of completion have been awarded.
- 70,700 hours of training and assessments have been delivered.
- A survey of more than 40 percent of the incumbent students indicates that they have received annual average wage increases of $1,337.00.
- A survey of 40 percent of the unemployed participants indicates they have received training-related employment, averaging a salary of $19,351 to start.

Danny Phillips, apprentice-chair of the local General Motors–UAW (International Union, United Automobile, Aerospace and Agricultural Implement Workers of America) believes that "This technology training is a must to keep up with competitive production."

What about the future? The Richland County Commissioners are leading a coalition of other county commissioners; economic development, job, and family services; and education and business officials in a nine-county-region effort. Their goal is to match the Ohio governor's discretionary funding to continue worker development not just in manufacturing, but in those fields that are most important to each county. Training Workers to Advance is a four-year $6.6 million program to expand earlier initiatives by also including IT training and health care education.

"With a lot of effort," says Zettler, "a little luck, and the tremendous support of friends and associates, we have prevailed. We've made a big difference, but we've only scratched the surface on the road to a more prosperous Mansfield by rebuilding our local talent pipeline."

Mansfield demonstrates what collaborative leadership is all about. "We know training and education are the answers. We keep plugging away to involve more businesses and students," says Zettler.[18] "By creating a workforce-building initiative to help themselves, they have highlighted the gigantic need for effective talent development in North Central Ohio, and started the long-term process to rebuild Mansfield."

North Carolina

In the state of North Carolina, a similar transformation of the talent pool has been under way, and it shows no signs of stopping.

During the 1980s, North Carolina's economic pillars—furniture and textile manufacturing and tobacco production—were already beginning to disappear. They have been replaced by pharmaceuticals, technology, viticulture, and tourism. The state has moved vigorously to attract foreign manufacturers by reinventing local-talent-creation systems. Both student career education and worker continuing education are the foundations on which the state is enticing outside investments and endeavoring to keep more of them coming. Let us briefly look at three pieces of this talent-creation picture.

"Napa is out. The new wines are from North Carolina!" said NBC's Phil Lempert on the March 27, 2008 *Today Show*. In the northwestern corner of the state, the Yadkin River Heritage Corridor Partnership has made viticulture a major piece of its economic development strategy. Over a four-county area, the emergence of the Yadkin Valley's wine industry's vineyards and wine-tasting rooms has led to an increase in tourism. New upscale accommodations and dining have followed. Further projects include hiking trails for ecotourism, as well as the development of Civil War historic sites. A local craft store has been opened as an outlet for regional artists of the Yadkin Valley Craft Guild. To support these efforts, Surry Community College offers degree programs in viticulture and enology (winemaking), as well as a craft-potters program.

University, business, and government collaboration created one of America's most successful economic development CBOs, the Research Triangle Park. Seven thousand acres were developed to attract pharmaceutical makers, technology giants, and financial service businesses. The park is located between North Carolina State University in Raleigh, Duke University in Durham, and the University of North Carolina at Chapel Hill. Nearly 40,000 people work there. The Charlotte-Raleigh areas now "are two of the stronger economies in the country," states Mark Vitner, senior economist at Wachovia Corporation in Charlotte.

This park has led to the expansion of hospital and clinical health care facilities and the growth of regional health care career-education programs. Local students are being prepared for careers in biotechnology with the pharmaceutical companies that are centered in the Raleigh-Durham area of the state.

North Carolina's BioNetwork is a statewide initiative that provides strategic assistance to local community colleges, including curriculum, equipment, and specialized training. The Capstone Center at North Carolina State University offers worker retraining and hands-on, short-course training for new hires and community college students. An effective outreach service is the BioNetwork bus. This is a self-contained, state-of-the-art mobile laboratory that travels anywhere with qualified, industry-experienced instructors providing local biotech companies with a variety of customized, hands-on training alternatives.

Companies such as Bayer, Bioger, Novo-Nordisk (NOVO), Purdue, and GlaxoSmithKline are creating 2,000 biotech jobs across the state, and recruiting qualified workers is a high priority for North Carolina. *The North Carolina Career Outlook Handbook* is a key informational tool for parents, students, and job seekers. "Knowing where the job openings are in the near future is the key to deciding on a postsecondary education that will prepare you for a rewarding career," says Christopher L. Droessler, the report's author and school-to-career coordinator for the Wake County Public School System.

The North Carolina Career Outlook Handbook has been published annually since 2003 and distributed widely throughout the state. The handbook is divided into twelve career clusters, including business technologies, engineering technologies, and the health sciences. Each career area lists the minimum education required, the outlook on the percentage of growth, the number of current workers in North Carolina, entry-level salary, and average salary. Also listed are the fastest-growing and declining occupations across the state.[19] (Please see the Resource A section for contact information on this and other schools and programs included in this chapter.)

CBOs ACROSS THE GLOBE

We have already seen how CBOs are taking the lead to develop local talent pools in California, North Dakota, Illinois, Ohio, and North Carolina. But CBOs are an international phenomenon, and they are providing solutions around the world. Let us look at some examples from the United Kingdom, Germany, and Brazil.

United Kingdom

England's Thames Valley Economic Partnership (TVEP) is a CBO of more than eighty companies, government agencies, and education institutions supporting existing companies and encouraging inward investment. One of the TVEP's major objectives is to develop the local talent pool across the region. Major companies such as BAA Heathrow, Cisco Systems, and Microsoft are represented on its board. The TVEP is funded primarily by the business community.[20]

Germany

The German Dual System is another example of a national agency partnering with CBOs to create a diversified, high-skill workforce. It is called a dual system because it combines classroom education and apprenticeship training programs inside community businesses.

These talent programs cover more than three hundred occupational areas. Federal and state governments finance part of the program. Businesses, through their local community chambers, invest billions of Euros annually on apprenticeship education. This business investment in the future workforce is the cornerstone of the German economy and its talent system.[21]

Brazil

In 2007 on a hilly site in Macaiba (northeastern Brazil), a CBO, the International Institute of Neuroscience of Natal, built the core elements of a "campus of the brain"—a research lab, a science school for four hundred local children, and a free health clinic. Another science school has been established in the large northeastern port of Natal. São Paulo also has a neuroscience lab at the Sirio-Libanés Hospital.

This is the beginning of Miguel Nicolelis' vision of a string of "science cities" to be built across Brazil's poorest regions. Dr. Nicolelis is widely recognized as one of the world's leading neuroscientists. Each city will have a world-class research institute concentrating on a specific aspect of science or technology. These knowledge cities will help spark new commercial scientific enterprises (mini-Silicon Valleys) that help jump-start regional development.

The main campus at Macaiba will have a 5,000-student science school, more labs, a sports facility, and an ecological park. Nicolelis' group is now working with Brazil's minister of education to create a new science curriculum for 254 new national technical high schools. "If this works, we'll be up to 1 million students in two years," Nicolelis predicts. The Brazilian government has pledged about $25 million toward finishing this campus.

Nicolelis' conviction is that promising young scientists can stay in Brazil to build such science parks and cities as they pursue their scientific development goals. This follows the lead of other local and national governments, especially in Asia (for example, in Singapore), that are pursuing this strategy.

The key is improving the quality of the child's regular school while offering supplemental classes at the institute's science schools. "Ninety-nine percent of scientific work doesn't require a Ph.D.," Nicolelis insists.

He is also careful to clarify that the Institute's vision is not to turn every student into a future scientist. "We are trying to create a generation of citizens capable of leading Brazil," Nicolelis explains. Whether or not the Natal model will work remains to be seen, but abundant national talent for a twenty-first-century Brazilian workplace is the laudable goal of this ambitious CBO.[22]

REBUILDING THE TALENT PIPELINE

U.S. education reform is essential for rebuilding the U.S. talent pipeline. CBOs and NGOs enable business to make a major impact on overall training-and-education quality and on updating the content and context of what is being taught. Though business cannot do this alone, it needs to make a far larger contribution to a total overhaul, first at the local, than at the state, and finally at the national level of the U.S. talent pipeline. At one time this was just another option to consider. Now business activism has become a necessity because the current talent crisis strikes at the heart of business sustainability across every U.S. community. Why now?

In 1983 the National Commission on Excellence in Education's report "A Nation at Risk" opened a bitter debate on the quality of American education that still rages on. Since then, has "the system" improved? For many years, overall results from the OECD's Programme for International Student Assessment (PISA) have shown the same nations in the lead: Singapore, Finland, South Korea, and Japan. American students trail their peers, ranking sixteenth of thirty countries in science and twenty-third in math as of 2007.

If you consider comparisons of U.S. students with international students to be unfair, consider the National Assessment of Educational Progress, also known as the "Nation's Report Card." Over the past thirty years, the results with few exceptions remain basically flat. U.S. spending on education has almost doubled since 1980, and class sizes are the lowest ever, yet student scores refuse to budge upward.

Successful new education policies and innovations have been developed over the past three decades. Some U.S. schools have been redesigned or created and have produced large achievement gains for students. But these achievements have not resulted in systemic change. They are unevenly spread across the United States.[23]

Since the 1980s the number of low-performing U.S. students has continued to rise. High school dropout rates have increased. The United States has not built into its system any equal access to education excellence, only pockets of excellence. There are no "silver bullets" left for easy, quick fixes.[24]

WHAT WORKS

Some countries do much better than the rest. What do the successful have in common?

McKinsey and Company, the international business consultancy firm, has tried to answer that question in its 2007 report "How the World's Best-Performing School Systems Come Out on Top." McKinsey used as a benchmark the top ten PISA-scoring school systems, and others whose recent reforms are rapidly improving student achievement. In brief, here are some of the components successful international schools share:

- Fewer curriculum goals and standards, clearly stated
- An emphasis on subject mastery
- Stronger teacher selection and preparation
- Stronger continuous professional development for teachers
- A longer school day and school year
- Comprehensive tutoring help for all students, given by specially trained teachers[25]

These findings can be summarized in three overarching policies: get the right people to become teachers, develop these people into effective teachers and principals, and foster quality instruction strategies that reach every student. Let us review each of these ideas and then consider how we can apply these policies everywhere.

Policy 1: Getting the Right People to Become Teachers

Over the next decade, how are we going to recruit even better people into teaching? The quality of an education system cannot exceed the quality of its teachers. The top-performing systems recruit their teachers from the top students: South Korea (top 5 percent), Finland (top 10 percent), and Singapore (top 30 percent). In contrast, the United States selects its teachers mostly from the bottom third of college graduates. How do the above nations do it? They use a careful combination of money, status, and selection.[26]

Attracting more of any society's best minds into teaching seems underpinned by strong selection and training processes and by frontloading salaries while increasing class size. These practices, in turn, elevate the cultural status of the teaching profession. As the McKinsey Report concludes, "The quality of an education system depends ultimately on the quality of its teachers."[27]

Higher salaries will clearly play a role in strengthening the teacher corps. Cities such as New York have also followed the alternative teacher certification route. The Teaching Fellows program attracts mature professionals to teaching; Teach for America, a national program, places top-achieving college graduates in difficult-to-staff inner-city schools. A 2008 New York Times editorial stated, "By emulating the New York model, America could finally give its children the high quality teachers that they desperately need."[28]

Policy 2: Developing These People Into Effective Instructors and Principals

The McKinsey Report emphasizes that the key to boosting student results is improving instruction. "Delivering this excellent instruction requires every teacher to develop a highly sophisticated set of skills." To do this, teachers need quality professional development programs throughout their teaching careers.[29]

Teachers need to build practical skills by doing teacher training in the teacher's own classroom, to have experienced teachers who mentor and coach beginning teachers, and to learn from each other via collaborative planning, observation, and peer counseling.

Singapore provides one hundred hours of professional development to teachers every year. In Boston a graduate teacher training program is based on a medical-residency model. Trainees have a one-year school apprenticeship: four days each week with an experienced teacher, and one day a week doing course work. In the second year, the new teacher has a mentor for two-and-a-half hours of in-class coaching each week. Chicago and Denver have established similar programs.

In Finland, university education programs manage their own fully operational training school. Students begin teaching there, with the content of their classroom training carried out in actual practice within this school. Faculty can observe, coach, and mentor each student more precisely.

Adam 12 School District near Denver has introduced coaches for math, as well as writing teachers. "We think the coaching model has been a critical component in the rise of student achievement," says superintendent Michael F. Paskewicz. He cites three ongoing years of growth in state test scores.

Coaching for teachers is fast becoming an effective development tool for other school districts. Examples of successful programs can be found in Dallas, Texas and Memphis, Tennessee. To be effective, the assistance must be sustained. Coaching must be made as much a part of a teacher's daily work as possible.[30]

Effective school leadership is second only to quality classroom teaching as an influence on daily student learning. Yet, too many principals are unable or unwilling to manage a culture of high expectations or strive for continuous improvement.

Programs in Singapore and Boston develop their school principals into drivers of improvement in instruction by doing three things:

Getting the "Right People": In Singapore, a leadership Assessment Center evaluates candidates' potential core competencies. If passed, a six-month training and assessment process prepares candidates for principalship. At its end, only candidates who are found to be ready are appointed as principals.

Developing Instructional Leadership Skills: Boston has a fellowship program that offers candidates an apprenticeship, three days a week working with an experienced principal. Its new support for principals includes a summer institute, mentoring by an experienced principal, networking, and just-in-time meetings. For ongoing development, the district lets deputy superintendents devote most of their time coaching principals.

Focusing Time on Instructional Leadership: As change managers, principals need to use most of their time working directly with teachers and students. Both Boston and Singapore let the principal *lead*.

School systems need to understand that effective principals have to become people managers and instructional leaders. Pushing paper for school administration needs to be done by somebody else who has not been given the key leadership role.[31]

Policy 3: High-Quality Instruction for All

The only way for a new talent system to reach peak performance is to raise the standard of every student. This means setting high expectations, then daily monitoring individual performance against these expectations, and developing effective instruction interventions at the school level. All children must have access to excellent instruction. This is a big challenge.

In the very best systems, these improvements come from building teacher and principal capacity and focusing on teacher and student motivation. What it does not mean is teaching to a test or just giving students more drill and practice.[32]

The U.S. Department of Education estimates that about 3 million students, ages six to twenty-one, have specific learning disabilities such as dyslexia. These disabilities require highly individualized instruction to help students stay focused on a learning task.[33]

Finland has gone further than any other system by providing universal access to effective high-quality instruction. Each Finnish school employs a large number of special-intervention teachers at a ratio of one for every seven regular classroom teachers. These special-intervention teachers provide one-to-one or small-group tutoring to any student who is at risk of falling behind. Thirty percent of all students in a school are given tutoring in any given year. All students have equal access to high-quality tutoring in any subject when they most need it. Teachers are given an additional year of tutor training at a university to prepare them for this special instructional role.

The high volume of universal tutoring has helped destigmatize the practice in Finland. Even the best students on occasion are sent for additional tutoring. This helps peers accept that tutoring is not necessarily a sign of underperformance. Quick intervention at the individual student level prevents early failure compounding into more long-term failure. Finland's aggressive tutoring program helps all schools maintain strong and consistently equitable individual student achievement.[34]

THE NEW SYSTEM

We have discussed how the old education-to-employment system worked very well in the United States for a long time. Then the system started to break down. It was a closed system that compartmentalized life into three separate segments: education, career preparation, and work. We built a filter between education and career preparation that pigeonholed students along a rude continuum from egghead to bonehead. The smarter kids went on to college from high school to prepare for white-collar careers. The supposedly "dumber" students continued on in vocational education or apprenticeships for blue-collar jobs.

The system then erected a high brick wall separating the "real world" of work from the "theoretical world" of education and career preparation. People openly talked about the year you "got out," as if high school or college were a prison. Apprenticeship education existed in its own limbo between these two worlds. Most people never crossed over that wall again. Yes, professionals, executives, salespeople, and advanced technicians did receive some training and development. But most workers were lucky even to receive on-the-job training. Historically, college tuition reimbursement has been the most underused U.S. employment benefit. This was basically a closed education-to-employment system for most workers.[35]

Now times have changed. As the world moves into the Cyber-Mental Age, it is the brains behind the technology that make innovation happen. Without this talent you are left with a pile of useless hardware and software.

White-collar vs. blue-collar job differences are blurring across much of the world's tech economy as part of a talent revolution. At the same time, many workers are being left behind. "Both the quality and quantity of the labor force are not keeping pace with the demands of a skill-based economy," contend two University of Chicago economists, James Heckman and Dimitriy Masterov, in their report for the Federal Reserve Bank. "Labor force quality as provided by education has stagnated."[36]

Business is beginning to worry that the global talent pool is too small for its growing needs. A 2006 joint survey of over four hundred Human Resources managers by the Conference Board and the Society for Human Resource Management offered an abysmal snapshot of entry-level workers. Forty-two percent of new high school hires were rated as "deficient." Only about 10 percent of community college and almost 24 percent of four-year-college hires were found to be "excellent."[37]

What will a new, more open education-to-employment system look like? (See Figure 3.) Business and communities can provide more people with the opportunities to develop their talent for multiple careers and jobs over a lifetime. In the Cyber-Mental Age the differences between jobs will be steeper, demanding a wider variety and greater depth of personal talent. The idea of "multiple intelligences" (varying individual aptitudes in verbal, mathematical, spatial, and other areas) has gained traction. Now education-to-careers is back in vogue.

Federal Reserve Chairman Ben Bernanke sees the real value of business investing in a new talent system that addresses the global talent showdown with "policies that boost our national investment in education and training." He points out, "A substantial body of research demonstrates that (these) investments . . . pay high rates of return."[38]

Business leaders are now more willing to make those investments if they result in a more talented workforce. A 2007 survey of more than 1,300 CEOs by the California Foundation for Commerce and Education found that 75 percent would pay more in business taxes if substantial systemic school reforms were mandated across the state. Even in the midst of the economic downturn of November 2008, 100 top CEOs of large corporations assembled by the Wall Street Journal ranked an educated workforce as their second highest priority (a fiscal stimulus for the United States was the top priority).[39] But what would we be investing in? Let us now take a walk through each part of the "New System." We can enlarge the world's talent pool by adopting a more open education-to-employment model.

Figure 3: The New System for the Twenty-First Century: Open Education-to-Employment Model

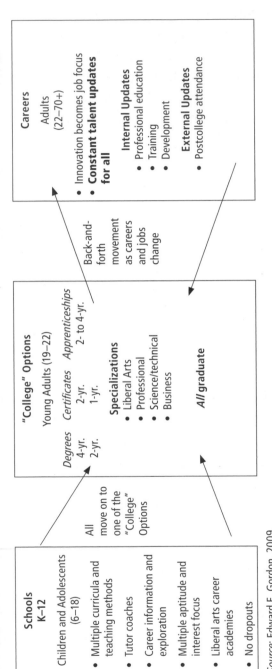

I. Education

II. Career Preparation

III. Employment

Schools K-12

Children and Adolescents (6–18)

- Multiple curricula and teaching methods
- Tutor coaches
- Career information and exploration
- Multiple aptitude and interest focus
- Liberal arts career academies
- No dropouts

All move on to one of the "College" Options

"College" Options

Young Adults (19–22)

Degrees	Certificates	Apprenticeships
4-yr.	2-yr.	2- to 4-yr.
2-yr.	1-yr.	

Specializations

- Liberal Arts
- Professional
- Science/technical
- Business

All graduate

Back-and-forth movement as careers and jobs change

Careers

Adults (22–70+)

- Innovation becomes job focus
- **Constant talent updates for all**

Internal Updates

- Professional education
- Training
- Development

External Updates

- Postcollege attendance

Source: Edward E. Gordon, 2009.

Back-to-Basics Elementary School

Everyone will receive higher-level academic content in reading, writing, math, and science, starting in first grade. In the past many educators, parents, and politicians assumed that children could "catch up" later when they reached middle school and high school. This is a flawed assumption. If a child falls behind on the basics in the early grades, their skills will often never catch up to the appropriate grade level in the future. To assure success, we need to employ highly qualified teachers throughout the elementary and secondary school learning years, and use teachers with specialized tutorial training to provide individualized instruction to students falling behind in the elementary grades.[40]

These talented teachers need to use multiple curricula, as well as teaching methods and flexible pedagogical styles adapted to the individual aptitudes and interests of each student.

Noted Harvard University psychologist Howard Gardner believes there are seven human abilities: linguistic, logical-mathematical, spatial, musical, bodily-fine-gross motor, interpersonal, and intrapersonal. Instruction in the classroom can be modified to emphasize a mixture of these areas rather than focus primarily on linguistic intelligence as school curricula do today.[41]

Different mental talents are spread universally across the population of the United States. Every individual is born with a mixture of these aptitudes, which are developed over a lifetime through personal education, training, and experience. But there remain individual differences.

Some people have strong aptitudes for the written word or verbal forms of intelligence. For others, their strongest skills center on mathematics, science, or languages. Still others have their intelligence centered in the design, construction, or maintenance of different technologies.

A person's career or job choices are driven by these different forms of human intelligence. However, culture remains a strong driving force over what a specific time period may consider highly desirable, prestige careers and those jobs that are not.

The nationally prominent psychologist Robert J. Sternberg argues that people with "successful intelligence" succeed in the real world because they possess a combination of practical, creative, and analytical skills. This is why schools across Europe and Asia now teach students using a variety of curricula for activating multiple intelligences.[42]

Career Education

Recently, a long row of students lined up at an indoor theme park. But they were not waiting to ride bumper cars or play video games. They were spending a day at Kidzania, an entertainment center dedicated to offering children a fun taste of what working life is like. Pavilions offer a dizzying range of occupations including pilot, gas station manager, dentist, package delivery messenger, and electrical engineer. This jobs theme park focuses on some seventy careers. It has been a huge success in Japan. But does it have a more serious side?[43]

Erik Russell led his class of twenty-seven students in a lesson on engineering. No, these were not college students; they were fourth-graders at Odyssey Elementary School in Colorado Springs, Colorado, involved in a career exploratory activity.

Actually the students were doing a hands-on project in chemical engineering, mixing combinations of flour, water, and salt and marking down what happened along the way. This may seem like child's play, but it was a lesson specifically aimed at inspiring students into thinking about becoming future engineers.

Currently a number of organizations—such as Intel and Project Lead the Way, a nonprofit corporation—have created exploratory engineering curricula for schools, and they are lobbying communities and states to add these preengineering career programs to their schools. (See the Resource A section of this book for examples of some these programs.)

Kids have long used hands-on experiments to learn basic scientific principles. The difference here is that these critical-thinking lessons are steeped in problem solving and design challenges that come from the real world, not just theory. These are the same qualities needed in the cyber-mental workplace.[44]

Experts agree that it is often in elementary school that students begin to think about adult careers. Children and their parents often conceptualize careers through an artificial filter of what the "hot" jobs are at any given time. In every decade the most popular occupations emerge through a biased structure of hierarchy, specialization, regulations, and control. Too often people discover the career of their dreams only later in life, after investing time and money preparing for other occupations.

Here is where businesses and CBOs or NGOs can step in and provide career information and exploration for both students and parents. These experiences will further drive a child's personal interests and help motivate him or her to better develop stronger abilities. Some of these career activities start in elementary school and continue in high school and postsecondary education. Here are some ideas to inspire you:

> *In-School Real-World Connection*: In support of a student's career awareness, career exploration, personal planning, and personal development, representatives from employers and community agencies may participate in developing skills, acting as role models, visiting classes, demonstrating projects, organizing hands-on projects, conducting lectures, and providing explanations of equipment design and use.

> *Tours*: Structured and meaningful visits to work sites are arranged to observe the workplace and workplace skills in action.

Job "Shadowing": A student spends time during the workday with an expert in a certain trade, craft, or profession, observing the expert's work-site skills and behaviors.

Structured Job: This is a part-time, paid, structured work experience designed to enhance a young person's understanding of the work site, work-site skills and behaviors, and the link between school and work. A mentor supports the student in mastering systems, processes, behavior, and skills.

Internship: As part of a work-site learning experience of several weeks or months, a student works on a specific task or project to become familiar with the work site and with work-site skills and behaviors and their application to academics (or vice versa).

Youth Work Study Course and Co-op: These are paid work experiences for credit in which students learn and perform occupational skills on the job.

Apprenticeship: This career preparation strategy combines supervised, structured on-the-job training in a bona fide and documented employment setting, with related theoretical instruction. It is sponsored by employers and labor management groups that have the ability to hire and train. This education and training strategy leads to the youth apprentice's high school graduation and counts toward advancement in an apprenticeship program, a postsecondary certificate or associate's degree program, or both.[45]

By combining a world-class liberal arts education and appropriate career-education components starting in elementary school, more students will develop multiple forms of intelligence to higher levels and begin discovering more long-term career interests. They will make a better transition into secondary education that will further complement this continuing process.

Parents—and CBOs/NGOs—Make the System Work

In 1994 the United States Congress decreed that by 2000 dropout rates would fall to 10 percent and U.S. students would rank "first in the world of mathematics and science achievement." It did not happen. Somebody forgot to tell the parents.[46]

As we have already seen, many parents still resist the idea of a technologically dominated job market. There is a big mismatch between what is taught and what is needed in the labor market.

Now some communities have ramped up parental education by providing understandable information on career content and job demand (see chapter 5). CBOs and NGOs will be essential in this effort to get parental groups engaged in updating the local education-to-employment system. Parents must understand that they greatly influence their children's attitudes toward school and their career choices and postsecondary schooling.

Home involvement increases motivation to learn. An Achievable Dream Academy in Newport News, Virginia mobilizes family participation by having parents pledge to take on responsibilities such as checking daily homework assignments and volunteering at the school. Family-focused evening classes offer parents the opportunity to study for the GED or to take classes in such subjects as parenting skills and financial management.

Practical Parenting Partnerships provides a system of training and home visits to build strong home-school relationships in twelve states and Canada. Other outreach programs through local schools send teachers into the home as tutors and parenting coaches.[47]

Too often, "students try to fit themselves into one of a series of career choices as defined by others, rather than using their interests to guide them in exploring the outer world," says Sue Shellenbarger in her *Wall Street Journal* article "Ways to Teach Your Children to Find the Work They Love."

What can parents do to better guide their child's thinking about careers?

- Avoid conveying unrealistic expectations about what jobs constitute "success."
- Foster the child's interests and aptitudes.
- Encourage visits to different types of workplaces.
- Do not load the child up with too many extracurricular activities.
- Give the child time to think, play, and read.

U.S. education is not going to fix itself. "If parents aren't willing to take drastic measures for their kids," says Joe Williams of the *New York Daily News*, "the status quo will surely prevail."[48]

CBO and NGO Pipelines

The CBO and NGO model offers a shared vision that can guide us through this major transition to a new education-to-employment system for the twenty-first century (see Figure 4).

In a republic, citizens need to constantly balance private interest

Figure 4: The CBO/NGO Shared Vision

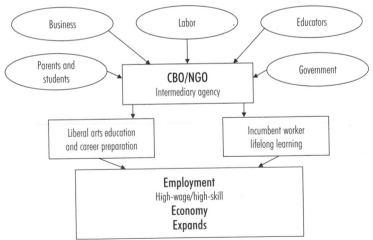

Source: Edward E. Gordon, 2009.

Figure 5: What NGOs Do

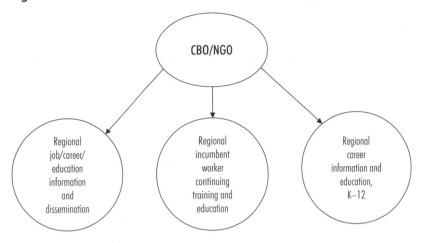

Other later activities:
- Welfare-to-work (single parent)
- Housing (low-cost, subsidized)
- Criminal justice employment
- Employment programs for the disabled
- Immigrant-education programs

Source: Edward E. Gordon, 2009.

and public virtue. Local community action through CBOs and NGOs can help develop the talent for a highly educated workforce, revitalize current businesses, and attract new companies to a city or region.

This is what CBOs and NGOs can accomplish for communities across the United States and much of the world (see Figure 5). We have a pool of people. What is missing is the "pipe" in between, which connects people to the opportunity. Talent is the United States' most renewable resource. The challenge facing all of us is to create more talented people from those who are not now participating in becoming part of the American dream.

2020 GOALS AND CHALLENGES

How can the United States double the number of well-educated people by 2020? Here are three ambitious yet attainable goals:

Goal 1: Fifty percent of all high school graduates will graduate reading at a twelfth-grade or higher level of reading comprehension.

Goal 2: Fifty percent of all high school graduates will complete a postsecondary "college" program of two- to four-year degrees, one- to two-year certificates, or two- to four-year apprenticeships.

Goal 3: The majority of all U.S. businesses will provide their employees with continuing training and education opportunities.[49]

Across much of the developing world, the next decade will see "the largest youth bulge in the history of the world," says Bill Reese, president and chief executive of the International Youth Foundation. According to the World Bank in 2007, by 2015 there will be three billion young people (ages twelve to twenty-four) in the world. In Africa, the Middle East, and South Asia, children and youth will make up 60 percent of the total population.

Most of the nations in these regions lack the resources to provide meaningful education to this vast population. They have large illiterate populations who barely eke out a subsistence living. Many are unemployed. These nations are tinderboxes of discontent that now threaten the peace and stability of the entire world. These issues can no longer be ignored by developed nations.

Some still may believe that centralized totalitarian regimes foster faster economic expansion in emerging economies. Robert Shapiro makes this argument in *Futurecast: How Superpowers, Populations, and Globalization Will Change the Way You Live and Work* (2008), saying that China's "absence of political freedom of virtually any kind has so far been one of its secret strengths." Robert Kagen also shares this view regarding both Russia and China in *The Return of History and the End of Dreams* (2008).

Across Europe, Russia, and Asia, the twentieth century provides stark testimony about the destructive, largely illusionary, economics of totalitarian governments. The mythical economic advances of Hitler's National Socialist Germany or Stalin's Communist Soviet Union were largely accomplished through widespread repression, bloodshed, and war. Spectacular short-term gains were followed by long-term collapse. The history of the twentieth century testifies that totalitarian economies fail to successfully compete with free, market-driven economies featuring moderate government regulation. It is my view, from my study of the current economies of Russia and China, that this verdict will not be reversed during the twenty-first century.[50]

THE ECONOMIC BENEFIT

But would expanding the current talent systems be a good business investment? The answer is an emphatic yes, say economists Eric A. Hanushek (Hoover Institution of Stanford University), Dean T. Jamison (University of California, San Francisco), Eliot A. Jamison (Babcock & Brown), and Ludger Woessmann (University of Munich), who conclude in a 2008 article titled "Education and Economic Growth" that "a highly skilled workforce can raise economic growth by about two-thirds of a percentage point a year."

The financial impact of a strong talent-creation system, they found, is far stronger for nations with "open economies." These are the countries more open to free trade and with fewer government controls over economic and business activity.

"Over the 20th century, the expansion of the U.S. education system outpaced the rest of the world." Combined with the freer nature of the U.S. economy, education fostered America's robust economic growth. But they conclude that this is now being jeopardized by the lagging performance of U.S. schools.[51]

WHAT'S NEXT?

Over the next decade and later, how will these events unfold? Here is a timeline of probable events as the global talent showdown unfolds over the next decade and beyond:

Year	*Events*
2010	Large-scale boomer retirements begin to have a major impact on the talent pool.
	Ten million U.S. positions are vacant.
	At the local level, CBOs and NGOs become acknowledged models to help reinvent the education-to-employment system.
2015	Fifteen million U.S. positions are vacant.
	CBOs and NGOs form across the United States.
	U.S. states begin updating talent-system mandates, including business training incentives.
	The U.S. Congress considers depreciating training investments.
	Europe and Japan increase their foreign direct investment in U.S. communities that have rebuilt the local talent pipeline.
2020	Seventy million boomers have retired.
	Twenty-four million U.S. positions are vacant.
	Most U.S. states have passed new talent mandates.
	The U.S. Congress passes legislation allowing the depreciation of training investments.
2025	Seventy-nine million boomers have retired.
	Generation Z (born after 2005) begins entering the workforce.
	All fifty U.S. states have mandated a new education-to-employment system.

Many of my predictions are based on the U.S. economy remaining open and flexible, which may or may not happen.

Today many American workers are hurting. The less-educated and those with outdated skills are unable to find "good-paying" jobs. They are angry about free-trade and globalization, because they see companies eliminating their jobs in the United States, and moving them abroad. At the same time, many better-educated Americans are profiting from globalization.

The primary source of trouble for many American workers has been inadequate schooling and training. Some Americans fear foreign competition. They think it profits others at our expense. Isolationism and trade wars will not address our root talent issues.

Talent creation is not a zero-sum game. It is not true that if some nations expand their talent pool, others will lose. Indeed, any nation can create a greater number of talented people through the processes we have considered, adjusted to their cultural, social, and economic circumstances. There are many reasons to believe that we are about to enter a new era of expanding talent, new ideas, and free trade that will help promote higher living standards for more people around the world.[52]

A decade of opportunities includes the shift of more service and production jobs to the United States from overseas. As the workforces in Europe and Japan shrink, businesses "see America as a great place to base their business units, whether it's an effort to attract skilled labor or to streamline operations," states the *Chicago Tribune*.

Such investment in the United States has been increasing over the past decade and will greatly expand throughout the next ten years. Workforce development will be the main driver of foreign direct investment across the United States. "Top executives of many international companies [are] strikingly upbeat about their capability to operate plants economically in the high-cost countries, often in tandem with other production centers in lower-cost regions," writes Peter Marsh in the *Financial Times*. But this is dependent on the high-skill labor "that can make specialized, high value-added products."[53]

THE U.S. ADVANTAGE

The United States does have a major advantage because of its highly flexible, diversified national economy. Spread over fifty states, the country is divided into distinctive geographic and cultural regions. The U.S. answer to the talent showdown will be distinctly local in flavor, with national policies coming only later.

Those states that are first out-of-the-gate with new mandated talent systems will be the big economic winners. They will attract a larger share of new tech start-ups and overseas foreign direct investment, while also helping their current businesses become more competitive.

Those states and regions that lag behind this talent change curve will continue to see population loss, business and jobs migration, and the shrinkage of their tax base. However, in the long run they too will adopt new talent-expansion systems. Citizens will demand these changes and elect political leaders who will deliver them across all fifty states. At the end of the day, the personal economic incentives are just too great to ignore in a free market economy.

WHAT YOU CAN DO NOW

No matter what your position in business or the local community, you need to consider your personal role in advancing the new talent system. Here is an action agenda to get you started:

Business

- Help form a local CBO or NGO "Gateway to the Future."
- Make talent creation a major organizational priority.
- Enhance links to public and private schools through contributions of time, talent, equipment, or funds.
- Invest in your employees' training and development.

- Facilitate "re-skilling."
- Use flexible work programs.
- Collaborate more with other community talent providers.
- Tap into underused talent sources in the community.
- Share future talent projections with the community.
- Support career-education programming.
- Consider internship and apprenticeship programs.
- Serve on a CBO or NGO Board, its committees, or both.
- Lobby to change the talent-system mandates in your state, as well as federal tax depreciation of employee training and development.

Trade Associations/Community Nonprofits/Service Agencies/Religious Organizations

- Help form a local CBO or NGO "Gateway to the Future."
- Enhance links with public and private schools.
- Make community talent improvement an organizational priority.
- Seek grants to support your activities as part of a new talent system.
- Collaborate more broadly with community talent partners.
- Help distribute talent information on jobs and careers.
- Serve on a CBO or NGO Board, its committees, or both.
- Lobby to change the talent-system mandates in your state.
- Support career-education programming.

Government Entities

- Help form a local CBO "Gateway to the Future."
- Seek grants that support a new local talent system.
- Make community talent expansion and improvement a nonpartisan issue.
- Share and distribute information on talent issues with the public.

- Serve on a CBO Board, its committees, or both.
- Make local talent-system improvement a major government priority.
- Support career-education programming.

Education Agencies

- Help form a local CBO or NGO "Gateway to the Future."
- Collaborate with community talent partners, both public and private.
- Increase professional development for teachers.
- Provide mentors and coaches to new teachers.
- Strengthen tutoring programs.
- Seek grant monies to support an improved local talent system.
- Serve on a CBO or NGO Board, its committees, or both.
- Provide career-education programming.

Parents

- Help form a local CBO or NGO "Gateway to the Future."
- Volunteer at a local public or private school through contributions of time, talent, and funds.
- Provide a home environment that supports your children's learning on a daily basis.
- Participate in family reading programs for yourself and your children.
- Help discover your children's career interests.
- Seek out appropriate information on specific careers and the education preparation for them.
- Serve on a CBO or NGO Board, its committees, or both.
- Act as a volunteer community mentor or tutor.
- Lobby to change the talent-system mandates in your state.

Unions

- Help form a local CBO or NGO "Gateway to the Future."
- Enhance links with public and private schools through contributions of time, talent, funds, or all of these.
- Offer preapprenticeship programs through local education institutions.
- Expand apprenticeship programs to underrepresented adults.
- Support career-education programs.
- Serve on a CBO or NGO Board, its committees, or both.
- Seek grants to strengthen the local talent system.
- Volunteer at local schools.

Citizens and Workers

- Help form a local CBO or NGO "Gateway to the Future."
- Volunteer at local public or private schools through contributions of time, talent, and funds.
- Serve on a CBO or NGO Board, its committees, or both.
- Act as a volunteer community mentor or tutor.
- Support career-education programs.
- Lobby to change the talent-system mandates in your state.
- Participate in employer education, training, and development to enhance your skills for current and future jobs or career changes.

The good news for Americans is that we are far stronger economically than one hundred years ago. Our people are better educated. The U.S. economy is by far the world's largest and most diverse. For more than two hundred years the can-do spirit of this republic and the continuity of its Constitution "gave Americans the pathway that has withstood the impact of changing times," economist Morris Beschloss reminds us.[54]

Globally we have also seen how expanding international trade has increased the wealth of a burgeoning middle class. We need to sustain this momentum by enlarging the talent pool of every country.

Let the ideas we have explored throughout *Winning the Global Talent Showdown* help renew the United States' resolve in a time of crisis. Let our determination and example inspire many other nations around the globe.

A DECADE OF OPPORTUNITY

Now you know what time it is, why it is time to take action, and how you can rebuild the talent system in your own business and community.

We are a transitional generation that has climbed up to the twenty-first-century watershed. We are now looking down the other side on a global workforce facing myriad challenges. But my vision of the future is that the United States and much of the world are now entering a new talent era. Continuous twenty-first-century techno-logical breakthroughs will necessitate major human capital invest-ment in new education-to-employment systems to revive and expand the world's labor economy.

In this I remain an optimist. Once the world recession ends I see a decade of opportunity. It can be a time of "more and better" if the United States mobilizes behind its sense of community and civic responsibility.

The night is far advanced. The dawn of a new Cyber-Mental Age, with its promise of continued economic advancement, is near. We must discard the education-to-employment system of the twenti-eth century and its outdated career aspirations for the world of work. We need to expand the pool of world talent that will improve eco-nomic opportunities for business, people, and nations.

NOTES

PREFACE

1. NASSCOM-McKinsey Report 2005, "Extending India's Leadership of the Global IT and BPO Industries," McKinsey Global Institute, 2005, http://www.nasscom.in/upload/10142/Mckinsey_study-2005.pdf (Accessed May 19, 2008); Diana Farrell, Martha Laboissiere, Jaeson Rosenfeld, Sascha Sturze, and Fusayo Umezawa, "The Emerging Global Labor Market: Part II—The Supply of Offshore Talent in Services," McKinsey Global Institute, June 2005, 24, http://www.mckinsey.com/mgi/reports (Accessed May 19, 2008); Diana Farrell and Andrew J. Grant, "China's Looming Talent Shortage," *The McKinsey Quarterly*, November 2005, 72, http://www.mckinseyquarterly.com/chinas-looming-talent-shortage-1685 (Accessed November 4, 2008).
2. Alicia Clegg, "In Hot Pursuit of the Best Brains," *Financial Times*, March 14, 2007, 8.

INTRODUCTION

1. National Federation of Independent Business, "SBET: Small-Business Optimism Blossomed in April," http://www.nfib.com/object/10_28213.html (Accessed January 10, 2008); *Wall Street Journal*, "The CEOs Top Priorities," November 24, 2008, sec. R, 4.
2. Manpower Inc., "2008 Talent Shortage Survey," http://www.manpower.com/research/research.cfm (Accessed June 12, 2008).
3. "Manpower Survey Shows Worldwide 'Talent Shortage'," *Reuters*, February 20, 2006, http://news.yahoo.com/s/nm/20060220/bs_nm/services_manpower_dc (Accessed February 21, 2006).
4. Patrick Dixon, "Wake up to Stronger Tribes and Longer Life," *Financial Times*, October 31, 2005, 6.
5. Chris Brown-Humes, "Demographics May Show the Consolations of Old Age," *Financial Times*, February 24–25, 2007, 12; Population Division of the Department of Economic and Social Affairs of the United Nations Secretariat, *World Population Prospects: The 2006 Revision*, http://esa.un.org.unpp (Accessed June 5, 2008).
6. Stephen Moore, "300,000,000," *Wall Street Journal*, October 3, 2006, sec. A, 26; Gerard F. Anderson and Peter Satir Hussey, "Population Aging: A

Comparison Among Industrialized Countries," *Healthy Affairs*, May/June 2000, 192; Robert Stowe England, *The Fiscal Challenge of an Aging Industrial World* (Washington, DC: Center for Strategic and International Studies, 2002), 6, 120–121.

7. David Ibison, "Firms Need More Growth in Jobs to Fund Their Pensions," *Financial Times*, March 14, 2007, 6; Andrew Taylor, "Asian Economies Near 'Demographic Cliff'," *Financial Times*, August 13, 2007, 4.

8. U.S. Department of Commerce, U.S. Bureau of the Census, "Population Projections for States, 1995–2025," http://census.gov/prod/2/pop/p25/p251131 .pdf (Accessed January 10, 2008); *Chicago Tribune*, "1st Boomer Applies for Social Security," October 26, 2007, sec. 1, 5; Arlene Dohm and Lynn Shniper, "Occupational Employment Projections to 2016," *Monthly Labor Review*, November 2007, 86; June Kronholz, "The Coming Crunch," *Wall Street Journal*, October 13, 2006, sec. B, 1; Korky Vann, "Centenarians Centerpiece of Geniworth's Ad Campaign," *Chicago Tribune*, September 10, 2006, sec. 5, 16; Sam Roberts, "Suburbs Are Graying Faster Than Big Cities," *New York Times*, June 12, 2007, sec. A, 12; William H. Frey, "Mapping the Growth of Older America: Seniors and Boomers in the Early 21st Century," http:// www3.brookings.edu/views/articles/200705frey.pdf (Accessed May 20, 2008).

9. Chris Brown-Humes, "Demographics"; "Baby Bonuses and Other Solutions," *Herman Trend Alert*, August 8, 2007, http://www.hermangroup .com/alert/archive_8-8-2007.html (Accessed March 26, 2008).

10. Joel Garreau, "300 Million and Counting," *Smithsonian*, October 2006, 104.

11. Martin Wolf, "A Bigger Playing Field Needs New Goal Posts," *Financial Times*, October 20, 2005, 4.

12. NASSCOM-McKinsey Report 2005, "Extending India's Leadership of the Global IT and BPO Industries"; Diana Farrell and Andrew J. Grant, "China's Looming Talent Shortage," 72.

13. Sundeep Tucker, "A Bidding War Makes for 'Crazy' Salaries Across Asia," *Financial Times*, May 7, 2007, 7; *The Economist*, "Deportation Order," April 28, 2007, 38.

14. Marcus Walker, "Just How Good Is Globalization," *Wall Street Journal*, January 25, 2007, sec. A, 10; *The Economist*, "Rich Man, Poor Man," January 20, 2007, 15–16.

15. Vance McCarthy, "Nanotechnology Matters," *Business Week*, March 26, 2007, 33; Richard Waters, "Why Nanotechnology Is the Next Big Thing," *Financial Times*, March 30, 2005, 9; James Flanigan, "Nanotechnology Near to the Point When It's Time to Go Public," *New York Times*, December 20, 2007, sec. C, 7; Kimi Yoshino, "Those Wireless Robots Try Not to Act Remote," *Los Angeles Times*, March 2, 2007, sec. C, 1; Salamander Davoudi, "Help—The Mechanical Variety—Is on the Way," *Los Angeles Times*, March 5, 2007, sec. C, 4; *The Economist*, "Starship Enterprise: The Next Generation," January 26, 2008, 12–13; *The Economist*, "Virgin Birth," January 26, 2008, 66–68; Peter Marsh, "Speaking Plastic Microchip May Be the Last Word in Technology," *Financial Times*, January 3, 2007, 1.

16. Laura Wides, "Widespread L.A. Blackout Blamed on Workers' Error," *Chicago Tribune*, September 13, 2005, sec. 1, 15; *Chicago Tribune*, "Thousands in New York Sweat in Blackouts," July 22, 2006, sec. 1, 3; Elizabeth Douglass, "Concern Grows on Refining Safety," *Los Angeles Times*, March 23, 2007, sec. C, 1; John Bacon, "Nationline—In K.C. Some New Homes Rotting Away," *USA Today*, December 14, 2006, sec. A, 3; William Neuman, "$1 Billion Spent and Elevators Fail," *New York Times*, May 19, 2008, sec. A, 1, 18.

17. Arnold Brown, "'Not with a Bang': Civilization's Accelerating Challenge," *The Futurist*, September–October 2007, 35.

18. Manpower, "2008 Talent Shortage Survey: Signs of a Tight Labor Market," *The Herman Trend Alert*, August 3, 2005, http://www.hermangroup.com/alert/archive_8-3-2005.html (Accessed March 26, 2008).

19. Marcus Walker, "Free-Trade Alert: A Warning on Globalization Backlash," *Wall Street Journal*, June 20, 2007, sec. A, 2; OECD *Employment Outlook* (Paris: Organisation for Economic Co-operation and Development, 2007), 85–90.

20. Quoted in Frank Levy and Richard J. Murnane, *The New Division of Labor: How Computers Are Creating the Next Job Market* (New York: Russell Sage Foundation, 2004), 1.

21. Frank Levy and Richard Murnane, *The New Division of Labor*, 149–157.

22. *Wall Street Journal*, "American Manufacturing," September 26, 2007, sec. A, 9; *The Economist*, "Industrial Metamorphosis," October 1, 2005, 69–70.

CHAPTER 1

1. "Understanding Human Capital Challenges in Canada," Deloitte & Touche Canada, http://www.deloitte.com/dtt/article/0,1002,sid%3D3630%26cid%3D104784,00.html (Accessed August 27, 2006); Norval Scott, "Alberta Worker Shortage Hampers Plans to Increase Oil-Sands Output," *Wall Street Journal*, April 24, 2006, sec. C, 4.

2. Arlene Dohm and Lynn Shniper, "Occupational Employment Projections to 2016," 86. According to U.S. Labor Department economists, future projections will show the same trends to at least 2020 or beyond.

3. *Wall Street Journal*, "American Brain Drain," November 30, 2007, sec. A, 16; During the 2004–2005 academic year, 565,000 foreign students were enrolled in U.S. higher-education institutions: 80,466 were Indian, of which 72 percent were enrolled in graduate courses largely in engineering, computer science, and mathematics; Vaishali Honawar, "Indians Top Foreigners Bound for U.S. Colleges," *Education Week*, November 30, 2005, 21.

4. Joel Leonard, "Think You're Smarter Than a Maintenance Technician?" http://www.plantservices.com/articles/2007/086.html (Accessed January 11, 2008).

5. Michael Lind, "A Labor Shortage Can Be a Blessing Not a Curse," *Financial Times*, June 9, 2006, 13; Jonathan Sapsford, "Japan Shifts Gears to Same Industrial Base," *Wall Street Journal*, June 9, 2006, sec. A, 4.

6. *A First Look at the Literacy of American Adults in the 21st Century* (Washington, DC: U.S. Department of Education, National Center for Education Statistics, 2006), 4, 15.

7. *Education at a Glance, 2007* (Paris: Organisation for Economic Co-operation and Development, 2007), 42, 54, 58, 67, 68.

8. National Center for Public Policy and Higher Education, "Measuring UP 2006: The National Report Card on Higher Education," 7–8, http://measuringup.highereducation.org (Accessed November 10, 2008).

9. N. Gregory Mankiw, "The Wealth Trajectory: Rewards for the Few," *New York Times*, April 20, 2008, 9; *A Nation at Risk* (Washington, DC: U.S. Department of Education, and the National Commission on Excellence in Education, 1983); *Reading at Risk* (Washington, DC: National Endowment for the Arts, 2004).

10. Michael E. Porter, *The Competitive Advantage of Nations* (New York: Free Press, 1990), 628–629.

11. Carlos Tejada, "Why Some Jobs Go Begging Despite Weak Labor Market," *Wall Street Journal*, September 2, 2003, sec. B, 1.

12. Demetri Sevestopulo, "Pentagon Calls a Truce with Mark of Globalization," *Financial Times*, July 6, 2007, 3.

13. Robert Samuelson, Adolfo Santos, Alexandra L. Montgomery, and James B. Caruthers, "Four Scenarios for the Future of Education," *The Futurist*, January–February 2005, 29.

14. Robert Balfanz and Nettie Legters, "Closing 'Dropout Factories,'" *Education Week*, July 12, 2006, 42–43.

15. *Straight A's* (Alliance for Excellent Education), "Demography as Destiny: How America Can Build A Better Future," October 2006, 4–5. Taken a step further, the U.S. Census Bureau projects today's minorities will become the majority by 2050. It is hoped that we will have taken concerted action by midcentury to prevent an ill-educated techno-peasant underclass from fundamentally reducing the capacity of the U.S. economy.

16. Jessica Twentyman, "IT Sector Faces Growing Skills Gap," *Financial Times*, November 21, 2007, 3; Stem Workforce Data Project, "STEM Employment Forecasts and Distribution Among Employment Sectors: Report No. 7," http://www.cpst.org/STEM/STEM7_Report.pdf (Accessed May 1, 2008).

17. Nanette Asimov, "Science Courses Nearly Extinct in Elementary Grades, Study Says," *San Francisco Chronicle*, October 25, 2007, sec. A, 1.

18. Pat Toensmeier, "The Amazing World of Advanced Manufacturing," *In Demand Magazine*, http://www.careervoyages.gov/indemandmagazine -advmanufacturing/pdf (Accessed May 16, 2008); Joel Leonard, "Think You're Smarter Than a Maintenance Technician?" http://www.plantservices .com/articles/2007/086.html (Accessed January 11, 2008); Michael Lind, "A Labor Shortage Can Be a Blessing Not a Curse," *Financial Times*, June 9, 2006, 13; Jonathan Sapsford, "Japan Shifts Gears to Same Industrial Base," *Wall Street Journal*, June 9, 2006, sec. A, 4.

19. G. Pascal Zachary, "Bell Labs Is Gone. Academia Steps In," *New York Times*, December 16, 2007, 4; *The Economist*, "Out of Dusty Labs," March 3, 2007, 74; Kathy Hafner, "Microsoft Adds Research Lab in East as Others Cut Back," *New York Times*, February 4, 2008, sec. C, 3.
20. Committee for Economic Development, *Built to Last: Focusing Corporations on Long-Term Performance*, Washington, DC, 2007, http://www.ced .org/docs/report-corpgov2007.pdf (Accessed February 20, 2008); Michael Reid, *Forgotten Continent*, 293–294.
21. *The Economist*, "Jam Today," July 24, 2007, 67; Stefan Stern, "Ride of 'Casino Capitalism' Shakes Faith of Moderate Monks," *Financial Times*, November 21, 2006, 8; Michael Reid, *Forgotten Continent*, 208–295.
22. Matthew Armstrong, Andrea Bourgeois, and Aneliese Debus, "Help Wanted: Long-Term Vacancies Grow for Canada's Entrepreneurs," *Canadian Federation of Independent Business*, March 2007, 1–9; Bernard Simon, "Surging Loonie Causes a Flap in US–Canada Border Trade," *Financial Times*, July 26, 2007, 3.
23. Morris Beschloss, "Canada Saves America's Energy Bacon," *Desert Sun*, February 10, 2008, sec. D, 2; Stephen Murgatroyd, "Canada's Innovation Challenge," in *Creating Global Strategies for Humanity's Future* (Bethesda: World Future Society, 2006), 363.
24. Julie Ann McMullin and Martin Cooke, *Labour Force Ageing and Skill Shortages in Canada and Ontario* (London, Ontario, Canada: Canadian Policy Research Networks, 2004), 5, 19–20, 22–26.
25. *The Economist*, "One Nation or Many?" November 18, 2006, 39; *The Economist*, "The Battle for Brainpower: A Survey of Talent," October 7, 2006, 12; Bernard Simon, "The United Colours of Canada, *Financial Times*, December 13, 2006, 8; *Globe and Mail*, "Canada in Brief: Immigration Largely Behind Population Growth," September 28, 2006, sec. A, 10.
26. Julie Ann McMullin and Martin Cooke, *Labour Force Ageing and Skill Shortages in Canada and Ontario*, 33–34; *Globe and Mail*, "Aging Dilemma," September 28, 2006, sec. A, 16; "Battle for Brainpower," 12–14; Marina Jimenez, "Canada Losing Its Appeal for Chinese Immigrants," *Globe and Mail*, October 18, 2006, sec. A, 1, 7; Sarah Efron, "Welcome to Canada," *Financial Post*, October 3, 2006, 78.
27. Deloitte & Touche Canada, "Understanding Human Capital Challenges in Canada," http://www.deloitte.com/dtt/article/0,1002,sid%3D3630%26cid %3D104784,00.html (Accessed August 27, 2006); Norval Scott, "Alberta Worker Shortage Hampers Plans to Increase Oil-Sands Output," *Wall Street Journal*, April 24, 2006, sec. C, 4; Geoffrey Scotton, "Paper Shufflers Blamed for Foreign Hiring Delays," *Calgary Herald*, July 13, 2005, sec. C, 1, 3; Douglas Belkin, "This Is the Life: Luxurious Digs on Frigid Oil Sands," *Wall Street Journal*, December 5, 2007, sec. A, 1; Heather Scofield, "Alberta, Newfoundland on Top," *Globe and Mail*, August 1, 2006, sec. B, 3; Bernard Simon, "Saskatchewan Rides Commodities Boom," *Financial Times*, January 2, 2008, 4; Bernard Simon, "Shell to Review Can-

ada Oil Sands Project," *Financial Times,* July 7, 2006, 1; *Wall Street Journal,* "Alberta's Oil Boom Drains Some Towns of Workers," February 1, 2008, sec. B, 3; *The Economist,* "Canada—Not Just a Breadbasket," June 7, 2008, 51.

28. Sinclair Stewart, "Why Cape Breton Shakes in the Echo of This Distant Boom," *Globe and Mail,* January 29, 2008, http://www.theglobeandmail. com/servlet/RTGAM.20080128.w-OS-main-29/BNStory/oilsands/feature -topic (Accessed November 13, 2008).

29. "International Adult Literacy and Skills Survey (IALSS)," *Literacy at Work,* (ABC Canada), no. 45, November 2005, 1–3; "Report Summary: Learning a Living: First Results of the Adult Literacy and Life Skills (ALL) Survey," ABC Canada Literacy Foundation, May 2005, http://www.abc-canada. org/media_room/news/all_survey_summary_shtml (Accessed August 30, 2006); The Conference Board of Canada, "Literacy, Life, And Employment: An Analysis of Canadian International Adult Literacy Survey (IALS) Microdata," January 2006.

30. Keynote presentation by Mary Ann Chambers, "Workplace Education and Learning Conference: Investing in People," Conference Board of Canada, Toronto, Canada, November 29, 2004.

31. Phillip S. Jarvis, "Talent . . . Opportunity Prosperity Requires Connecting the Dots," National Life/Work Centre, Ottawa, Canada, 2006.

32. Stephen Murgatroyd, *Canada's Innovation Challenge,* 372; Edward E. Gordon, "Smart Worker Deficit Impacts Canadian Economy," *Employee Benefit News Canada,* January/February 2005, 19; Mark Goldenberg, "Employer Investment in Workplace Learning in Canada," Canadian Policy Research Networks, September 2006, http://cprh.com/download.cfm ?doc=15298&file=45354_en.pdf (Accessed May 10, 2008).

33. http://www.cia.gov/library/publications/the-world-factbook (Accessed September 27, 2008).

34. Michael Reid, *Forgotten Continent,* 1–29, 243.

35. Roger Cohen, "New Day in the Americas," *New York Times Week in Review,* January 6, 2008, 12; Colin McMahon, "Breaking the Cycle," *Chicago Tribune,* sec. 2, 1, 3; *The Economist,* "Adios to Poverty," 22–23.

36. Bob Davis and John Lyons, "Globalization's Gains Come With a Price," *Wall Street Journal,* May 24, 2007, sec. A, 12.

37. *The Economist,* "Brazil–Lula's Leap," March 4, 2006, 33; Michelle Kessler, "U.S. Tech Companies Give Brazil a Go," *USA Today,* sec. B, 1; Michael Reid, *Forgotten Continent,* 197.

38. *The Economist,* "Brazil–Lula's Leap," 34; UNESCO Institute for Statistics, "UIS Statistics in Brief: Education in Brazil," http://stats.uis.unesco.org; Michael Reid, *Forgotten Continent,* 144, 218.

39. *The Economist,* "Chile's Schools—How to Make Them Better," October 7, 2006, 44.

40. *The Economist,* "Child Playground Harmony," December 15, 2007, 46; UNESCO Institute for Statistics, "UIS Statistics in Brief"; Adam Thom-

son, "Chile's State Education System Could Do Better," *Financial Times*, January 26, 2005, 9.

41. Lygia Navarro, "Penguin Revolution Pays Off," *Chicago Tribune*, July 5, 2006, sec. 1, 9; Adam Thomson, "Chile's State Education System"; Michael Reid, *Forgotten Continent*, 180–183.

42. Liam Julian, "Note to Mexico: Education Instead of Emigration," *The Education Gadfly*, July 13, 2006, http://www.edexcellence.net/gadfly/index .cfm?issue=249 (Accessed August 20, 2006); Bob Davis and John Lyons, "Globalization's Gains Come With a Price," *Wall Street Journal*, May 24, 2007, sec. A, 12; Joel Kurtzman, "Mexico's Job-Creation Problem," *Wall Street Journal*, August 3, 2007, sec. A, 9.

43. Joel Kurtzman, "Mexico's Job-Creation Problem," *Wall Street Journal*, August 3, 2007, sec. A, 9; UNESCO Institute for Statistics, "UIS Statistics in Brief: Education in Mexico," available at http://stats.uis.unesco.org.

44. Bob Davis and John Lyons, "Globalization Gains," A12; Adam Thomson, "Maquiladora: Skills and Technology Add Value to Product," *Financial Times: Mexico—Business & Infrastructure*, May 9, 2007, 3.

45. Joel Kurtzman, "Mexico's Job-Creation Problem," sec. A, 9.

46. Stephen Franklin, "Mexico Faces Own Job Drain," *Chicago Tribune*, December 23, 2007, sec. 3, 1, 4; Reid, *Forgotten Continent*, 208–209.

47. Marla Dickerson, "Costa Rica Rides High Tech Wave," *Los Angeles Times*, March 18, 2006, sec. C, 1–3; UNESCO Institute for Statistics, "UIS Statistics in Brief: Education in Costa Rica," available at http://stats.uis.unesco .org; U.S. Department of State, Bureau of Western Hemisphere Affairs, "Background Note: Costa Rica Profile," http://www.state.gov/r/pa/ei/bgn .2019.html (Accessed January 24, 2008). *Costa Rica Guide*, "Costa Rica Economy," http://www.incostaricaguide.com/economy/economy_2.html (Accessed January 24, 2008).

48. Andres Oppenheimer, "Latin American Economy Improving but Lagging," *Miami Herald*, December 23, 2007, http://www.miamiherald.com/ news/columnists/andres_oppenheimer/story/354754.html (Accessed January 24, 2008); United Nations Economic Commission for Latin America and the Caribbean, "Latin American and Caribbean Economies Grow 5.6% in 2007; Slight Downturn Viewed for 2008," http://www.eclac.org/cgi -bin/getProd.asp?Xml=/prensa/noticias/comunicados/9/32019/P32 (Accessed January 24, 2008).

49. Roger Cohen, "New Day in the Americas," *New York Times Week in Review*, January 6, 2008, 12; Bob Davis and John Lyons, "Globalization Gains," A12; Michael Reid, *Forgotten Continent*, 29.

CHAPTER 2

1. Robyn Meredith, *The Elephant and the Dragon* (New York: W.W. Norton, 2007), 160; Chris Patten, "Saddled with the Worst of Both Worlds," *Financial Times*, June 12, 2006, 14.

2. Kohzem Merchant, "Shrines to Knowledge and Wealth," *Financial Times*, September 7, 2004, 10; *Chicago Tribune*, "Motorola to Build India Factory," June 8, 2006, sec. 3, 3; Simon London, "Accenture Aims for 30,000 Jobs to Expand Offshore," *Financial Times*, July 8, 2005, 17; Philip Stephens, "A Future for Europe Shaped by Museums and Modernity," *Financial Times*, September 8, 2006, 15.

3. *The Economist*, "Capturing Talent," August 18, 2007, 59; Guy De Jonquieres, "Asia Cannot Fill the World's Skills Gap," *Financial Times*, June 13, 2006, 15; Herman Trend Alert, "Brain Drain," May 10, 2006, http://www.hermangroup.com/alert/archive_5-10-2006.html (Accessed July 20, 2006).

4. Sundeep Tucker, "A Bidding War Makes for 'Crazy' Salaries Across Asia," 7.

5. *The Economist*, "India Overheats," February 3, 2007, 11; Amartya Sen, "Can Life Begin at 60 for the Sprightly Indian Economy?" *Financial Times*, August 14, 2007, 11; Meredith, *The Elephant and the Dragon*, 38–46; Matthew Rees, "The Boom Beyond Our Borders," *Wall Street Journal*, July 18, 2007, sec. D, 10; Jo Johnson, "A Confident New Country," India Special Report, *Financial Times*, August 15, 2007, 1; Martin Wolf, "A Waking Giant Tugging Hard at its Chains," *Financial Times*, January 25, 2008, 3.

6. *The Economist*, "The New Titans: A Survey of the World Economy," September 16, 2006, 14.

7. Bob Goldstein, "India's Manpower Shortage in Skilled Labor Threatens Expansion," *Bloomberg News*, August 21, 2007, http://www.bloomberg.com/apps/news?pid=20601109&sid=aNtGr9ytmeYI &refer=news (Accessed May 20, 2008).

8. Population Division of the Department of Economic and Social Affairs of the United Nations Secretariat, "World Population Prospects: The 2006 Revision," http://esa.un.org/unpp (Accessed November 10, 2008).

9. Robyn Meredith, *The Elephant and the Dragon*, 132–133; Paul Beckett and Krishma Pokhared, "India's Surging Economy Lifts Hopes and Ambitions," *Wall Street Journal*, November 28, 2007, sec. A, 1, 20.

10. *Chicago Tribune*, "Investments in India to Triple to 6 Billion," June 7, 2006, sec. C, 1; Francesco Guerrera and Richard Waters, "IBM Chief Wants End to Colonial Companies," *Financial Times*, June 12, 2006, 1.

11. *Financial Times*, "IBM/India," The Lex Column, June 7, 2006, 14; John Willman, "Poll Finds Nine out of 10 Top Executives Optimistic," *Financial Times*, January, 17, 2007, 6.

12. Scott R. Bayman, "Thirteen Years on the Inside: A Perspective on India," Presentation to the Chicago Council on Global Affairs and the Confederation of Indian Industry, Chicago, IL, September 8, 2006.

13. NASSCOM-McKinsey Report 2005, "Extending India's Leadership of the Global IT and BPO Industries," McKinsey Global Institute, 2005, http://www.nasscom.in/upload/10142/Mckinsey_study-2005.pdf (Accessed May 19, 2008); Sundeep Tucker, "A Bidding War," 7.

14. *The Education Gadfly*, "A Subcontinental Divide," January 24, 2008, http://www.edexcellence.net/institute/gadfly/issue.cfm?id=324&edition=#3281

(Accessed May 19, 2008); Meredith, *The Elephant and the Dragon*, 128, 156; India's illiteracy is so pervasive that Citigroup rolled out a network of biometric automatic cash machines that will recognize account holder's thumbprints and have color-coded screen instructions and voiceovers to guide illiterates through transactions, Joe Leahy, "Citigroup Gives India's Poor a Hand with Thumbprint ATMs," *Financial Times*, December 3, 2006, 1.

15. Bob Goldstein, "India's Manpower Shortage in Skilled Labor Threatens Expansion," Bloomberg News, August 21, 2007, http://www.bloomberg.com/apps/news?pid=20601109&sid=aNtGr9ytmeYI &refer=news (Accessed May 20, 2008); Jo Johnson, "India PM on Science Failings," *Financial Times*, July 12, 2006, 3.

16. NASSCOM-McKinsey Report 2005; Somini Sengupta, "Skills Gap Threatens Technology Boom in India," *New York Times*, October 17, 2006, sec. A, 1, 6; Jo Johnson, "How India Raises an Army," *Financial Times*, May 22, 2007, 12; NASSCOM's Education Initiatives, http://www.nasscom.in/Nasscom/templates/NormalPage.aspx?id=51761 (Accessed July 6, 2007); Jon Larkin, "India's Talent Pool Drying Up," *Wall Street Journal*, January 4, 2006, sec. A, 9; Wayne Simmons, "The Risks Ahead: India," Kata Consulting, November 1, 2007, http://www.kataconsulting.com/docs/Risks %20Ahead%20-%20India.pdf (Accessed May 15, 2008); *New York Times*, "Skills Gap Hurts Technology Boom in India," November 30, 2006, sec. A, 12; *World Bank Development Policy Review*, "India—Inclusive Growth and Service Delivery: Building on India's Success," 2006, 17; *The Economist*, "Economics Focus—Light and Shade," August 12, 2006, 64.

17. Pratham Annual Status of Education Report 2007, http://www.pratham.org/aser07/aser2007.php (Accessed January 30, 2008); UNESCO Institute for Statistics, "UIS Statistics in Brief, Education in India," available at http://stats.uis.unesco.org.

18. Saritha Rai, "Outsourcers Struggling to Keep Workers in the Fold," *New York Times*, November 12, 2005, sec. A, 21; *The Economist*, "Now for the Hard Part: A Survey of Business in India," June 3, 2006, 5; Sundeep Tucker, "A Bidding War," 7; *The Economist*, "The World is Our Oyster: A Survey of Talent," October 7, 2006, 9; Amy Yee, "Soaring Salaries to Hit India IT Group Margins," *Financial Times*, September 12, 2007, 18; *Chief Financial Officer*, "Outsourcing Passing on India?" June 2006, 17; Jackie Range, "India's Technology Firms Arrive at a Critical Hour," *Wall Street Journal*, April 13, 2007, sec. B, 4; *The Economist*, "India Overheats," February 3, 2007, 11; Jehangir S. Pocha, "Booming Indian Economy Luring Many Back," *Press-Enterprise* (Riverside, CA), February 11, 2007, A16; *The Economist*, "Deportation Order," April 28, 2007, 38.

19. Pui-Wing Tam and Jackie Range, "Some in Silicon Valley Begin to Sour on India," *Wall Street Journal*, July 3, 2007, sec. A, 15.

20. Jo Johnson, "A Tether that Keeps Potential in Check," *Financial Times: India Infrastructure Special Report*, May 8, 2007, 1; Joe Leahy, "Mumbai Battles against Blackouts," *Financial Times*, June 22, 2007, 5; Sumathi

Vaidyanthan, "India's Plague of Power Outages Crimps Business," *Wall Street Journal*, May 10, 2005, sec. A, 1; Somini Sengupta, "Electricity Crisis Hobbles an India Eager to Ascend," *New York Times International*, May 21, 2007, sec. A, 6; Somini Sengupta, "Thirsting for Energy in India's Boomtowns and Beyond," *New York Times International*, March 2, 2008, 4; Eric Bellman, and Jackie Range, "Shortage of Laborers Plagues India," *Wall Street Journal*, May 1, 2008, sec. A, 1, 4.

21. Jo Johnson, "India's Great Hope for Prosperity," *Financial Times Life & Arts*, June 7–8, 2008, 2.

22. Mark Leonard, "China's Long and Winding Road," *Financial Times Weekend*, July 9–10, 2005, sec. W, 1–2; Howard Birnberg, "Travel Notes—A Visit to China," *On and Off the Cliff: Newsletter of the Cliff Dwellers*, July/August 2005, 2–4; Howard Birnberg in discussion with the author, September 23, 2005; David Moser (President DFT, Inc.) in discussion with the author, February 11, 2008; *The Economist*, "Survey of China: Coming Out," March 25, 2006, 3–18; Ian Bremmer, "Uncertainty Surrounds Stamina of China's Economic Expansion," *Financial Times*, March 21, 2005, 24.

23. Keith Bradsher, "Wages Are on the Rise in China as Businesses Court the Young," *New York Times*, August 29, 2007, sec. A, 1, 9.

24. Martin Wolf, "China Cracked," *Financial Times Weekend*, February 3–4, 2007, sec. W, 7; U.S. Congress, Joint Economic Committee, "Five Challenges that China Must Overcome to Sustain Economic Growth," July 2006, 8–9, http://www.house.gov/jec/studies/2006/07-27-06china_economy .pdf (Accessed January 10, 2008); Mure Dickie, "China Looks to Ease its One Child Policy," *Financial Times*, February 29, 2008, 6; Jim Yardley, "China to Reconsider One-Child Limit, an Official Suggests," *New York Times*, February 29, 2008, sec. A, 4; Meredith, *The Elephant and the Dragon*, 153; Loretta Chao, "China to Retain Its One-Child Policy," *Wall Street Journal*, March 11, 2008, sec. A, 4; Bruce D. Liegel and Stephen K. Bossu, "Emerging Market Fairy Tales: A Message from the Currency Markets," *The LCM Perspective*, February 10, 2008, 10.

25. Richard McGregor, "Economists Cast Doubts on China's GDP Data," *Financial Times*, October 24, 2005, 6; Guy De Jonquires, "Lies, Damn Lies, and China's Economic Statistics," *Financial Times*, November 22, 2005, 19; *The Economist*, "Economics Focus: An Aberrant Abacus," May 3, 2008, 85.

26. Albert Keidel, "The Limits of a Smaller, Poorer China," *Financial Times*, November 14, 2007, 11; *The Economist*, "Clipping the Dragon's Wings," December 22, 2007, 68.

27. *The Economist*, "Balancing Act—A Survey of China: No Time Like the Present," March 25, 2006, 19–20.

28. *The Economist*, "The Technology Industry: Different Strokes," October 7, 2006, 72–73; *The Economist*, "The New Titans," 14; Graeme Maxton, "Not Enough People in China," *The Economist: The World in 2008*, 128.

29. *Financial Times*, "Struggle to Retain Staff in China," September 1, 2006, 2; Nicholas Timmins, "Employers Suffer Talent Shortages," *Financial*

Times, October 20, 2006, 6; *The Economist*, "Briefing Manpower—The World of Work," January 6, 2007, 57–58; *People's Daily*, "Chinese Manufacturing Slowed by Skilled Worker Shortage," September 8, 2002, http://english.people.com.cn/200209/08/eng20020908_102840.shtml (Accessed June 3, 2007); *Knowledge@Wharton*, "Does a Growing Worker Shortage Threaten China's Low-Cost Advantage?" May 10, 2006, http://knowledge.wharton.upenn.edu/article.cfm?articleid=1473&specialid=53 (Accessed June 3, 2007); Tom Mitchell and Geoff Dyer, "Heat in the Workshop," *Financial Times*, October 15, 2007, 7; Mure Dickie, "Competition Is Hot for Dalian Outsourcing Services," *Financial Times*, June 12, 2007, 4; *The Economist*, "One to Watch," February 24, 2007, 79; *The Economist*, "Industry in China: Where Is Everybody?" March 15, 2008, 77–78.

30. *Financial Times*, "China's Weakest Link," October 7, 2005, 14; Geoff Dyer and Khozen Merchant, "Graduates 'May Fail Chinese Economy,'" *Financial Times*, October 7, 2005, 8; Andrew Baxter, "Preaching Best Practice," *Financial Times*, November 27, 2007, 4; Farrell, et al., "The Emerging Global Labor Market"; Martin Wolf, "A Colossus With Feet of Clay," *Financial Times*, January 24, 2007, 6; Martin Wolf, "Industry in China," *Financial Times*, January 24, 2007, 78.

31. Martin Wolf, "China Changes the Whole World," *Financial Times*, January 23, 2008, 2; Tom Mitchell, "China's Factory Heartland Set for Big Rise in Minimum Wage," *Financial Times*, April 19, 2006, 1; David Barboza, "China Inflation Exacting a Toll across the US," *New York Times*, February 1, 2008, sec. A 1, 8; Tom Mitchell, "Margins Squeeze Bites into China Textile Sector," *Financial Times*, March 3, 2008, 5.

32. Don Lee, "Job Hopping Is Rampant as China's Economy Chases Skilled Workers," *Los Angeles Times*, February 21, 2006, sec. C, 1, 8; "Mapping Global Talent," Heidrick & Struggles and Economist Intelligence Unit, September 2007, 12.

33. Don Lee, "Job Hopping," sec. C, 1; Elaine Kurtenbach, "Rising Costs Pinch Factories in China," *Desert Sun*, February 22, 2008, sec. E, 2.

34. Jun Wang, "The Return of the 'Sea Turtles': Reverse Brain Drain to China," *China Daily*, September 27, 2005, http://www.chinadaily.com.cn/english/doc/2005-09/27content_481163.htm (Accessed February 10, 2008); Don Lee, "Returning Chinese Find a Tough Market," *Los Angeles Times*, March 5, 2006, sec. C, 1, 5.

35. Tucker, "A Bidding War Makes for 'Crazy' Salaries Across Asia," 7.

36. *The Economist*, "Silicon Valley Deportation Order," April 28, 2007, 38; *The Economist*, "Opening the Doors: A Survey of Talent," October 7, 2006, 13; *Financial Times*, "Torn Between the Claims of Two Generations," June 9, 2005, 11; Don Lee, "Research Follows Factories to China," *Los Angeles Times*, January 14, 2007, sec. C, 10; Peter Cochrane, "The Reverse Brain Drain that Fueled China's Rise," *Financial Times*, May 9, 2007, 2.

37. *The Hechinger Report*, "Lessons from China: What the U.S. Can Learn—and What It Shouldn't," Fall/Winter 2007, 3.

38. Gary Gereffi and Vivek Wadhwa, "Framing the Engineering Outsourcing Debate: Placing the United States on a Level Playing Field with China and India," Duke University School of Engineering, December 2005, 2, 5, 9; Gary Gereffi, Vivek Wadhwa, and Ben Rissing, "Framing the Engineering Outsourcing Debate: Comparing the Quantity and Quality of Engineering Graduates in the United States, India, and China," paper prepared for the SASE Conference, Trier, Germany, June 30–July 2, 2006, 13–14; *The Economist*, "Survey of the World Economy 2006," 14.

39. Farrell, et al., "The Emerging Global Labor Market."

40. David Lague, "1977 Exam Opened Escape Route Into China's Elite," *New York Times International*, January 6, 2008, 4; Ann Hulbert, "Re-Education," *New York Times Magazine*, April 1, 2007, 39–40; *New York Times Magazine*, "Lessons From China," April 1, 2007, 3.

41. UNESCO Institute for Statistics, "UIS Statistics in Brief, Education in China," http://stats.uis.unesco.org; *Wall Street Journal*, "Is China Stumbling in Fight Against Illiteracy?" June 11, 2007, sec. B, 6.

42. Clive Cookson, "Academia Seeks to Join Global Elite," *Financial Times*, July 8, 2005, 11; *The Economist*, "China: Chaos in the Classroom," August 12, 2006, 32–33; Meredith, *The Elephant and the Dragon*, 72.

43. Richard McGregor, "Debate Rages on Nations Place in the World," *Financial Times Special Report: World Economy*, October 8, 2005, 5; *The Economist*, "Missing the Barefoot Doctors," October 13, 2007, 27; Richard McGregor, "OECD Warning on Rural China," *Financial Times*, November 15, 2005, 4; Leslie T. Chang, "A Migrant Worker Sees Rural Home in a New Light," *Wall Street Journal*, June 8, 2005, sec. A, 1, 12; Howard W. French, "Lives of Grinding Poverty, Untouched by China's Boom," *New York Times International*, January 13, 2008, 4; Hulbert, "Re-Education," 41; Yasheng Huang, "What China Could Learn From India's Slow and Quiet Rise," *Financial Times*, January 24, 2006, 13; Yasheng Huang, "The Brains Business," *Financial Times*, January 24, 2006, 16.

44. *Financial Times*, "China and India: The Two Differ in Business as Much as They Do in Politics," December 12, 2006, 8; U.S. Congress, "Five Challenges that China Must Overcome," 12.

45. Ching-Ching Ni, "5 Girls' Deaths Highlight Child-Labor Woes in China," *Chicago Tribune*, May 22, 2005, sec. 1, 8.

46. Howard W. French, "Child Slavery Revelations Shock China," *Chicago Tribune*, June 16, 2007, sec. 1, 8; David Lague, "China Tries to Contain Scandal Over Slave Labor With Arrests and Apology," *New York Times*, June 23, 2007, sec. A, 6; Jamil Anderlini and Geoff Dyer, "Wary Welcome for China Labour Law," *Financial Times*, July 2, 2007, 6; David Barboza, "Chinese Factories, Flouting Labor Laws, Hire Children From Poor, Distant Villages," *New York Times International*, May 10, 2008, sec. A, 5, 7; Alexandra Harney, *The China Price* (New York: Penguin Press, 2008), 1–42, 106–147; Morgen Witzel, "The Hidden Cost of 'Cheap' Chinese Goods," *Financial Times*, April 3, 2008, 10.

47. U.S. Congress, Joint Economic Committee, "Five Challenges that China Must Overcome to Sustain Economic Growth," 31–33; Seymour N. Lotsoff, "China, India, the United States, and Iraq: Ten Years Hence," *The LCM Perspective*, August 2006, 1–6; Meredith, *The Elephant and the Dragon*, 154.

48. Morris Beschloss, "Japan's Economy Resists Stimulation," *Desert Sun*, April 11, 200, sec. E, 2.

49. David Pilling, "Japan's Recovery Lures Back Workers," *Financial Times*, May 2, 2006, 4; Joseph Coleman, "Japan Opening for Foreigners," *Desert Sun*, January 31, 2007, sec. A, 23; *The Economist*, "Briefing: Japan's Changing Demography," July 28, 2007, 24–26; David Turner, "Japan's Jobless Rate at Lowest in Eight Years," *Financial Times*, April 1–2, 2007, 5; *New York Times International*, "World Briefing Asia–Japan: Warning Over Declining Work Force," April 23, 2008, sec. A, 9.

50. *The Economist*, "Briefing: Japan's Changing Demography," 26; Sebastian Moffett, "Fast Aging Japan Keeps Its Elders on the Job Longer," *Wall Street Journal*, June 15, 2005, sec. A, 1, 8; *The Economist*, "How to Deal With a Falling Population," July 28, 2007, 11.

51. *The Futurist*, "Promoting Parenthood in Japan," May–June 2007, 9; David Turner, "Japan Pay Deals Offer Workers Baby Bonus," *Financial Times*, March 22, 2007, 6.

52. *The Economist*, "Better Than People," December 24, 2005, 58–59; Clive Cookson, "How Humanoids Won the Hearts of Japanese Industry," *Financial Times*, July 3, 2006, 8; *Wall Street Journal*, "The Future of Health Care?" June 26, 2006, sec. R, 7, 8; Hiroko Tabuchi, "Japanese Robot Technology Takes Hold," *Desert Sun*, March 2, 2008, sec. A, 10, 11.

53. David Pilling, "Japan's Fight to Stay Ahead," *Financial Times*, June 26, 2005, 11; Edward E. Gordon, *The 2010 Meltdown: Solving the Impending Job Crisis* (Westport, CT: Praeger, 2005), 32.

54. Micheline Maynard, "At Toyota a Giant Strives to Show Its Agility," *New York Times*, February 22, 2008, sec. C, 1, 4.

55. *Financial Times*, "Inculcating Culture the Toyota Way," January 21, 2006, 11; Edward E. Gordon, *The 2010 Meltdown*, 153–154, 183–184.

56. *Chicago Tribune*, "Nissan Training Takes a New Spin," December 1, 2006, sec. 3, 2; Jathon Sapsford, "Japan Shifts Gears to Save Industrial Base," *Wall Street Journal*, June 9, 2006, sec. A, 4.

57. UNESCO Institute for Statistics, "UIS Statistics in Brief, Education in Japan," http://stats.uis.unesco.org; Richard G. Neal, "Extended School Day and Year Are Under Review Across the Country," *School Reform News*, February 2008, 17; Martin Fackler, "As Japan Ages, Universities Struggle to Fill Classrooms," *New York Times International*, June 22, 2007, sec. A, 3.

58. Martin Fackler, "High-Tech Japanese, Running Out of Engineers," *New York Times*, May 17, 2008, sec. A, 1, sec. B, 4.

59. Guy De Jonquires, "If Korea Is So Cool, Why Is Seoul in a Lather?" *Financial Times*, September 13, 2005, 17; Anna Fifield, "Bright Outlook in Spite of Setbacks," *Financial Times: Investing in South Korea*, December 4, 2006, 1.

60. United Nations, World Population Prospects, http://esa.un.org/unpp (Accessed September 27, 2008); Euromonitor International, http://euromonitor .com/Ageing_South_Korea (Accessed September 27, 2008).

61. Anna Fifield, "Bright Outlook," *Financial Times*, December 4, 2006, 2; Anna Fifield, "Seoul Sleepwalk: Why an Asian Export Champion Is at Risk of Losing Its Way," *Financial Times*, March 19, 2007, 9.

62. Anna Fifield, "Bright Outlook in Spite of Setbacks," 1–2; Tariq Hussain, *Diamond Dilemma* (New York: Random House, 2006), 52, 191; Anna Fifield, "Flaws in Korea in Spite of a Cutting Edge," *Financial Times*, January 31, 2007, 7.

63. Sebastian Moffett and SungHa Park, "South Korea Looks to Put Pep Back into Economy," *Wall Street Journal*, February 26, 2008, sec. A, 6.

64. UNESCO Institute for Statistics, "UIS Statistics in Brief, Education in the Republic of Korea," http://stats.uis.unesco.org; Edward E. Gordon, *The 2010 Meltdown*, 181.

65. Jin Ah Yoo, "Korean Youth Driven Onward by Degrees," *Chicago Tribune*, November 25, 2005, sec. 1, 24; Evan Ramstad, "Korean Equality Starts Early," *Wall Street Journal*, December 26, 2007, sec. A, 5; *Program for International Student Assessment (PISA) 2005* (Paris: Organisation for Economic Co-operation and Development, 2005), 118.

66. Norimitsu Onishi, "For Studies in English Learn to Say Goodbye to Dad," *New York Times International*, June 8, 2008, 1, 16.

67. Anna Fifield, "Bright Outlook in Spite of Setbacks," 2; Anna Fifield, "Seoul Sleepwalk," 9; Anna Fifield, "Increase in Medical Students Bodes Ill for South Korea," *Financial Times*, July 17, 2007.

68. *The Economist*, "Singapore's Economy–High Flyer," October 27, 2007, 51; Frances Williams and John Burton, "Singapore Overtakes US to Lead World in New IT," *Financial Times*, March 10, 2005, 6.

69. John Burton, "Singapore Goes Back to Its Roots for Skilled Staff," *Financial Times*, August 2, 2007, 2; Nicholas Timmins, "Employers Suffer Talent Shortages," *Financial Times*, October 24, 2006, 6; "Singapore's Economy-High Flyer," 51.

70. *The Economist*, "The Battle for Brainpower: A Survey of Talent," October 7, 2006, 12; John Burton, "Singapore Goes Back," 2; "Singapore's Economy-High Flyer," 51.

71. UNESCO Institute for Statistics, "UIS Statistics in Brief, Education in Singapore," http://stats.uis.unesco.org; Richard G. Neal, "Extended School Day and Year Are Under Review Across the Country," 17; Richard Lee Colvin, "Singapore Students Surpass Our Own in Math, Science," *The Hechinger Report*, Fall/Winter 2007, 2; John Burton, "Stellar Results Mask a Lack of Flexibility," *Financial Times*, October 18, 2006, 3; Michael Barber and Mona Mourshed, "How the World's Best Performing School Systems Come Out on Top," McKinsey & Company, September 2007, 17–19 http://www.mckinsey.com/clientservice/socialsector/resources/pdf/Worlds _school_systems_final.pdf (Accessed November 10, 2008).

72. *The Economist*, "The Problem With Made in China," January 13, 2007, 68–69.

73. *Herman Trend Alert*, "Reverse Migration of Manufacturing Base," August 30, 2006, http://www.hermangroup.com/alert/archive_8-30-2006.html (Accessed September 12, 2006); Martin Wolf, "A Glimpse of a Prosperous 2030 and What Can Foster It," *Financial Times*, December 20, 2006, 11; "Competitive Advantage of 'Low Wage' Countries Often Exaggerated," The Conference Board, Executive Action No. 212, October 2006, http://conference-board.org.

CHAPTER 3

1. *Key Facts and Figures About Europe and the European* (Luxembourg: Office for Official Publications of the European Communities, 2005), 3–13; *How the European Union Works* (Luxembourg: Office for Official Publications of the European Communities, 2005), 5, 36–37, 42, 50; Jeffrey Fleishman, "At 50, EU Faces an Identity Crisis," *Los Angeles Times*, March 27, 2007, sec. A, 9.

2. European Commission, "Spring Economic Forecast 2007–2008: Unemployment and Public Accounts to Improve Further as Growth Stays Solid," July 5, 2007, http://ec.europa.eu/economyfinance/publications/europeaneconomy/forecasts.en (Accessed March 3, 2008); *Work Permit News*, "Economic Growth, Skills Shortages Remain Strong in New EU States," September 28, 2007, http://review.workpermit.com/news/2007-09-28/europe/world-bank-report-new-european-union-states-strong-economy-skills-shortage.htm (Accessed March 2, 2008); Chris Giles, "Immigrants Boost British and Spanish Economies," *Financial Times*, February 20, 2007, 3.

3. *Key Facts and Figures About Europe and the European*, 14–15; Tom Hundley, "Europe Battles Its Baby Bust," *Chicago Tribune*, July 23, 2006, sec. 1, 12.

4. European Centre for the Development of Vocational Training, "Future Skill Needs in Europe Medium-Term Forecast Synthesis Report" (Luxembourg: Office for Official Publications of the European Community, 2008), 12–14.

5. European Centre for the Development of Vocational Training, "Future Skill Needs in Europe Medium-Term Forecast Synthesis Report," 54–56.

6. Ifo Institute, "EU Immigration," 2008, http://www.cesifo-group.de/ (Accessed March 3, 2008).

7. Jean Pisani-Ferry, "Europe's Eroding Wealth of Knowledge," *Financial Times*, August 23, 2006, 9.

8. Ralph Atkins, "Eurozone Wakes Up to Changing Face of Labor," *Financial Times*, June 2–3, 2007, 2; *The Economist*, "Job Vacancies in Europe," August 18, 2007, 85.

9. Jon Boone, "Immigrant Pupils 'Lag Behind' at School," *Financial Times*, May 16, 2006, 4; *Education at a Glance 2007* (Paris: Organisation for Economic Co-operation and Development, 2007), 104–115.

10. Jon Boone, "OECD Attacks Wasting of Schools Cash," *Financial Times*, September 19, 2007, 6.

11. *The Economist*, "Universities—How Europe Fails Its Young," September 10, 2005, 14.

12. Andrew Taylor, "OECD States Host 75 Million Migrants," *Financial Times*, February 21, 2008, 2; *The Economist*, "Europe's 'Blue Card' Plan—Not the Ace in the Pack," October 27, 2007, 60; John W. Miller, "EU's New Tack on Immigration," *Wall Street Journal*, February 10, 2006, sec. A, 8; Laura Dixon, "Brussels Plans to Woo Skilled Migrants," *Financial Times*, October 24, 2007, 2.

13. *The Economist*, "Europe and Immigration—The Trouble With Migrants," November 24, 2007, 56–57; Jean-Christophe Dumont and George Lamaitre, *Counting Immigrants and Expatriates in OECD Countries: A New Perspective* (Paris: Organisation for Economic Co-operation and Development, 2007), 6–13, 21; *The Economist*, "European Migration—The Brain-Drain Cycle," December 10, 2005, 57–58; Joellen Perry and Stephen Power, "Shortage of Skilled Labor Pinches Eastern Europe," *Wall Street Journal*, July 10, 2007, sec. A, 1, 14.

14. European Commission, "Funding Programmes in Education and Training," April 25, 2007, http://ec.europa.eu/education/programmes/programmes_en.html (Accessed March 3, 2008); Linda Anderson, "Worthy Cause Gains Momentum," *Financial Times: Business Education Management Section*, September 17, 2007, 5; *The Economist*, "Winning by Degrees," May 5, 2007, 67; Ursula Milton, "Skills Translation Comes Closer," *Financial Times Special Report: Professional Development*, November 12, 2007, 3.

15. Mark Landler, "Germany Posts—Month 21 of Declining Jobless Rate," *New York Times*, January 4, 2008, sec. C, 5; Bertrand Benoit, "Slow German Growth Sounds Poverty Alert," *Financial Times*, May 5, 2008, 2.

16. Bertrand Benoit, "Germans Turn to Demographic Robbery as Jobs Go Unfilled," *Financial Times*, November 28, 2006, 2; Joellen Perry, "Exodus of Skilled Workers Leaves Germany in a Bind," *Wall Street Journal*, January 3, 2007, sec. A, 2.

17. Bertrand Benoit, "Overhauled: Why Germany Is Again the Engine of Europe," *Financial Times*, March 30, 2007, 9; *The Economist*, "Back Above the Bar Again," July 14, 2007, 80–82.

18. *The Economist*, "The Problem With Solid Engineering," May 20, 2006, 71–73; Hugh Williamson, "Job Creation Still a Vital Challenge," *Financial Times Special Report: Germany*, December 4, 2007, 4; Bertrand Benoit, "Germans Turn to Demographic Robbery," 2; Bertrand Benoit, "Germany's Skills Gap Costs $27 Billion a Year," *Financial Times*, August 21, 2007, 30.

19. Erik W. Robelen, "The Great Divide," *Education Week*, May 11, 2005, 32, 34; *The Economist*, "Waiting for a Wunder—A Survey of Germany," February 11, 2006, 7; *The Economist*, "Two Unamalgamated Worlds," April 5, 2008, 32.

20. Wilfried Preno, "The Sorcery of Apprenticeship," *Wall Street Journal*, February 12, 1993, sec. A, 22.
21. Erik W. Robelen, "The Great Divide," *Education Week*, May 11, 2005, 32, 34; *The Economist*, "Waiting for a Wunder—A Survey of Germany," February 11, 2006, 13; Marcus Walker, "Berlin Cracks Immigrant Door," *Wall Street Journal*, August 27, 2007, sec. A, 5; Hugh Williamson, "Germany Looks East as Skills Shortage Bites," *Financial Times*, July 26, 2007, 3.
22. Robelen, "The Great Divide," 33—34; "Two Unamalgamated Worlds," 33.
23. Hans Schieser in discussion with the author, March 15, 2008; *The Economist*, "Waiting for a Wunder—A Survey of Germany," 7; Bertrand Benoit, "Different Divide," *Financial Times*, September 18, 2007, 9.
24. United Kingdom, Office of National Statistics, http://www.statistics.gov (Accessed September 29, 2008).
25. *Financial Times*, "The UK Skills Gap," September 11, 2007, 10.
26. Chris Giles, "A Tale of Two Valleys, the Tee and Thames," *Financial Times*, September 19, 2006, 13; Frances Williams, "UK Overtakes China as FDI Destination," *Financial Times*, September 30, 2005, 8; Bob Sherwood, "Heart and Soul of the U.K. Economy," *Financial Times Special Report: Doing Business in the Thames Valley*, April 24, 2008, 1; Bob Sherwood, "New Brew Helps Region Achieve Prosperity," *Financial Times Special Report: Doing Business in the Thames Valley*, April 24, 2008, 2; Phillip Stafford, "Home for Technology Giants and Minnows," *Financial Times Special Report: Doing Business in the Thames Valley*, April 24, 2008, 4.
27. Andrew Bolger, "Narrow Victory Leaves All to Play For," *Financial Times Special Report: Doing Business in Scotland*, September 20, 2007, 1, 4; Andrew Bolger, "Workforce: Better Educated but Lower Paid," *Financial Times*, October 12, 2005, 27.
28. *Wall Street Journal, Special Section: Investing in Wales*, "Government Backs a Fast Growing Bio-Science Sector," March 29, 2007, sec. A, 11.
29. *The Economist*, "Britannia Redux: A Special Report on Britain," February 3, 2007, 7.
30. *New York Times*, "Britain: Unemployment Is Down," December 13, 2007, sec. C, 8; The Institution of Engineering and Technology, "Wage Inflation on the Rise," June 27, 2007, http://www.ieeconferences.org/OnComms/Circuit/benefits/Editorials/News&Views/ (Accessed June 27, 2007).
31. Gill Plimmer, "The Jobs Puzzle Is Hard to Solve," *Financial Times Professional Development*, November 14, 2005, 1–2; Miranda Green, "Drive Focuses on Both Young and Old," *Financial Times Professional Development*, November 14, 2005, 4; Bob Sherwood, "UK's Stubborn Wealth Divide Highlights a Tale of Two Cities," *Financial Times*, December 23, 2006, 24; Alicia Clegg, "In Hot Pursuit of the Best Brains," *Financial Times*, March 14, 2007, 8.
32. *The Economist*, "Do Better Next Term," February 19, 2005, 53–54; *The Education Gadfly*, "Doing Choice Right Across the Pond," June 16, 2005,

1, http://www.edexcellence.net/institute/gadfly/issue.cfm?id=1978&edition =#2354 (Accessed January 10, 2008); *The Economist,* "Who Wants a New Classroom?" October 7, 2006, 64–65; Jon Boone, "Britain Slips Down Global League Table of Graduates," *Financial Times,* September 19, 2007, 6.

33. Andrew Bolger, "A Degree of Concern Over Funding and Connections," *Financial Times Special Report: Doing Business in Scotland,* September 20, 2007, 6; Edward E. Gordon, *Skill Wars: Winning the Battle for Productivity and Profit* (Boston: Butterworth-Heinemann, 2000), 193–194; *The Economist,* "Scottish Development International," November 17, 2007, 91.

34. *The Economist,* "Britannia Redux," 16; Edward E. Gordon, *The 2010 Meltdown,* 97–98.

35. Marc Coleman, "The Celtic Tiger Can Come Roaring Back," *Financial Times,* January 29, 2008, 11; Quentin Fottrell, "A Jam in Ireland's Open Door," *Wall Street Journal,* October 25, 2005, sec. A, 8.

36. R. F. Foster, *Luck and the Irish* (New York: Oxford University Press, 2008), 7–13.

37. R. F. Foster, *Luck and the Irish,* 14; John Murray Brown, "How Ireland Freed Its Economy," *Financial Times,* May 27, 2005, 11.

38. Eamon Quinn, "Ireland Learns to Adapt to a Population Growth Spurt," *New York Times International,* August 19, 2007, 3; R. F. Foster, *Luck and the Irish,* 34, 36, 188–189; *EIR Jobs.com,* "Irish Job News," February 3, 2008, http://www.eirjobs.com/news/Ireland-unemployment-rate-at-a-75-year-high/ (Accessed May 10, 2008).

39. David Ibison, "All Is Not as It Appears in Frozen Land," *Financial Times Special Report: Finland,* September 4, 2007, 1; Robert Anderson, "Baby Boom Retirement Aftershock Looms," *Financial Times Special Report: Finland,* September 4, 2007, 6; Leif Fagermas, "Labor Shortage Is Primary Challenge," *Financial Times Special Report: Finland,* September 4, 2007, 6; Robert Anderson, "Focus on a Knowledge Economy," *Financial Times Special Report: Finland,* September 4, 2007, 11; Paivi Munter, "Finnish Success—Small Nation Focuses on Wider Picture," *Financial Times,* September 29, 2005, 6; Sean Cavanagh, "Finnish Students Are at the Top of the World Class," *Education Week,* March 16, 2005, 8; *Education at a Glance 2007,* 36–40; *The Economist,* "Where Bosses Will Be Your Friends," April 5, 2008, 56.

40. Paivi Munter, "Norway's Economic Dream Being Fueled by Oil and Gas," *Financial Times,* April 5, 2006, 24; Morris Beschloss, "Norway Emerges as a Financial Power," *Desert Sun,* March 9, 2008, sec. D, 5; Robert Anderson, "Jobs Without Borders," *Financial Times,* October 25, 2007, 9.

41. Marcus Walker, "For the Danish, a Job Loss Can Be Learning Experience," *Wall Street Journal,* March 21, 2006, sec. A, 1, 11; *The Economist,* "Flexicurity," September 9, 2006, 29; Robert Anderson, "Jobs Without Borders," 9; Joel Sherwood, "Danish Jan Unemployment Rate 2.1," *Data Snap,* February 28, 2008, http://www.fxstreet.com/news/forex-news/article

.aspx?StoryId=92242984 (Accessed March 8, 2008); *Education at a Glance 2007*, "Where Bosses Will Be Your Friends," 56; *The Economist*, "Economic and Financial Indicators—Denmark," February 23, 2008, 119.

42. Robert Anderson, "Jobs Without Borders," 9.

43. Jeffrey Fleishman, "Looking for Work," *Los Angeles Times*, January 21, 2007, sec. C, 1, 10.

44. Stefan Wagstyl, "Where Have All My Workers Gone?" *Financial Times Special Report: Poland*, December 30, 2006, 3; Jeffrey Fleishman, "Looking West for Work," sec. C, 1, 10.

45. CIA, "Economy—Romania," *The World Factbook*, http://www.cia.gov/library/publications/the-world-factbook/geos/ro.html (Accessed March 9, 2008); Ana-Maria Smadeanu, "Talking the Same Language," *The Diplomat Bucharest*, June, 2006, http://www.thediplomat.no/features_0606_3 .html (Accessed March 10, 2008); Larive Romania, "Foreign Direct Investment in Romania," *Romanian Business Digest*, 2007, 45–49; Guy Dinmore, "Romanians in Italy—Europe Caught Out by Migration, Says Prodi," *Financial Times*, November 7, 2007, 3; Tracy Wilkinson, "Have a Baby, Get a Bonus," *Los Angeles Times*, February 9, 2005, sec. A, 1, 5.

46. *Thomson Financial News*, "Hungary Nov–Jan Unemployment Up to 8.1 pct vs 7.7 pct," February 28, 2008, http://www.fxstreet.com/news/forex-news/article.aspx (Accessed March 9, 2008); Stefan Wagstyl, "A Protracted Course of Bitter Medicine," *Financial Times Special Report: Hungary*, October 25, 2007, 2.

47. Thomas Escritt, "Supply of Graduates Makes for High-Value Back Offices," *Financial Times Special Report: Hungary*, October 25, 2007, 5.

48. Thomas Escritt, "Supply of Graduates Makes for High-Value Back Offices."

49. *Thomson Financial News*, "Hungary Nov–Jan Unemployment Up to 8.1 pct vs 7.7 pct"; CIA, "Economy—Hungary," *The World Factbook Hungary*, http://www.cia.gov/library/publications/the-world-factbook/geos/hu/html (Accessed March 9, 2008); Stefan Wagstyl, "A Protracted Course of Bitter Medicine," 2; Thomas Escritt, "Second City Hungry for Skills," *Financial Times Special Report: Hungary*, October 25, 2007, 3; Thomas Escritt, "Supply of Graduates Makes for High-Value Back Offices," *Financial Times Special Report: Hungary*, October 25, 2007, 5.

50. Stefan Wagstyl and Jan Cienski, "One Nation: Three Realities," *Financial Times Special Report: Poland*, December 30, 2006, 1, 6; Stefan Wagstyl, "Where Have All My Workers Gone?" 3; *International Herald Tribune*, "Poland's Unemployment Rate Nudges Up to 11.7 Percent in January," February 25, 2008, http://www.iht.com/bin/php?id=10353936 (Accessed March 9, 2008); CIA, "Economy Poland—Economy Overview," *The World Factbook*, http://www.cia.gov/library/publications/the-world-factbook/geos/pl.html (Accessed March 9, 2008); Jan Cienski, "Red Tape Forces Companies Across the Border," *Financial Times*, March 20, 2008, 4; Guy Dinmore, "Romanians in Italy—Europe Caught Out by Migration, Says

Prodi"; Stefan Wagstyl, "Skills Exodus Worries Polish Employers," *Financial Times*, February 8, 2006, 2; Jeffrey Fleishman, "Looking West for Work," sec. C, 1, 10.

51. Justyna Pawlak, "Nokia Finds Romania's Hidden Labour Force," *Globe and Mail*, January 25, 2008, http://www.theglobeandmail.com/servlet/story/RIGAM.20080125.wgtromania0125/BNStory/Business/ (Accessed March 1, 2008).

52. *The Economist*, "Russian Health and Demography—A Sickness of the Soul," September 9, 2006, 51–52.

53. Kimberly Blandhard-Cattarossi and Irina Pshenichnikova, "Focus on Russia," *Training*, June 2008, 20; *The Economist*, "Russian Health and Demography—A Sickness of the Soul," 51–52; Joel Garreau, "300 Million and Counting," 101; *New York Times*, "Russia: UN Warning on Population," April 29, 2008, sec. A, 6.

54. Stefan Wagstyl and Neil Buckley, "Russian Revival Plagued by a Shortage of Skills," *Financial Times*, April 18, 2008, 7.

55. *The Economist*, "Yeltsin's Moment," April 28, 2007, 18; *The Economist*, "Smoke and Mirrors," March 1, 2008, 27; *Wall Street Journal*, "How Putin's Policies Hurt Economic Growth," January 2, 2008, sec. B, 8; Stephan Sestanovich, "Russia by the Numbers," *Wall Street Journal*, December 17, 2007, sec. A, 21; Stefan Wagstyl, "Display of Strength is Part Illusion," *Financial Times Special Report: Investing in Russia*, October 11, 2005, 13.

56. Jodi Koehn, "Russian Education and National Security," Woodrow Wilson International Center for Scholars, http://www.wilsoncenter.org/index.cfm?fuseaction=events.event_summary&event_id=3846 (Accessed March 13, 2008).

57. *The Economist*, "Face Value: The Reluctant Briber," November 4, 2006; "Smoke and Mirrors," 29; Alex Rodriguez, "A Silicon Valley in Siberia?" *Chicago Tribune*, July 25, 2007, sec. 1, 12; Neil Buckley, "Industry's Vanguard," *Financial Times*, November 15, 2007, 15.

58. Alex Rodriguez, "Russia's Stability Called Frail," *Chicago Tribune*, October 15, 2007, sec. 1, 10.

CHAPTER 4

1. Beverly Goldberg, "Improving Performance With an Older Work Force," in *Business: The Ultimate Resource* (New York: Basic Books, 2006), 23–24.

2. Loretta Chao, "For Gen Xers, It's Work to Live," *Wall Street Journal*, November 29, 2005, sec. B, 6.

3. Adecco S.A. and Harris Interactive, "Adecco Workplace Insight Survey," August 30, 2007, http://www.adeccousa.com (Accessed September 20, 2007).

4. Bernadette Kenny (Chief Career Office, Adecco S.A) in discussion with author, August 24, 2007.

5. Loretta Chao, "For Gen Xer's, It's Work to Live," sec. B, 6; *Chicago Tribune*, "Generation Y Bother?," March 5, 2006, sec. 6, 1; Robert D. Atkinson, "Building a More-Humane Economy," *The Futurist*, May–June, 2006, 48.

6. Angela Rozas, "Devil Wears Prada: Why Some Never Will," *Chicago Tribune*, July 16, 2006, sec. 2, 1; *The Economist*, "The Boomers' Babies," August 11, 2007, 68; Constance Alexander, "Understanding Generational Differences Helps You Manage A Multi-Age Workforce," *The Digital Edge*, July 2001, http://digitaledge.org/monthly/2001_07/gengap1.html (Accessed March 5, 2007); Haya El Nasser and Paul Overberg, "Millions More Are Changing States," *USA Today*, November 30–December 2, 2007, sec. A, 1.

7. Cathleen Benko and Anne Weisberg, *Mass Career Customization: Aligning the Workplace With Today's Nontraditional Workforce* (Boston: Harvard Business School Press, 2007), 76, 90–102, 102–107, 188; Barbara Prose, "Workers Selecting Own Career Track," *Chicago Tribune*, September 9, 2007, sec. 5, 2; P.J. Forman and Lynn Carlin, "The Age of Change: Multiple Generations in the Workforce," *We Connect*, October 15, 2005, http: globallead.com/WeConnect/Oct05/ageofchange.html (Accessed May 4, 2008).

8. Barbara Prose, "Workers Inventing New Types of Career Models," *Chicago Tribune*, May 28, 2007, sec. 3, 2; Barbara Prose, "Group Helps Mom With Job Re-Entry," *Chicago Tribune*, June 4, 2007, sec. 3, 2; Sylvia Ann Hewlett, "Focus on the Female Talent in the Backyard," *Financial Times*, May 12, 2008, 17.

9. Sue Shellenbarger, "The Mommy Drain: Employers Beef Up Perks to Lure New Mothers Back to Work," *Wall Street Journal*, September 28, 2006, sec. D, 1; "More New Mothers Are Staying Home Even When It Causes Financial Pain," *Wall Street Journal*, November 30, 2006, sec. D, 1; *Wall Street Journal*, "Time On Your Side: Rating Your Boss's Flexible Scheduling," January 25, 2007, sec. D, 1; *Wall Street Journal*, "Reason to Hold Out Hope for Balancing Work and Home," January 11, 2007, sec. D, 1; *Wall Street Journal*, "What's Ahead for Volunteering, Flextime and Working Moms," December 20, 2007, sec. D, 1; Each year the Alfred P. Sloan Foundation issues company awards for business excellence in workplace flexibility. For information on current company winners, visit http:www.whenworkworks.org.

10. *The Futurist*, "Promoting Parenthood in Japan," May–June 2007, 9; David Turner, "Japan Pay Deals Offer Workers Baby Bonus," *Financial Times*, March 22, 2007, 6.

11. David Wessel, "Older Staffers Get Uneasy Embrace," *Wall Street Journal*, May 15, 2008, sec. A, 2; Erin White, "The New Recruits: Older Workers," *Wall Street Journal*, January 14, 2008, sec. B, 3; "Retiring Baby Boomer Talent Shortage Already Felt by Some Employers," BenefitsLink, June 12, 2007, http: benefitslink.com; Molly Selvin, "Boomer Retirements Could Cripple Middle Management," *Chicago Tribune*, November 4, 2007, sec. 5, 5; Lynn Gresham, "The New SMB Workforce: Retaining and Recruiting

Veteran Workers," February 1, 2008, *SMB/Human Resources*, http://smbhr .benefitnews.com.

12. "The Business Case for Workers Age 50+," December 2005, http://www .aarp.org/research/work/employment/workers_fifty_plus.html (Accessed May 15, 2008); Barbara Prose, "AARP Retain Older Workers," *Chicago Tribune*, December 11, 2005, sec. 5, 1, 4.

13. Patricia Bathurst, "Boomer, Younger Workers Find Common Ground," *Arizona Republic*, May 5, 2008, http://azcentral.com/business/news/articles/ 2008/05/05/20080505career-generationboomer0506.html.

14. David Wessel, "Older Staffers Get Uneasy Embrace," sec. A, 2; Beverly Goldberg, "Improving Company Performance With an Older Work Force," in *Business: The Ultimate Resource* (New York: Basic Books, 2006), 23–24; Patricia Bathurst, "Boomers, Younger Workers Find Common Ground," *Arizona Republic*, May 5, 2008, 12; *Wall Street Journal*, "Older Minds Face Trade-Off: Duller Here, Sharper There," November 5, 2007, sec. B, 10; Alison Maitland, "Stereotype Under Scrutiny," *Financial Times*, July 5, 2005, 7.

15. Ken Dychtwald, "Ageless Aging: The Next Era of Retirement," *The Futurist*, July–August, 2005, 19; Gail Marks Jarvis, "Working Beyond 65 Becomes Growing Trend," *Chicago Tribune*, June 15, 2007, sec. 3, 5; Michael Skapinker, "The Age of Entitlement," *Financial Times Life and Arts*, April 19–20, 2008, 6; Andrew Taylor, "Aging Populations Threaten to Overwhelm Public Finances," *Financial Times*, October 11, 2005, 6; *AARP Bulletin*, "The Poll–Older Workers," September 2007, 6; William D. Novelli, "Valuing Older Workers, Major Reasons for Working in Retirement," *AARP Bulletin*, January 2006, 31.

16. Tamara Erickson, *Retire Retirement: Career Strategies for the Boomer Generation* (Boston: Harvard Business Press, 2008), 1–3, 41–47.

17. Elizabeth Pope, "They Won't Let Me Retire," *AARP Bulletin*, March 2008, 12–13; Barbara Prose, "Seniors Still Sidelined as Skill Drought Approaches," *Chicago Tribune*, August 31, 2005, sec. 3, 8; Jennifer Youssef, "Older Workers Take to the Road," *Chicago Tribune*, October 2, 2006, sec. 3, 1.

18. Phred Dvorek, "Set to be Put Out to Pasture? Think Again," *Wall Street Journal*, February 21, 2006, sec. B, 8.

19. Joyce M. Rosenberg, "Keeping Boomers on the Job With a Few Concessions," *Chicago Tribune*, July 3, 2006, sec. 3, P3; *Herman Trend Alert*, "For Some Older Workers, It Is Prime Time," June 7, 2006, http://www.hermangroup. com/alert/archive_6-7-2006.html (Accessed July 8, 2006); *AARP Magazine*, "AARP Best Employers for Workers Over 50," November–December, 2005–2007. Experience Works is a forty-year-old national nonprofit organization that offers training and employment opportunities for older workers. For more information, see http://www.experienceworks.org or call 866-397-9757.

20. Sebastian Moffett, "Fast-Aging Japan Keeps Its Elders on the Job Longer," *Wall Street Journal*, June 15, 2005, sec. A, 1, 8.

21. Sarah E. Needleman, "Employers Tap Executives for Temporary Jobs," *Wall Street Journal*, May 13, 2008, sec. D, 6; *Herman Trend Alert*, "U.S. Employee Confidence Index Declines," April 2, 2008, http//www.hermangroup.com/alert/archive_4-2-2008.html (Accessed April 10, 2008); Amy Zipkin, "A Trend toward Putting Consultants on Payrolls," *New York Times*, March 22, 2008, sec. B, 2.

22. Kristi Essick, "Help Wanted," *Wall Street Journal*, June 26, 2006, sec. R, 9.

23. Edward E. Gordon, "Retiring Retirement: Mastering the Workforce Generation Gap," *Benefits and Compensation Digest*, July 2007, 18; Diana Farrell, Eric Beinhocker, Ezra Shukla, Jonathan Ablett, and Geoffrey Greene, "Talkin' 'Bout My Generation: The Economic Impact of Aging U.S. Baby Boomers," McKinsey Global Institute, 2008, 17–21, http://mckinsey.com/mgi/reports/pdfs/Impact_Aging_Baby_Boomers/MGI_Impact_Aging Baby_Boomers_full_report.pdf (Accessed June 23, 2008); Steve Lohr, "For a Good Retirement, Find Work. Good Luck," *New York Times Week in Review*, June 22, 2008, 3.

24. Amy Merrick, "Erasing 'Un' From 'Unemployable'," *Wall Street Journal*, August 2, 2007, sec. B, 1; *Herman Trend Alert*, "Hiring People with Disabilities Makes Business Sense," January 23, 2008, http://www.herman-group.com/alert/archive_1-23-2008.html (Accessed January 28, 2008); Edward E. Gordon, *The 2010 Meltdown*, 216.

25. Kevin Hollenbeck and Jean Kimmel, "The Returns to Education and Basic Skills Training for Individuals with Poor Health or Disability," Upjohn Institute Staff Working Paper 01–72, August 2001, http://ssrn.com/abstract =292230.

26. U.S. Department of Labor. Office of Public Affairs, News Release, "Employers Gain Access to Database of 2,000 Job Candidates With Disabilities," March 29, 2007, 1.

27. Edward E. Gordon, *The 2010 Meltdown*, 216–217.

28. David E. Hale (Program Manager, American Association of People with Disabilities) in discussion with the author, March 12, 2008; Andrew J. Inparato, "Time to Get Equal!" *AAPD News*, Summer 2007, 2.

29. *Herman Trend Alert*, "Hiring People With Disabilities Makes Business Sense."

30. Adam Liptak, "More Than 1 in 100 Adults Are Now in Prison in U.S.," *New York Times*, February 28, 2008, sec. A, 14; Adam Liptak, "Inmate Count in U.S. Dwarfs Other Nations," *New York Times*, April 23, 2008, sec. A, 1.

31. Dan Bloom, *Employment-Focused Program for Ex-Prisoners* (New York: MDRC, 2006), iii; *The Economist*, "Packing Them In," August 12, 2006, 23; Robert K. Elder, "Beyond License Plates," *Chicago Tribune*, May 22, 2007, sec. 5, 1.

32. Paul VanDeCarr, "Call to Action—How Programs in Three Cities Responded to the Prisoner Reentry Crisis," *Public/Private Ventures*, March, 2007, 1–2, http://www.ppv.org/ppv/publications/assets/211_publication.pdf (Accessed May 12, 2008).

33. Ron Rubbin, "Fidelity Bond Program for At-Risk Job Seekers," *NAWDP Advantage*, August 2006; U.S. Department of Labor, Federal Bonding Program, *A Best Practice Guide to Fidelity Bonds: The Power Tool in the Employment Toolbox*. For more information, see http://www.bonds4jobs .com or call 800-233-2258.

34. Elizabeth Greenberg, Eric Dunleavy, Mark Kutner, and Sheila White, *Literacy Behind Bars—Results From the 2003 National Assessment of Adult Literacy Prison Survey* (Washington, DC: U.S. Department of Education, 2007), vi; Prisoner Reentry Institute, *Venturing Beyond the Gates: Facilitating Successful Reentry With Entrepreneurship* (New York: City University of New York, 2007), 11.

35. Robert I. Lerman, "Are Skills the Problem?" in Timothy J. Bartik and Susan N. Houseman, eds., *A Future of Good Jobs? America's Challenge in the Global Economy* (Kalamazoo: W.E. Upjohn Institute for Employment Research, 2008), 49.

36. Dan Bloom, *Employment-Focused Programs for Ex-Prisoners*, 10.

37. David Heinzmann, "Parolees' Jobs Hard to Snag," *Chicago Tribune*, December 14, 2005, sec. 2, 2; Rex W. Huppke, "A Rough Road: Jail Cell to Job," *Chicago Tribune*, January 29, 2006, sec. 4, 1–2; Prisoner Reentry Institute, *Venturing Beyond the Gates*, 15.

38. Susan Dawe, ed., *Vocational Education and Training for Adult Prisoners and Offenders in Australia: Research Readings*, National Centre for Vocational Education Research, 2007, 12, 16, http://www.ncver.edu.au/research/proj/ nd4200b.pdf (Accessed May 20, 2008); Amy L. Solomon, Jenny W.L. Osborne, Stefan F. Lo Burglio, Jeff Mellow, and Debbie A. Mukamal, *Life After Lockup: Improving Reentry From Jail to the Community*, 2008, 38, 50, http:// www.urban.org/UploadedPDF/411660_life_after_lockup.pdf (Accessed May 20, 2008). This report features successful programs from many parts of the United States; John Leland, "As Job Surplus Grows in Iowa, Workers Are Calling the Shots," *New York Times*, May 31, 2008, sec. A, 1, 10.

CHAPTER 5

1. *Philadelphia Business Journal*, "Philadelphia Academies, Inc.," July 28, 2006, http://www.philadelphia.bizjournals.com/Philadelphia/stories/2006/ 07/31/story4.html (Accessed January 14, 2008); Philadelphia Academies, Inc., Annual Report, 2007; John Gehring, "School-to-Work Seen as Route to More Than Just a Job," *Education Week*, April 11, 2001, 21; Edward E. Gordon, *The 2010 Meltdown*, 124–125.

2. Todd G. Buchholz, "What Color Is Your Collar?" *Wall Street Journal*, September 30, 2005, sec. W, 11.

3. "Career Academy National Standards of Practice," *National Career Academy Coalition*, 2005, 2–4; Lynn Olson, "Vocational Programs Earn Mixed Revenues, Face Academic Push," *Education Week*, May 24, 2006, 21.

4. Lynn Olson, "Economic Trends Fuel Push to Retool Schooling," *Education Week*, March 22, 2006, 1.

5. Lemelson-MIT Program, "Survey Shows U.S. Teens Confident in Their Inventiveness; More Hands-On, Project-Based Learning May Be Needed," January 16, 2008, http://web.mit.edu/inventn-pressreleases/n-press-08 index.html (Accessed March 27, 2008).

6. Carol G. Schneider, "Liberal Education: Slip-Sliding Away?" in Richard H. Hersh and John Merrow, eds., *Declining by Degrees: Higher Education at Risk* (New York: Palgrave Macmillan, 2006), 64–65; Mitchell Landsberg, "Vocational Ed Is Favored, Poll Says," *Los Angeles Times*, April 6, 2006, sec. B, 3; Lemelson-MIT Program, "Survey Shows U.S. Teens Confident in Their Inventiveness: More Hands-On, Project-Based Learning May Be Needed."

7. Rhea R. Borja, "Brave New Science," *Education Week*, September 17, 2003, 27–30; Thomas Markham III (Director of Community Relations and Development, Minuteman High School) in discussion with the author, July 15, 2004; *The Education Innovator*, "Center for Advanced Research and Technology Puts Students on a Fast Academic and Professional Track," September 28, 2005, http://www.ed.gov/newsletters/innovator/ 2005/0927.html (Accessed January 14, 2008).

8. V. Dion Hayes, "In California, Experimental School Bids to Turn Out High-Tech Workers," *Chicago Tribune*, December 26, 2000, sec. 1, 20; Susan Fisher (Chief Operating Officer CART) in discussion with the author, June 23, 2008.

9. Dennis Littky, Nancy Diaz, Chris Hempel, Charlie Plant, Phil Price, and Sam Grabell, "Moment to Moment at the Met," *Educational Leadership* 61 (May 2004): 39–43; Phil Price (Met Building Principal) in discussion with the author, June 20, 2008. The Big Picture Network that began the Met also opened seventy other high schools across the United States.

10. Joel Rubin, "Auto Tech Academy Helps Put Teens Back on Track," *Los Angeles Times*, May 24, 2004, sec. B, 2; Jonathan Fahey, "Bumper-to-Bumper Education," *Forbes*, September 6, 2004, 77, 80; Robert McCarroll (Academy Director, San Clemente High School) in discussion with the author, July 15, 2004.

11. *The Education Innovator*, "The California Academy of Mathematics and Science (CAMS)," March 29, 2007, http://www.ed.gov/newsletters/innovator/2007/0329.html (Accessed January 14, 2008).

12. *The Education Innovator*, "Two Years of High School and Six of College: The Early College Model," June 20, 2005, http://www.ed.gov/newsletters/ innovator/2005/0620.html (Accessed January 14, 2008); Dahleen Glanton, "Getting a Head Start on College," *Chicago Tribune*, May 9, 2007, sec. 1, 3; Richard G. Neal, "North Carolina Program Allows Students to Combine High School and College Coursework," *School Reform News*, January, 2008, 18; Nancy Hoffman, "Challenge, not Remediation: The Early College High School Initiative," in Richard Kazis, Joel Vargas, Nancy Hoffman, eds., *Double the Numbers* (Boston: Harvard Education Press, 2004), 213—220.

13. Joan Wren (President, Hudson Precision Products) in discussion with the author, February 4, 2008; Lori Olaszewski, "11 High Schools Join Reforms," *Chicago Tribune*, May 9, 2007, sec. 2, 1, 9; "Austin Polytechnical Academy," http://www.austinpolytech.com.

14. Ana Beatriz Cholo, "Hard Work Paying Off for Students and School," *Chicago Tribune*, May 21, 2003, sec. 1, 1, 7; Ann Therese Palmer, "Cristo Rey Crafts a School Model That Works," *Chicago Tribune*, December 26, 2003, sec. 3, 1, 3; Kristy Black More (Director of Communications, Cristo Rey Network Office) in discussion with the author, June 20, 2008; *Viva!*, "10 Years of Dreams at Work," Spring, 2007, 1, http://www.cristoreynetwork.org.

15. Jon Boone, "Private Money Adds to Mix in State System," *Financial Times*, October 18, 2006, 3; *The Economist*, "Trying Harder," September 17, 2005, 58; *Education Week*, "England's Teacher Unions Fight Blair's 'Academies'," April 20, 2005, 8.

16. *The Economist*, "Education in Germany, The Next Generation," August 20, 1996, 44.

17. Hedrick Smith, *Rethinking America* (New York: Random House, 1995), 137, 140.

18. Bertrand Benoit, "A Germany Seeking Skills Warms up Its Welcome," *Financial Times*, July 15, 2008, 9; Richard Milne, "Sector That Catches Them Young," *Financial Times*, June 17, 2008, 14; *Financial Times*, "German Groups Seek Next Crop of Engineers in the Kindergarten," June 17, 2008, 1.

19. Jeff Barbian, "Get 'Em While They're Young," *Training*, January 2004, 44; David Wessel, "Workers Get Dessert: Bigger Slice of Pie," *Wall Street Journal*, April 19, 1999, sec. A, 1.

20. Mary Ann Roe, "Cultivating the Gold-Collar Worker," *Harvard Business Review*, May 2001, 33.

21. Learning Circuits, "Survey Shows U.S. Teens"; Amy Christen, "The Way We Learn Now," May 2008, http://www.learningcircuits.org/0608_christen.

22. Rosanne T. White (National Executive Director, Technology Student Association) in discussion with the author, April 2, 2008.

23. Sean Cavanagh, "Scientists Nurture Teacher's Growth in Math and Science," *Education Week*, November 28, 2007, 10.

24. Don Resnick (Director, Z Series Academic Workforce Development Program, IBM) and Kevin Faughnan (Director, IBM Academic Initiative) in discussion with the author, April 23, 2008.

25. Erik W. Robelen, "AT&T Commits $100 Million to Dropout Prevention," *Education Week*, April 23, 2008, 8.

26. Michelle Miller-Adams (Visiting Scholar, W.E. Upjohn Institute) in discussion with the author, March 5, 2008; *The Economist*, "A Promising Future," February 9, 2008, 32.

27. Nancy Tichy (Senior Director of Human Resources, the Cleveland Clinic) in discussion with the author, March 17, 2008; *The Economist*, "Mayo With Everything," February 23, 2008, 44; *The Economist*, "Back From the

Dead," October 27, 2007, 43; "Rochester, Minnesota Community," Rochester Area Economic Development, Inc., http://www./raedi.org/economic_overview.html#rochester (Accessed May 4, 2008); Shirley S. Wang, "Cleveland Clinic's Medical School to Offer Tuition-Free Education," *Wall Street Journal*, May 15, 2008, sec. D, 3.

28. Jack Schultz, *Boom Town USA: The 7 1/2 Keys to Big Success in Small Towns* (Herndon, VA: National Association of Industrial and Office Properties, 2004), 166.

29. Peter D. Hart Research Associates, Inc., and Civic Enterprises, *The Silent Epidemic: Perspectives of High School Dropouts*, March 2006, 1–5, http://www.civicenterprises.net/pdfs/thesilientepidemic3-06.pdf (Accessed February 12, 2008); Catherine Gervertz, "H.S. Dropouts Say Lack of Motivation Top Reason to Quit," *Education Week*, March 8, 2006, 1, 14; Piedad F. Robertson, "Dual Enrollment," *Education Week*, July 13, 2005, 38–48.

30. Bob Wise, *Raising the Grade—How High School Reform Can Save Our Youth and Our Nation* (San Francisco: Jossey-Bass, 2008), 5.

31. Mat Herron, "States Allow High Schoolers to Choose Majors, Coursework," *School Reform News*, September, 2006, 12.

32. ACT, "Crisis at the Core," 2005, iii, http://www.act.org.crisisathecore_report.pdf (Accessed May 14, 2008); James E. Rosenbaum, "Prepared for What?" *Education Week Report: Ready for What?* June 12, 2007, 36; Harry J. Holzer and Robert I. Lerman, "America's Forgotten Middle-Skill Jobs: Education and Training Requirements in the Next Decade and Beyond," *Workforce Alliance*, November, 2007, 3–7, http://www.skills2compete.org/atf/cf/%7B8E9806BF-4669-4217-AF74-26F62108EA68%7D/Forgottenjobs Reports%20Final.pdf (Accessed May 12, 2008); James Howlett and Brad Huff, "Industrial Arts/Technology: What Are We Doing?" *Phi Delta Kappan* 88, June 2007, 764–767; James Howlett, "Industrial Arts: Call It What You Want, the Need Still Exists," *Phi Delta Kappan* 89, March 2008, 522–524.

33. Larry Gordon, "What's Your Major? Try Multiple Choice," *Chicago Tribune*, June 8, 2008, sec. 1, 9.

34. *Economist.Com*, "Survey: The Near Future—The Next Society," November 1, 2001, http://www.economist.com/.

35. *Training Magazine Annual Industry Reports*, March 1990, 2000, 2008.

36. Amin Rajan, "Self-Discovery the Socrates Way," *Financial Times Special Report on Professional Development*, November 13, 2006, 6.

37. Andrew Baxter, "Training Takes Center Stage," *Financial Times Special Report on Professional Development*, November 12, 2007, 1–2.

38. *Training*, "Training Top 100," March 2006, 4, 8, 40–41, 45, 49, 60, 61, 72; *Training*, "Training Top 125," February 2008, 8, 40–59, 76–111; *Chicago Tribune*, "Paying for Worker's Tuition: An Investment," August 6, 2007, sec. 3, 3; Robert I. Lerman, "Are Skills the Problem?" in Timothy J. Bartik and Susan N. Houseman, eds., *A Future of Good Jobs? America's Challenge in the Global Economy* (Kalamazoo, MI: W.E. Upjohn Institute for Employment Research, 2008), 56–58.

39. Peter M. Senge, *The Fifth Discipline* (New York: Doubleday Currency, 1990), 14.

40. Jon Boone, "Corporate Universities—Boardroom to Mortarboard," *Financial Times Special Report on Professional Development*, November 13, 2006, 4; Sarah Murray, "E-Learning at Cisco's College," *Financial Times Special Report on Professional Development*, November 13, 2006, 4; Rebecca Knight, "GE's Corporate Boot Camp—Talent Spotting Venue," *Financial Times Special Report Business Edition*, March 20, 2006, 2.

41. Alan Cane, "Skills and Learning How Best to Train the Dispersed Workforce?" *Financial Times*, January 24, 2007, 5; Mary K. Tallent-Runnels, Julie A. Thomas, William Y. Lan, Sandi Cooper, Terence C. Ahern, Shana M. Shaw, and Xiaoming Liu, "Teaching Courses Online: A Review of the Research," *Review of Educational Research* 76, Spring 2006, 93–155; Michael W. Allen, "Designing Outside the Box," *T & D*, February 2008, 30–33; *Training*, "2008 Industry Report," November–December 2008, 24.

42. Edward E. Gordon, "Balance Short-Term Profit With Long-Term Investment in Human Capital," *Benefits and Compensation Digest*, July 2006, 24–29; Stephen Covey, "Talks About the 8th Habit: Effective Is No Longer Enough," *Training*, February 2005, 18; Fiona Czerniawska, "Tomorrow's People, Managing Talent in a Diverse World," Hay Group and the Management Consultancy Association, 2007, http://www.haygroup.com/uk/Research/detail.asp?PageID=10084 (Accessed June 8, 2008).

43. Edward E. Gordon, *Skill Wars*, 85–92. Internal Revenue Service Ruling 96–62 states, "Training costs must be capitalized only in the unusual circumstances where training is intended primarily to obtain future benefits significantly beyond those associated with training provided in the ordinary course of a taxpayer's trade or business."

44. Edward E. Gordon, *Skill Wars*, 75–83. The Human Capital ROI Nine-Step Worksheet and software is available free of charge at http://www.imperialcorp.com.

45. Martyn Sloman, "Knowledge Rests on Wanting to Learn," *Financial Times Special Report on Professional Development*, November 12, 2007, 4; Candace Zacher, "Is Training a 'Bad' Word?" *Training Today*, Spring 2006, 14; Simon London, "Guided by Experience," *Financial Times*, January 10, 2005, 7; Stefan Stern, "Why Businesses Get Stuck in Their Ways," *Financial Times*, July 12, 2007, 10.

46. Holly Dolezalek, "Wall Street Is Bad for Your Business," *Training*, February 2006, 10–14; Candace Browning, "Companies Should Drop Quarterly Earnings Guidance," *Financial Times*, March 20, 2006, 3; Francesco Guerrera, "Call to Cut Quarterly Guidance," *Financial Times*, June 27, 2007, 15; Dan Roberts, "Opposition Grows to Earnings Forecasts," *Financial Times*, March 13, 2006, 1; Francesco Guerrera, "Call to End Quarterly Guidance 'Obsession,'" *Financial Times*, July 24, 2006, 1; Francesco Guerrera, "The Wrong Focus? How the Race to Meet Targets Throws Corporate America Off Course," *Financial Times*, July 24, 2006, 9.

47. *Financial Times*, "Quarterly Guidance Misses the Mark," April 18, 2008, 10.
48. Martyn Sloman, "Knowledge Rests on Wanting to Learn"; Stuart Crainer and Des Dearlove, "Whatever Happened to Yesterday's Bright Ideas?" *Across the Board*, May/June 2006, 33–40; *Financial Times*, "Quarterly Guidance Misses the Mark," April 18, 2008, 10; Edward E. Gordon, *The 2010 Meltdown*, 174–179.
49. Peter M. Senge, *The Fifth Discipline*, 6–13, 139–233, 373–377.
50. Gail Johnson, "Good to Great," *Training*, July/August 2003, 38–42.
51. Hedrick Smith, *Rethinking America*, xvii.
52. *The Economist: Special Report by Peter Drucker*, "Trusting the Teacher in the Grey-Flannel Suit," November 19, 2005, 72; Peter Drucker, *Concept of the Corporation* (New York: John Day & Co., 1945).

CHAPTER 6

1. *The Economist*, "The Great Jobs Switch," October 1, 2007, 13–14.
2. David Manning, "Why We Need a World Education Bank," *Financial Times*, March 3, 2008, 9; Hedrick Smith, *Rethinking America*, 417; Michael Skapinker, "Virtue's Reward? Companies Make the Business Case for Ethical Initiatives," *Financial Times*, April 28, 2008, 8.
3. Michael Skapinker, "Only the Strong Survive," *Financial Times Weekend*, June 11–12, 2005, sec. W, 1.
4. *The Economist*, "Just Good Business—A Special Report on Corporate Social Responsibility," January 19, 2008; Michael Skapinker, "Corporate Responsibility Is Not Quite Dead," *Financial Times*, February 12, 2008, 1.
5. Sarah Murray, "A Fair Division of Charity's Spoils," *Financial Times*, February 21, 2008, 13; Ross Tieman, "Building Capacity Is Still the Challenge," *Financial Times Special Report: Corporate Citizenship and Philanthropy*, July 5, 2007, 8.
6. Heath Prince, ed., "Strategies for Financing Workplace Intermediaries: Working Papers," National Fund for Workforce Solutions and Jobs for the Future, 2007, http://www.jff.org/documents/Financing/WI.pdf (Accessed May 12, 2008); National Center on Education and the Economy, *Tough Choices in Tough Times* (San Francisco: Jossey-Bass, 2007), 26–28.
7. Peter Willets, "What Is a Non-Governmental Organization?" *Encyclopedia of Life Support Systems*, 2002, http://www.eolss.net; Olena P. Maslyukivska, "The Role of Non-Governmental Organizations in Development Cooperation," Research Paper, UNDP/Yale Collaboration Program, 1999 Research Clinic, New Haven, 1999; International Center for Non-Profit Law, *The Handbook on Good Practices for Laws Relating to Non-Governmental Organizations* (Washington, DC: World Bank, 1997).
8. Ed Morrison, "New Models of Economic Development," White Paper, May 2006, 1–7, http://www.i-open.org/_Media/I-Open_White_Paper_2.pdf (Accessed March 25, 2008); Ed Morrison, founder of Institute for Open Economic Networks, in discussion with the author, May 14, 2008.

9. Ed Morrison, "New Models of Economic Development," 8–9.

10. Edward E. Gordon, *The 2010 Meltdown*, 191–194.

11. Sarah Murray, "Partnerships on the Rise," *Financial Times Special Report: Business & Development*, June 24, 2004, 5; *Education Week*, "Major Gates Foundation Grants to Support High Schools," June 16, 2004, 28–29.

12. Mark Dixon, "School District Must Focus on Closing Widening Gaps," *News-Leader* (Springfield, MO), August 28, 2007, 4A.

13. Albert O. Hirschman, *Shifting Involvements: Private Interest and Public Action* (Princeton: Princeton University Press, 2002), 126.

14. Dale Ward (Executive Vice President, Santa Ana Chamber of Commerce) in discussion with the author, March 17–18, 2008.

15. Michael Metzler (President, Santa Ana Chamber of Commerce) in discussion with the author, March 17–18, 2008; Michael Metzler, "Dealing With a National Leadership Vacuum," *City Line*, July/August 2007, 2; Lynn Gresham, "The New SMB Workforce: Training the Next Generation," *SMB Human Resources*, February 25, 2008, http://smbhr.benefitnews.com; Scott Duke Harris, "Hardship City," *Los Angeles Times Magazine*, October 5, 2005, 18–21; Fermin Leal, "Students in Vocational Classes Grasp the Concepts," *Orange County Register*, February 2, 2008; Jennifer Delson, "Santa Ana Touting English Classes," *Los Angeles Times*, April 9, 2007, sec. B, 1, 6; Edward E. Gordon, *The 2010 Meltdown*, 109–113. To learn more about High School Inc. and English Works, see http://www.santaanaalliance.com.

16. David Martin (President, Fargo-Moorehead Chamber of Commerce) in discussion with the author, May 10, 2007; Don Morton (Manager, Microsoft Great Plains) in discussion with the author, November 20, 2007, and March 26, 2008; Morris Beschloss, "North Dakota Taps Into Its Sweet Crude," *Desert Sun*, March 23, 2008, sec. D, 4; Monica Davey, "As Oil Flows in North Dakota, Job Boom and Burdens Follow," *New York Times*, January 1, 2008, sec. A, 1, 14; *The Bridge*, "National Publications Reinforce What We Already Know," May 2007, 21; Timothy Aeppel, "Still Built on the Homefront," *Wall Street Journal*, October 24, 2006, sec. B, 1–2; Edward E. Gordon, *The 2010 Meltdown*, 113–116; *The Economist*, "The Great Plains Drain," January 19, 2008, 35.

17. Vicki Haugen (President, CEO, Vermilion Advantage) in discussion with the author, April 4, 2008; Jack Schultz, *Boom Town USA*, 105; *Vermilion Advantage*, "2007–2008 Educational Workforce Programs," http://www.vermilionadvantage.com.

18. Robert Zettler (Workforce Consultant to Richland County on Employee and Family Services) in discussion with the author, April 12, 2007 and March 21, 2008; Robert Zettler, "Training Workers in Advanced Technology: A Community Success Story in Workforce and Economic Development," Richland County Job and Family Services, April, 2007, Unpublished Progress Report. To learn more, contact Robert Zettler at rzettler@ncstatecollege.edu.

19. Marion Venable (Executive Director, Surry Community College Foundation Grant Coordinator) in discussion with the author, March 31, 2008; Yadkin River Heritage Corridor Partnership, *Yadkin River Heritage Coordinator Master Plan* 2008; Chris Allisbury (Associate Director, North Carolina Community College Bio-Network) in discussion with the author, March 17, 2008; Robert J. Witchger (Associate Director for Tech Prep, North Carolina Community College System) in discussion with the author, March 17, 2008; Christopher L. Droessler (School-to-Career Coordinator, Wake County Public School System) in discussion with the author, March 2008; Christopher L. Droessler, *North Carolina Career Outlook Handbooks* available at http://www.nccareeroutlook.com; Edward E. Gordon, *2010 Meltdown*, 122–124.

20. Thames Valley Economic Partnership, http://www.businessinberkshire.co .uk/tvep (Accessed September 28, 2008).

21. The German Workforce Development System, Briefing Paper, http://www .portjobs.org/resources/research/german_workforce_system.doc (Accessed September 28, 2008).

22. Christine Soares, "Building a Future on Science," *Scientific American*, February 2008, 80–85.

23. Kathleen Kennedy Manzo and Sean Cavanagh, "A Nation at Risk 25 Years Later—American Scouts Overseas to Boost Education Skills," *Education Week*, April 23, 2008, 1, 14–15.

24. Edward B. Fiske, "A Nation at a Loss," *New York Times*, April 25, 2008, sec. A, 27; Chester E. Finn, Jr., "Twenty-Five Years Later, a Nation Still at Risk," *Wall Street Journal*, April 25–26, 2008, sec. A, 7.

25. Michael Barber and Mona Mourshed, *How the World's Best-Performing School Systems Come Out on Top*, McKinsey and Company, September, 2007, 1–45; Sam Dillon, "Imported From Britain: Ideas to Improve Schools," *New York Times*, August 15, 2007, sec. A, 21.

26. Michael Barber, *How the World's Best-Performing School Systems Come Out on Top*, 16–23; Nam-Hwa Kang and Miyoung Hong, "Achieving Excellence in Teacher Workforce and Equity in Learning Opportunities in South Korea," *Educational Researcher*, May 2008, 202.

27. Michael Barber, "How the World's Best-Performing School Systems Come Out on Top," 23.

28. Bess Keller, " 'Residencies' Set Up to Train Urban Teachers at School Sites," *Education Week*, November 1, 2006, 14; *New York Times*, "Better Quality Teachers," June 23, 2008, sec. A, 24.

29. Michael Barber, "How the World's Best-Performing School Systems Come Out on Top," 26.

30. Bess Keller, "Coaching Teachers to Help Students Learn," *Education Week*, December 12, 2007, 22.

31. Michael Barber, *How the World's Best-Performing School Systems Come Out on Top*, 30–31; Daniel L. Duke, "Turning Schools Around," *Education Week*, February 21, 2007, 35, 37; Patricia M. Cunningham, "High-Poverty

Schools That Beat the Odds," *The Reading Teacher* 60, No. 4, December 2006/January 2007, 382–385.

32. Michael Barber, *How the World's Best-Performing School Systems Come Out on Top*, 34–37.

33. Jeffrey A. Trachtenberg, "Simplified Classics? Educators Are Divided," *Wall Street Journal*, May 23, 2005, sec. B, 1, 4.

34. Michael Barber, *How the World's Best-Performing School Systems Come Out on Top*, 38. Extensive research and best practices on high-quality tutoring programs can be found in Edward E. Gordon, Ronald R. Morgan, Charles O'Malley, and Judith Ponticell, *The Tutoring Revolution: Applying Research for Best Practices, Policy Implications, and Student Achievement* (New York: Rowman & Littlefield Education, 2007).

35. Bob Sipchen, "Work Skills Winning New Respect," *Los Angeles Times*, March 3, 2007.

36. James J. Heckman and Dimitriy V. Masterov, "The Productivity Argument for Investing in Young Children," NBER Working Paper Series 13016, April 2007, http://nber.org/neew_archive; Barton Kunstler, "An Educational Approach for an Era of Profound Technological Change," in Cynthia G. Wagner, ed., *Foresight, Innovation, and Strategy: Toward a Wiser Future* (World Future Society, 2005); Robert I. Lerman, *Are Skills the Problem?* 68; David Brooks, "The Cognitive Age," *New York Times*, May 2, 2008; Edward E. Gordon, *The 2010 Meltdown*, 231; Bill Barnhart, "U.S. Needs to Fix Education, Bernanke Says," *Chicago Tribune*, February 15, 2007, sec. 3, 5.

37. Jill Casner-Lotto and Linda Barrington, *Are They Really Ready to Work? Employer's Perspectives on the Basic Knowledge and Applied Skills of New Entrants to the 21st Century U.S. Workforce*, The Conference Board, Partnership for 21st Century Skills, Corporate Voices for Working Families, and Society for Human Resource Management, October 2006, 13–14, 57, http://www.21stcenturyskills.org/documents/FINAL_REPORT_PDF09-29-06.pdf (Accessed May 12, 2008).

38. Ben S. Bernanke, "The Level and Distribution of Economic Well-Being," Remarks before the Greater Omaha Chamber of Commerce, Omaha, Nebraska, February 6, 2007, http://www.federalreserve.gov/newsevents/speech/Bernanke20070206a.htm (Accessed January 14, 2008).

39. *California Foundation for Commerce and Education*, "Business Leader Attitudes on California Education System," March 2007, http://calchamber.com/NR/rdomlyres/FDA12C87-DC89-45B5-99C7-AGA82ACC97D5/0/31207surveysummary.doc (Accessed January 14, 2008); Juliet Williams, "Business Leaders: Raise Taxes to Help Pay for Better Schools," *Desert Sun*, March 13, 2007, sec. A, 5; *Wall Street Journal*, "The CEOs Top Priorities," November 24, 2008, sec. R, 4.

40. ACT and The Education Trust, "On Course for Success," http://www.act.org/path/policy/pdf/success_report.pdf (Accessed March 10, 2008); Harold Pratt, "Science Education's 'Overlooked Ingredient'," *Education Week*, October 10, 2007, 26, 32.

41. Howard Gardner, *Frames of Mind: The Theory of Multiple Intelligences* (New York: Basic Books, 1983).

42. Debra Viadero, "Ideas on Creative and Practical IQ Underlie Tests of Giftedness," *Education Week*, May 21, 2008, 1, 16.

43. Miko Inada, "Playing at Professions," *Wall Street Journal*, February 9, 2007, sec. B, 1–2.

44. Anne Marie Chaker, "Reading, Writing . . . and Engineering," *Wall Street Journal*, March 13, 2008, sec. D, 1–2.

45. Ideas Adapted from the Rochester, NY School District and the National Center on Education and the Economy.

46. George Will, "A Nation Still at Risk, Still Failing at Schooling," *Chicago Tribune*, April 28, 2008, sec. 1, 19.

47. *Education Week*, "Parent's Aid at Home Benefits Preschoolers," January 19, 2005, 12; *The Education Innovator*, "Newport News Magnet School Makes All Dreams Achievable for Its Students," April 13, 2006, 1; Edward E. Gordon, *The 2010 Meltdown*, 204. For more information on Practical Parenting Partnerships, see http://www.ppctr.org; Edward E. Gordon et al., *The Tutoring Revolution*, 169–173.

48. Sue Shellenbarger, "Ways to Teach Your Children to Find the Work They Love," *Wall Street Journal*, August 2, 2007, sec. D, 1; Kenneth R. Ginsburg, "The Importance of Play in Promoting Healthy Child Development and Maintaining Strong Parent-Child Bonds," *American Academy of Pediatrics*, 2006, http://www.aap.org/pressroom/playFinal.pdf (Accessed May 2, 2008); Lawrence Baines, "Learning From the World: Achieving More by Doing Less," *Phi Delta Kappan* 89, October 2007, 98–100; Nancy Padak and Timothy Rasinski, "Family Involvement: Is Being Wild About Harry Enough? Encouraging Independent Reading at Home," *The Reading Teacher*, December 2007/January 2008, 350–353; Joe Williams, *Cheating Our Kids: How Politics and Greed Ruin Education* (New York: Palgrave Macmillan, 2005), 239.

49. Richard Kazis, Joel Vargas, and Nancy Hoffman, eds., *Double the Numbers: Increasing Postsecondary Credentials for Underrepresented Youth* (Boston: Harvard Education Press, 2004), 1–35.

50. Sarah Murray, "Gearing Up For a New Battle of the Bulge," *Financial Times Special Report Investing in Young People*, January 26, 2006, 1; "Businesses Learn Lessons As Ties Get Closer Worldwide," *Financial Times Special Report Investing in Young People*, January 26, 2006, 3; Robert Shapiro, *Futurecast. How Superpowers, Populations, and Globalization Will Change the Way You Live and Work* (New York: St Martin's Press, 2008), 1–22; Robert Kagan, *The Return of History and the End of Dreams* (New York: Alfred A. Knopf, 2008), 12–36, 53–80.

51. Eric A. Hanushek, Dean T. Jamison, Eliot A. Jamison, and Ludger Woessmann, "Education and Economic Growth," *Education Next*, Spring 2008, 62–70, http://www.media.hoover.org/document/ednext_20082_62.pdf; Debra Viadero, "Researchers Gain Insight Into Education's Impact on Nation's Productivity," *Education Week*, April 23, 2008, 17–19.

52. Tyler Cowen, "This Global Show Must Go On," *New York Times*, June 8, 2008, 5.

53. *New York Times Week in Review*, "Is Trade the Problem?," April 27, 2008, 11; *Chicago Tribune*, "Over Here: Forget Outsourcing—Certain Companies Looking for Employees for U.S. Sites," July 1, 2007, sec. 6, 1; Ralph Atkins, "Everyone Wakes Up to Changing Face of Labor," *Financial Times*, June 2, 2007, 2; Peter Marsh, "The Alloy Approach: How Industry in the West is Learning Again to Compete," *Financial Times*, December 12, 2006, 11; David J. Lynch, "Economy 'Open' for Business," *USA Today*, May 11, 2007, sec. B, 1–2.

54. Morris Beschloss, "On Easter Weekend, Hope Springs Eternal," *Desert Sun*, March 22, 2008, sec. E, 3.

RESOURCE A

In this section you will find a mix of solutions being used to tackle the global talent shortage.

CAREER ACADEMIES

Across the United States a wide spectrum of secondary education career initiatives is rebuilding the local education-to-employment talent pipeline. You will find more information about a cross-section of these schools here.

Austin Polytechnical Academy, http://www.austinpolytech.com

California Academy of Mathematics and Science, http://www.californiaacademy.org

Center for Advanced Research and Technology, http://www.cart.org

Cristo Rey, http://www.cristoreynetwork.org

Minuteman Regional High School, http://www.minuteman.org

National Career Academy Coalition, http://www.ncacinc.com

Philadelphia Academies, Inc., http://www.academiesinc.org

The Met, http://www.metcenter.org

EXPLORING ENGINEERING CAREERS

The following programs are examples of innovative ways to encourage students to explore careers in engineering.

Figure 6: Engineering Career Exploration Examples

Curriculum/ Developer	Grade Level	Approach
Engineering Is Elementary www.mos.org/eie Museum of Science, Boston	1–5	Engineering concepts taught through storybooks and activities
Project Lead the Way www.pltw.org Project Lead the Way, Inc.	6–12	No textbooks; hands-on activities and open-ended problem solving directed by teachers
Stuff That Works! citytechnology.ccny.cuny.edu City College of New York	K–12	Professional development guides for teachers
Children Designing & Engineering www.childrendesigning.org	K–5	Each curricular unit comes with lesson plans and kits of consumable materials for a class of 24 children
Infinity Project www.infinity-project.org Southern Methodist University, Dallas	9–12	Includes textbooks, hardware, engineering-design software, and a mandatory teacher-training program

Source: Edward E. Gordon, 2009.

THE NORTH CAROLINA CAREER OUTLOOK HANDBOOK

The North Carolina Career Outlook Handbook, published annually since 2003, is a key resource for parents, students, and job seekers. It offers detailed information about a wide variety of career clusters, including business technologies, engineering technologies, and the health sciences. You can download a free copy at http://www.nccareeroutlook .com.

EXPANDING THE TALENT POOL

A number of organizations' Webs sites offer both private business and government access to qualified disabled job candidates or free postings of open positions. Some of these include

- Disabled People Looking for Work, Disabled Career Center (www.Disaboom.com)

- National Association of People with Disabilities (www
.peopleresources.org)
- National Business and Disability Council, Job Listings,
National Resume Database (www.nbdc.com)
- National Council for Support of Disability Issues, Employment Job Listings (www.peopleresources.org)
- Workforce Recruitment Program for College Students
with Disabilities, co-sponsored by the U.S. Labor Department and Department of Defense [(866) 327-6669]

RESOURCE B

How to Establish a CBO or NGO

Step 1 Building a Framework

- Mission Statement
- Board of Directors = community members who
  Know the issues
  Are connected to the CBO or NGO's mission
- Bylaws of the Board
- Conflict-of-Interest Statement
- Financial Management Practices

Step 2 Program Planning and Evaluation

- Describe the problem to be addressed.
- Identify strategies to address the problem.
- Describe the individual activities for each strategy.
- Establish monitoring procedures to determine if a project is on track or if revisions are needed.
- Plan periodic evaluation of CBO or NGO programs.

Step 3 Coalition Building

- Develop partnerships with other community players.
- Adopt coordinated long- and short-term programs.
- Look for common activities with other groups.
- Determine if a coalition is temporary for a specific issue or permanent if missions and interests are compatible.

Step 4 Developing Sustainable Benchmarks

- Early Transition (Examples)
  Develop clear mission and strategic plan.

Dialogue with key players: business, government, unions, schools, etc.

- Mid-Transition (Examples)

  Clearly define the roles of the board and staff.

  Lobby and advocate at local and state levels.

  Develop a diversified funding base.

  Fully involve community and staff in strategic planning.

- Consolidation (Examples)

  Attract public support and engage decision-makers through clarity of vision and purpose.

  Enlist the board in fundraising, public relations, and lobbying activities.

  Adapt the strategic plan to ongoing changes.

Step 5 Fundraising

- Diversify activities and donor base.
- Build partnership with donors.
- Ensure a continuous process of grant seeking.

Adapted from Peter Willets, "What Is a Non-Governmental Organization?" in *Encyclopedia of Life Support Systems*, 2002; Olena P. Maslyukivska, "The Role of Non-Governmental Organization in Development Cooperation," Research Paper, UNDP/Yale Collaboration Program, 1999, and Research Clinic, New Haven, 1999; and *The Handbook on Good Practices for Laws Relating to Non-Governmental Organizations*, International Center for Non-Profit Law, Washington, DC: World Bank, 1997.

ACKNOWLEDGMENTS

There are hundreds of people who shared their knowledge with me as I researched *Winning the Global Talent Showdown*. Among those to whom I am particularly grateful are

Eunice Askov, Distinguished Professor Emerita, The Pennsylvania State University

Ronald Bird, Chief Economist, U.S. Department of Labor

Morris Beschloss, Economist

Anita Bullin, Surry Community College

Michael Bloom and Linda Scott, The Conference Board of Canada

Joyce Gioia, President, The Herman Group

Joanna Greene, Acting Executive Director, Chicago Workforce Board

Lynn Gresham, Senior Editor, *Employee Benefit News*

Kevin Hollenbeck, Assistant Director, W. E. Upjohn Institute for Employment Research

Suzanne Knell, Literacy Expert

Mary Anne Kelly, Vice President, Metropolitan Chicago Healthcare Council

William Leslie, Youth Services Specialist, Illinois Department of Commerce and Economic Opportunity

Henry J. Lindborg, Marian University

Peggy Luce, Vice President, Chicagoland Chamber of Commerce

Jim McShane, Executive Director, Crossroads Workforce Investment Board

Ed Morrison, Economic Development Consultant

Connie Majka, Philadelphia Academies, Inc.

James T. Parker, Literacy Consultant

Martin von Walterskirchen, Director, Swiss Business Hub, Minister, Consulate General of Switzerland

Holly Wade, Policy Analyst, National Federation of Independent Business

Dale Ward, Executive Vice President, Santa Ana Chamber of Commerce

Robert J. Witchger, Associate Director for Tech Prep, North Carolina College System

Robert B. Zettler, Workforce Consultant, Richland County Ohio OneStop

I also want to thank the readers of my previous workforce books. Many of you have encouraged me to continue to research and develop pragmatic solutions to the growing talent crisis.

Additionally, I am grateful to the people at hundreds of my presentations on these issues for their many positive comments, thoughtful questions, and useful suggestions. You have helped to sustain me in this quest for answers.

This book would never have reached fruition without the long-term support of John Willig, my literary agent. His encouragement over the past decade has provided me with essential opportunities to develop my thoughts. John's ideas about this project and his low-key, patient approach to marketing made this book a reality. Thanks very much, John.

Throughout the publishing process, Johanna Vondeling, editorial director at Berrett-Koehler; Sharon Goldinger, development editor; and their colleagues have provided many useful ideas to improve this work. I am very grateful to all of them.

Both Valerie J. Collier and Bonnie Cloer were essential in assisting me with their computer skills in preparing the manuscript for publication. I deeply appreciate their invaluable efforts.

Above all, Elaine Gordon, a professional writer and researcher and former university librarian, provided constructive suggestions and gave of herself untiringly in the entire process of researching and editing this book. After many years of joint collaboration, she is the enlightened foundation for all these publications and remains a very dear wife. However, for any factual errors this book may contain, I take sole responsibility.

EDWARD E. GORDON
Chicago, Illinois

INDEX

233

ABOUT THE AUTHOR

Edward E. Gordon is an internationally recognized writer, researcher, speaker, and consultant on the future of the workforce both in the United States and around the world. As President of Imperial Consulting in Chicago and Palm Desert, California, his clients have ranged from Fortune 500 companies to government agencies in the United States, Canada, and Europe; workforce boards; economic development/industrial commissions; business trade associations; museums; health care organizations; research groups; and colleges and universities.

Dr. Gordon's prior business titles include *The 2010 Meltdown: Solving the Impending Jobs Crisis, Skills Wars*, and *FutureWork*. His research on current business issues has appeared in the *New York Times, Wall Street Journal, Los Angeles Times, Washington Post*, and *Chicago Tribune*, as well as such business publications as *Business Week, Management Review, Employee Benefit News, Training, T & D*, and *M World*. He has appeared on CBS, CNN, NPR, and other substantive discussion programs.

Dr. Gordon taught for twenty years at three Chicago universities: DePaul, Loyola, and Northwestern. He serves on the board of the Better Business Bureau of Chicago and Northern Illinois. He is also a member of the Education Quality Workforce Committee of the Chicagoland Chamber of Commerce, the Youth Council of the Chicago Workforce Board, and chairs the Board of Trustees of the Better Business Bureau Foundation of Chicago and Northern Illinois.

IMPERIAL CONSULTING CORPORATION

Imperial is a research and consulting organization based in Chicago and Palm Desert, California. Its focus is real-world solutions for creating talent through the provision of compelling presentations, policy analysis, systems design, and coaching for business, education, government, and many other entities. Imperial was founded in 1968 by Edward E. Gordon. Many of the seventeen books and over two hundred articles authored by Dr. Gordon and his associates feature best practices and case studies on significant aspects of global workforce development related to Imperial's consulting services.

For more information, please visit www.imperialcorp.com.

THE *ASTD* MISSION:

Through exceptional learning and performance, we create a world that works better.

The American Society for Training & Development provides world-class professional development opportunities, content, networking, and resources for workplace learning and performance professionals.

Dedicated to helping members increase their relevance, enhance their skills, and align learning to business results, ASTD sets the standard for best practices within the profession.

The society is recognized for shaping global discussions on workforce development and providing the tools to demonstrate the impact of learning on the organizational bottom line. ASTD represents the profession's interests to corporate executives, policy makers, academic leaders, small business owners, and consultants through world-class content, convening opportunities, professional development, and awards and recognition.

Resources
- *T+D (Training + Development)* Magazine
- ASTD Press
- Industry Newsletters
- Research and Benchmarking
- Representation to Policy Makers

Networking
- Local Chapters
- Online Communities
- ASTD Connect
- Benchmarking Forum
- Learning Executives Network

Professional Development
- Certificate Programs
- Conferences and Workshops
- Online Learning
- CPLP™ Certification Through the ASTD Certification Institute
- Career Center and Job Bank

Awards and Best Practices
- ASTD BEST Awards
- Excellence in Practice Awards
- E-Learning Courseware Certification (ECC) Through the ASTD Certification Institute

Learn more about ASTD at www.astd.org.
1.800.628.2783 (U.S.) or 1.703.683.8100
customercare@astd.org

About Berrett-Koehler Publishers

Berrett-Koehler is an independent publisher dedicated to an ambitious mission: Creating a World That Works for All.

We believe that to truly create a better world, action is needed at all levels—individual, organizational, and societal. At the individual level, our publications help people align their lives with their values and with their aspirations for a better world. At the organizational level, our publications promote progressive leadership and management practices, socially responsible approaches to business, and humane and effective organizations. At the societal level, our publications advance social and economic justice, shared prosperity, sustainability, and new solutions to national and global issues.

A major theme of our publications is "Opening Up New Space." They challenge conventional thinking, introduce new ideas, and foster positive change. Their common quest is changing the underlying beliefs, mindsets, institutions, and structures that keep generating the same cycles of problems, no matter who our leaders are or what improvement programs we adopt.

We strive to practice what we preach—to operate our publishing company in line with the ideas in our books. At the core of our approach is *stewardship*, which we define as a deep sense of responsibility to administer the company for the benefit of all of our "stakeholder" groups: authors, customers, employees, investors, service providers, and the communities and environment around us.

We are grateful to the thousands of readers, authors, and other friends of the company who consider themselves to be part of the "BK Community." We hope that you, too, will join us in our mission.

BE CONNECTED

VISIT OUR WEBSITE

Go to www.bkconnection.com to read exclusive previews and excerpts of new books, find detailed information on all Berrett-Koehler titles and authors, browse subject-area libraries of books, and get special discounts.

SUBSCRIBE TO OUR FREE E-NEWSLETTER

Be the first to hear about new publications, special discount offers, exclusive articles, news about bestsellers, and more! Get on the list for our free e-newsletter by going to www.bkconnection.com.

GET QUANTITY DISCOUNTS

Berrett-Koehler books are available at quantity discounts for orders of ten or more copies. Please call us toll-free at (800) 929-2929 or email us at bkp.orders@aidcvt.com.

HOST A READING GROUP

For tips on how to form and carry on a book reading group in your workplace or community, see our website at www.bkconnection.com.

JOIN THE BK COMMUNITY

Thousands of readers of our books have become part of the "BK Community" by participating in events featuring our authors, reviewing draft manuscripts of forthcoming books, spreading the word about their favorite books, and supporting our publishing program in other ways. If you would like to join the BK Community, please contact us at bkcommunity@bkpub.com.